AROUND
THE
WORLD
IN 80
MINUTES

AROUND THE WORLD IN 80 MINUTES

IN SEARCH OF RUGBY GREATNESS

ROBERT KITSON

BLOOMSBURY SPORT

LONDON • OXFORD • NEW YORK • NEW DELHI • SYDNEY

BLOOMSBURY SPORT
Bloomsbury Publishing Plc
50 Bedford Square, London, WC1B 3DP, UK
29 Earlsfort Terrace, Dublin 2, Ireland

BLOOMSBURY, BLOOMSBURY SPORT and the Diana logo are trademarks of
Bloomsbury Publishing Plc

First published in Great Britain 2023

Text copyright © Robert Kitson, 2023

A catalogue record for this book is available from the British Library

Library of Congress Cataloguing-in-Publication data has been applied for

ISBN: HB: 978-1-3994-0358-0; eBook: 978-1-3994-0357-3; ePdf: 978-1-3994-0354-2

2 4 6 8 10 9 7 5 3 1

Typeset in Adobe Garamond Pro by Deanta Global Publishing Services, Chennai, India
Printed and bound in Great Britain by CPI Group (UK) Ltd., Croydon, CR0 4YY

All plate section images © Getty Images, unless otherwise stated.

To find out more about our authors and books visit www.bloomsbury.com
and sign up for our newsletters

For Dad, Mum & CK,
with much love

The evening air was pale and chilly and after every charge and thud of the footballers the greasy leather orb flew like a heavy bird through the grey light.
James Joyce, *The Portrait of the Artist as a Young Man*

'Brilliant! Oh, that's brilliant . . .'
Cliff Morgan, BBC commentator,
Barbarians v New Zealand, 27 January, 1973

CONTENTS

PREFACE

Rugby can be a bittersweet addiction. Driving home on cold, wintry nights, I often hear my mother's scepticism – 'I don't know what you see in that awful game' – echoing in the motorway darkness. Few team sports have so many brutal imperfections or demand such unsparing commitment. Even sofa-bound fans need to be aware their viewing pleasure could be blood-spattered, bone-breaking or, potentially, worse.

But hang on. Rugby, for me, is primarily about the men and women who play it. It bursts into life as a consequence of the emotions they feel – their collective passion, their inner drive – and the reciprocal love shown by the communities they represent. Bravery, fellowship, loyalty, risk, reward. Along with all the pain, it has the capacity to enrich the soul.

Not everyone appreciates this inherent contradiction. Some people prefer life to be smooth, others love a bit of friction. Rugby union's split personality is further complicated by the collision of two very different tribes. The biggest of them are called 'forwards' and think the world revolves around them. The rest are called 'backs' and believe otherwise. Rugby *union*? Having spent decades reporting on it, *disunion* might be more accurate.

It is also a game played seriously in 132 countries, according to World Rugby, its governing body. Contrasting characters, colliding cultures, the same oval-shaped ball. The other unifying link? You need to have something about you – or a point to prove – even to set foot on a rugby field. Once you do, other team games start to feel tame and lacking in rugby's intangible shared joy.

The colour and range of the backdrops can be just as enticing. The Six Nations remains the classic example. Steamed-up train windows, prematch sharpeners, instant new friends; the rugby almost becomes secondary because the experience is everything. Once, catching the ferry over to Ireland from Holyhead in the late 1980s, we bumped into a Dublin-bound contingent from Preston Grasshoppers. Their rendition of 'Molly

Malone' – 'We've come down from Barr-ow, Down the M6 so narr-ow!' – still makes me smile. So does the memory of staying at a guest house near Lansdowne Road. Our landlady was serving us our breakfast when she mentioned that her son would be going to the game that afternoon.

'Lucky old him to get a ticket.'

'Oh, he hasn't.'

Sure enough, around 90 minutes before kick-off, an ambulance pulled up outside the front door. The back doors were thrown open and in jumped the aforementioned son. Quick as a flash, he lay down on the stretcher and the doors slammed shut again. Moments later, the same vehicle was being ushered through the main gates to the stadium. Different times.

A desire to capture some of that fun and warmth was the spur for embarking on this book. Maybe my own undistinguished, injury-prone playing career was a further subconscious motivation. As a teenager I suffered so many fractures and dislocations my medical file was thicker than my biceps. One midweek afternoon in Edinburgh, aged 19, the final curtain fell. We were playing a team of medical students and, just before the interval, I went in to make a tackle. Instantly I felt something go in my right wrist. In the absence of a team doctor, I wandered over to our opponents' half-time huddle to ask for a rough diagnosis. There was a brief, hushed discussion before the captain turned apologetically back to me. 'I'm awfully sorry,' he said. 'We haven't reached that part of the course yet.'

I took a long, solitary walk over to the Western General Hospital, where my latest broken bone was eventually confirmed. 'Not bad for my first time,' the nurse told me, straight-faced, once she had sorted everything out. But that was me removed from our upcoming scheduled tour to France. By the following season I was learning how to be a sports journalist in London and was required to work at weekends. Somehow the game managed to limp on without me.

How fortunate have I been, therefore, to stay clinging to its fuselage for the subsequent 40-odd years, including almost a quarter of a century as the *Guardian*'s rugby union correspondent. If you don't mind a life spent in perpetual winter, rubbing shoulders with plenty of people taller, stronger and more talented than yourself, writing about rugby around the globe is a pretty tough gig to beat.

And on the eve of the highest-profile, most competitive Rugby World Cup in history, this felt like a timely moment to pause and reflect on a host of memorable people, teams and places. It was also exactly 200 years since William Webb Ellis allegedly picked up the ball and ran with it at Rugby School in 1823 (spoiler alert: this legend is not supported by overwhelming evidence). Most of all, though, I wanted to seek out those who had either made me fall in love with the sport or stood out in more recent years. To look north, south, east and west and celebrate those who made a genuine difference. Even if it was not entirely obvious to everyone at the time.

On my way, I discovered why relatively few authors have attempted to scale this specific Everest. Who would be mad enough to strap on their metaphorical crampons and go looking for something as subjective as rugby greatness? But one day the mists cleared just enough to glimpse a possible route to the summit. Could the distant peak be reached via the first-hand testimonies of those who blazed some kind of trail over the past half-century? Might their individual stories serve as beacons, starting with the day when rugby caught my imagination 50 years ago? And could they help to shed fresh, intriguing light on some key milestones in the sport's history?

The result is an eclectic bunch of individuals and teams. Some of the people in this book have shaped and defined modern rugby. Others deserve more recognition than they have received to date. It is important to stress, however, that this is not a definitive list of gods and goddesses. If your personal favourites are missing, they are in decent company. The late Jonah Lomu probably deserved three chapters to himself. I also opted to leave Jonny Wilkinson in peace, while the chronological and geographical requirements of the book counted against modern legends such as Richie McCaw, Dan Carter, Siya Kolisi, Sergio Parisse and Johnny Sexton. Another time, perhaps.

The reader will also be left to decide whether today's professionals are hugely different to their amateur predecessors. As one or two of the ensuing chapters will underline, the sport has its wider problems. In places there is darkness where, even five years ago, there was light. Yet, all around the world, millions of people continue to find rugby maddeningly irresistible and endlessly compelling. This book is for them, whether they are forwards or backs. And for anyone else wondering where the appeal lies.

1

DAVID DUCKHAM AND OTHER ANIMALS

Oh, that fellow Edwards. Who can touch a man like that?

Misty-eyed nostalgia is only ever a newsflash away these days. When a childhood sporting hero dies, a chunk of your youthful self goes with them. Suddenly we have to grow up and accept we are no longer the carefree kids we used to be. Which is why it comes as such a jolt, on a Sunday evening in June, to hear of Phil Bennett's passing at the age of 73. If anyone should have had the ability to sidestep adversity, it was surely him?

It is the same story on a damp Tuesday in January at a motorway services near Coventry. Stopping off to write up the day's rugby events for the *Guardian,* a message pops up on my mobile phone. David Duckham has died, aged 76. Oh no. Please, no. When our most cherished national icons depart, they crush our most vivid hopes and dreams.

At least we have their fabulous highlight reels to console us. And the comforting knowledge that, even 50 years on, their greatness still infuses the sport. Because if modern rugby union had its own Big Bang, it took place on Saturday, 27 January, 1973. Barbarians v New Zealand, Cardiff Arms Park. 'If the greatest writer of the written word would've written that story no one would have believed it.' Cliff Morgan's melodic, chapel-infused voice in the commentary box echoed the sense of wonderment the rest of us were feeling at home.

Such days change your life. And fundamentally shape your outlook. I would probably never have become a sportswriter had Dad and I not nipped home early from my brother Charlie's sixth birthday party in the village hall that fateful afternoon. Muhammad Ali's Rumble in the Jungle in Zaire?

Brazil stroking it around at the World Cup in Mexico? The gymnastic genius of Olga Korbut and Nadia Comăneci? The 1970s had some all-time great sporting spectacles, but for some of us there is no contest. For sheer unfettered joy, the Barbarians v All Blacks game still stands alone.

As luck would have it, we timed our escape from the Victoria Hall perfectly. Within a minute we were back across the road and in front of the telly. We'd missed something called the haka, but how good was this?

'If the greatest writer of the written word would've written that story no one would have believed it.'

It was the first full live, televised rugby match I'd ever seen. We had not long had a colour TV set, which added further to the novelty. Aged eight, I felt as if a window to another galaxy was being opened.

The Barbarians' black and white hooped jerseys, in particular, made football look second division. The Baa-Baas (cool name!) were also sporting an intriguing range of different-coloured socks, intensifying the sense of mystery. The mean, moody All Blacks, who had already beaten Wales, Scotland and England and drawn with Ireland in that winter of 1972–73, had the facial hair and brooding menace of proper pantomime villains.

Our sense of sofa-bound anticipation seemed to be shared by those in the stadium. Even before Bryan Williams hoisted that high, right-footed cross-kick from near the touchline, the opening couple of minutes had been frenetic. We watched as the diminutive Barbarians no. 10, in his distinctive scarlet socks, chased back towards his own line to retrieve the loose, bouncing ball. In retrospect, I was hooked even before 'Benny' stooped to pick it up off his bootlaces.

What happened next sealed it. One, two, three sidesteps and – *whooah!* – the little genius was suddenly scampering free in the shadow of his own posts. Seeking help, he found J.P.R. Williams who, with his namesake Bryan hanging around his neck, offloaded to John Pullin. Sensibly the England hooker identified a speedier teammate and shovelled the ball on to his captain John Dawes. Was that really a dummy from Dawes? If the blessed Morgan thought so, it must have been.

The late, great Dawes – who passed away in 2021 – was a consummate midfield craftsman. Readjusting his feet like a class steeplechaser approaching a fence, he expertly drew his man to put his compatriot Tom David away. 'David, Tom David, the halfway line . . .' The Welsh flanker made a few crucial yards before flinging the most outrageous one-handed pass just prior to being flattened by Graham Whiting. Somehow big Derek Quinnell managed to cling on – 'Brilliant by Quinnell . . .' – as he thundered up in valiant support. A minor miracle, both then and now.

Let us not wreck the sporting poetry. Did Quinnell's scoring pass float forward? Who cares? Because Gareth Edwards had arrived to lend an already dazzling move another surge of electricity. Even the full-stretch tackle of Joe Karam could not prevent the scrum half, with the athleticism of the gymnast he used to be, from rounding off the breathtaking move with a stunning dive past Grant Batty. 'WHAT A SCORE!' By now, Morgan, a late replacement for Bill McLaren, was purring into the microphone. 'Oh, that fellow Edwards. Who can touch a man like that?'

How could it not be love at first sight for us mortals? Courage, speed, skill, deftness, derring-do, defiance. And that was just Batty with his buttoned-up collar and peppery manner. It even felt special to others far better equipped to judge. 'I would suggest we've seen more quality rugby in the first 16 minutes of this game than we've seen for a long, long time,' confirmed Morgan.

Thus were my winter leisure choices instantly transformed. No one else in our village played or even spoke about rugby. No matter. I had only really played football and cricket until that point, so even running a few yards with ball in hand and the wind in my hair (those were the days) felt liberating. Re-enacting Edwards' brilliant score was logistically tricky, but Bennett's sidestep? Suitably inspired, I also spent hours trying to copy his kicking style. I particularly loved the way he could torpedo a ball sweetly into touch upfield, bouncing momentarily on his standing left leg in his follow through. Even with wellies on, it was sometimes possible to catch our deflated brown plastic rugby ball just right and spiral it into the vegetable patch. Maybe, if I kept practising, I might follow him into international rugby one day . . .

* * * * *

3

Which is why it is such a pleasure to meet Sir Gareth Edwards 50 years on. By chance, we end up sitting together at the Rugby Union Writers' Club annual lunch in London. This book was starting to take shape and a retrospective chat with the game's all-time best player would, clearly, be a privilege. Would he be prepared to chat in more detail at some stage? The world seemed to stop turning, as it does when people propose to their partners or await that crucial final lottery ball. To his credit, Sir Gareth did not roll his eyes too much.

And when we do finally reconvene, it is well worth the wait. Edwards has both a sharp memory and a nice line in wry humour. He tells a particularly good story about a fishing trip he took to a remote part of Russia in the early 1990s. 'Perestroika had just happened and the Russian interior was opening up. We were staying about a three-hour helicopter ride from Murmansk, right in the wilderness. The town was basically built out of wood and looked like a Western set. The only guy who was missing was John Wayne. It turned out the local mayor had been the commander of a Soviet nuclear submarine and was delighted to welcome us. After a while he says to me, "I have something to show you." We went back to his house and he puts this DVD on. And there it was. Barbarians v New Zealand, 1973. It just showed you how far it travelled.'

Reminiscing about a dim and distant snapshot in time is not necessarily everyone's idea of fun. 'I've spent the last 30 years trying to forget that bloody game,' sighed Ian Kirkpatrick from his Gisborne farm back in 2003 when I rang the former All Black skipper to gather a few recollections. Edwards has had it even worse. Imagine how often he has been asked, over the years, to wind back the 1973 Barbarian clock.

Soon enough, though, we are back in Cardiff on that day of days. As he sets the scene, citing the importance of two factors – the 1971 British & Irish Lions tour to New Zealand and the visionary coaching of Carwyn James – I feel like I'm listening to a celebrated composer explaining how he created a classic symphony. 'One thing Carwyn said still rings in my ears 50 years later. "The ball moves faster than the man." That was his philosophy. He would have us endlessly practising our passing and trying to catch someone out. It set us up to do that under pressure. Mike Gibson,

Barry John, Gerald Davies . . . it's not being sycophantic, but when I see some of the old films I think, *Bloody hell's bells*. I can still remember the pleasure it gave us. Even some of the local fans, when they reflected on it, would probably agree some of that rugby in 1971 was mesmerising.'

These Lions were the first side to conquer New Zealand, taking the series 2–1, and the tourists returned home feeling a couple of feet taller. 'The Barbarians game came with a certain extra pressure attached. We were concerned because it was the first opportunity the British public would have to see it. We wanted to show them how we played – and the opposition had every incentive in the book to have a bit of revenge,' recalls Edwards. 'There was a little bit of trepidation.'

There was also the small matter of preparation time. 'The All Blacks had been together for three months. The Barbarians met up on the Thursday when Tommy David arranged for them to have a beer or two in Pontypridd, followed by a single run-out in Penarth on the Friday. With the strictures of amateurism still firmly in place, they also had strictly limited access to their master coach. 'We asked to have Carwyn to coach us and you could see the Barbarians committee going pale, the blood draining from their faces. Eventually they said he could come along but couldn't stand on the field. He was only allowed to be on the touchline. Having him in our midst, though, gave us all confidence and great delight.'

Then, to everyone's chagrin, the brilliant Gerald Davies pulled a hamstring in training and had to withdraw. Worse was to follow. 'I was sharing a room with Mervyn Davies. When I awoke on the Saturday morning, he says to me, "Gar, I'm not feeling well. I think I've got the flu." I said I didn't believe him. "No," he said, "I'm honestly not feeling well."' Sure enough, he was also forced to pull out, with Derek Quinnell switching position and David coming into the starting XV.

In the first couple of minutes, even Edwards was beginning to wonder what he had let himself in for. The pace of the game was intense before Williams kicked long and Bennett scurried backwards to retrieve it. 'I was cursing having to run all the way back and I thought Phil would kick to touch. But suddenly our players were coming towards me. I remember thinking: What the hell's he doing now? I had to get out of the way and put my hands up to show I wasn't interfering with play.'

Had he stopped to catch his breath, rugby history would have been very different. Instead, Edwards turned around and silently cursed to himself again. There was no other option but to follow the collective charge, if only for appearance's sake. *I'd better chase after this or they'll be complaining I'm not trying.*

There was plenty of ground to make up, but suddenly he was up on the inside of Quinnell and roaring at his teammate in Welsh. 'Derek has a smattering of Welsh and I shouted at him, "Throw it here."' Was it slightly forward? It did not feel that way to the recipient. 'I never thought for one minute it was anything but a flat pass.'

Edwards' sudden arrival caught the All Black defence by surprise. 'Out of the corner of my eye I could see Joe Karam was caught in two minds. He had John Bevan in his eyeline and then I came through. Maybe it was those kinds of things that made it happen.' One other significant issue had also struck him: *Please, God, don't let my hamstring go now.*

And the final flourish? 'It's peculiar. You sense the crowd around you. It was uplifting. And I could see Grant Batty coming across. At which point you grasp at things you were taught in school. My schoolmaster always used to say, "If you're going for the line, dive in underneath them. That makes it harder for you to be tackled." As I got to the try line, that's what I tried to do.'

No still image of his iconic dive, amazingly, has ever existed. 'There was no photograph, no other television angle. Today you've got loads of cameras dotted around the ground. Then there were only two, I think. One on the halfway line hanging off the South Stand and one other on the far side, but none behind the posts at the River End, as we used to call it.'

The 'Magnificent Seven' stampede, nevertheless, has gloriously stood the test of time. Fifty years on more than 1,000 guests gathered for lunch just outside Newport to pay renewed homage and to hear Edwards' theory on its enduring spell. 'I don't watch it every day or every week, but it still gives us a little tingling at the back of the neck when you see it. That was the way the game was supposed to be played. The beauty of it was that we played what was in front of us. In today's game I don't suppose they would try to run it. It's far more stereotyped and defences are much tighter. How we were able to improvise under pressure is probably why it still stands up. Over the years, wherever I've gone, people have said to me, "I saw that game." There must have been half a million people in the ground that day . . .'

Comparative statistics, interestingly, suggest there are now five times more rucks and mauls in a typical modern rugby Test. On the other hand, the 1973 fixture contained a whopping 94 scrums and line-outs as well as 96 kicks out of hand. The other big difference was the absence of any television match officials to interrupt the fun. 'Looking back, we couldn't believe how many times it could have gone wrong. But there was no Television Match Official and it was allowed to flow. Some of Dai Duckham's running, Phil's darts . . . everybody had their moment in the sun somewhere along the line. I remember Ray McLoughlin holding up a couple of All Blacks who were trying to score. He was like a pit prop in a mine, holding up the roof. That was every bit as important as the try. Everybody played their part.'

In retrospect, Edwards has also come to appreciate something else. 'People say, "Is it the best try you scored?" The truth is, I've scored tries from a yard out that were just as important. But years later I was at a dinner in Hamilton in the company of the All Black flanker Alistair Scown. He turned to me and said, "You must be very pleased – and rightly so – because it was a fantastic try. But just think about me sometimes. I was the one who missed Phil Bennett."'

Edwards, though, was the man who elevated the sport to new athletic heights. Wales was the most passionate rugby nation on the planet and the miner's son from the village of Gwaun-cae-Gurwen was its shining jewel. No scrum half, before or since, has had the same coruscating mix. As a kid he had been lucky to come under the influence of the great Bill Samuel, who did his best to nurture Edwards' raw talent. Edwards wanted to play centre, but Samuel soon put him straight. 'You don't want to be a centre,' he told Edwards sternly. 'That's for people with Brylcreem on their hair and their hands in their pockets.'

At other times he would encourage his protégé to aim that little bit higher in terms of fitness. 'After a games lesson he'd say, "Where are you going?" I'd tell him I had to catch a bus, otherwise I'd have to walk home. He'd say, "Don't worry, I'll take you home. Go and do 6 × 200 metres to build up your stamina."' Alternatively, Samuel would try and play the part of aggressive opponent. 'He'd go into the line-out, tap the ball back awkwardly towards me and then come through and give me a bit of a shoulder if I didn't get it away quickly enough. "That's what you've got to be prepared for," he'd say.'

Edwards was also lucky to be surrounded by generous-spirited teammates such as David Watkins, his first Wales half-back partner. Before his first international against France in 1967 the papers were full of questions about the young man's passing ability, so he rang up Watkins and suggested they squeezed in a little extra practice session before the team departed for Paris. "Oh, I work in Cardiff, Gareth. Why don't we meet at the Arms Park?" Edwards was suitably grateful – until he got caught in traffic driving over from Neath where he was working. 'By the time I got there David was standing there waiting for me with his jacket slung over his shoulder, talking to his then girlfriend who later became his wife. I apologised and explained why I'd been delayed. "It's all right," replied David. "The groundsman won't give us a ball anyway."'

The 19-year-old Edwards, not surprisingly, began to feel a creeping dread in the pit of his stomach. A Five Nations debut in Paris alongside an experienced fly half to whom he had never thrown a pass? With his Test future on the line, he decided to try his luck with the groundsman one more time.

'I'm playing for Wales on Saturday, could you lend us a ball?'

'I don't care who you're playing for, nobody's told me about it.'

And that would have been that had Watkins not slipped his jacket off his shoulder, rolled it into a ball and tied the sleeves together to form a makeshift ball. 'The first pass I ever threw to him was his coat tied up in a bundle,' laughs Edwards, sounding incredulous even now. 'At least I knew where he was going to stand. Then we saw this distant figure. It was the groundsman. Looking embarrassed, he kicked a ball towards me saying, "You might as well have this."'

Ah, the good old amateur days. Edwards went on to win 53 Wales caps in total and graced one of the all-time greatest Welsh sides, but there were tough times as well. 'Not every match we played was as exciting as the Baa-Baas v New Zealand game. There were some bloody miserable games.' He still believes, even so, that some of yesteryear's stars would compare favourably with the modern greats. 'There's lots of lovely rugby today. Great conditions, good balls, not the slippery leather ones. But the quality of those days – some of the movement, some of the passing – has stood the test of time. Lots of it would live with anything played today. To be fair, defences are much tougher these days, but we had some exceptional tacklers, too.'

> 'Phil didn't have a clue where he was going, so what chance did the opposition have?'

More pertinent, perhaps, is Edwards' belief that not all his teammates would have played rugby nowadays. Football is more popular, rugby more physically demanding. 'Most of us played rugby for the school in the morning and football for the village in the afternoon. I loved football. And if rugby then was as physical as it is today they might well have said, "I'm going to go and play football."'

It is one of those conversations you wish could go on for ever. 'Who can touch a man like that?' It remains true: Sir Gareth is a gent and a timeless role model for us all. Sadly there is only time for one last problematic question. How does he think Phil Bennett would have fared in today's game? 'Phil would still have contributed somewhere along the line. But I wouldn't like to have seen his little frame carrying an extra two stone. He would still be in there, mind. Brave as hell, tackling anyone he had to.'

There is a momentary silence as Sir Gareth seeks to find the right words, eager to do justice to his friend. 'Phil didn't have a clue where he was going, so what chance did the opposition have? You were sometimes mesmerised by the ability of those guys. Today it's more a case of *What a huge crunch tackle*. The game has moved on and I suppose you have to move with the times. But when Phil passed away, it was the end of an era.'

* * * * *

If English rugby possessed a similarly bright comet during a bleak decade in which they failed to win a single Five Nations title, it was unquestionably the much-loved Duckham. When we met up near Stratford-upon-Avon for the purposes of this book a few months before he died, it was a joyous experience from the moment he pulled into the pub car park in his bright red Audi with its personalised numberplate: DUK. Unfortunately, this most dashing of players was not immune to the curse of arthritis. 'I can walk quicker than I can run now,' he murmured, apologetically.

From the outside looking in, the most-capped English back of his time had it all: charisma, a sense of adventure and enough pace to worry anyone. Sadly, like every other English player in those days, he also retired with a few regrets. Back in the day, he told me, he would wake up most mornings fully expecting the selectors to drop him. 'One bad game and you were out. We were all paranoid about losing our places.'

After a while it began to sap the confidence of the most gifted English attacker of his generation. The sidesteps that lit up Cardiff became rarities at Twickenham. 'At one stage John Pullin and I were the only two regulars in the side. Because of that I didn't risk things. With hindsight, I wish I had done.' When he was first picked by England he did not even regard himself as an elite athlete. 'I didn't see myself as a star player, but the media seemed to think I was because I had such a meteoric rise. I hated track and field at school. Hated it.' Why was that? 'Because I was afraid to lose more than I enjoyed to win. It wrecked my confidence.'

Luckily he had been part of an outstanding team at grammar school in his native Coventry – Peter Preece and Peter Rossborough also went on to represent their country – and he also had a compelling local role model to study. Peter Jackson was a star for Coventry, England and the British & Irish Lions and the youthful Duckham was a huge fan. 'He was my real hero. As a schoolboy I'd go to Coundon Road to watch him play. I'd live for the moment when he got the ball.'

Suddenly, in what felt to him like the blink of an eye, the long-striding Duckham was playing for England and the Lions himself. Like Edwards, he could scarcely believe the quality of the company he was keeping on the 1971 tour of New Zealand. 'They became my mates. But I also had the benefit of seeing these guys play at close quarters. If you'd picked a World XV in those days, the majority would have come from the UK. At least four or five of Wales' team would have been in it. They were that good, they really were.'

To the end of his days Duckham also retained vivid memories of the 1973 Barbarians classic, not least the prematch reshuffle which forced him to switch over to the right wing to accommodate Bevan on the left. Training was rudimentary – 'It was a farce, an absolute joke. We just messed around' – but the mood changed utterly when Carwyn Jones entered the dressing room before kick-off.

'He had been given special dispensation by the Barbarian committee to say a few words. "Remember what happened 18 months ago?" he said to us. "We won the Test series by taking New Zealand on at their game. Now we're on our patch. Just go out and play. Let's play Barbarian rugby." That's all he said, but it was enough for me. *Right, just give me the goddam ball.*'

According to Duckham, the Barbarians would have won by even more had Gerald Davies – 'The best winger I've ever seen, no doubt' – been involved. His other most cherished memory was the freedom with which he and his friends chose to play. 'We just cast caution to the winds and played on pure instinct. If something didn't work, you knew you had support behind you.' Neither Duckham nor the great Irish centre Mike Gibson anticipated Bennett doing what he did. 'When he was running back, both of us were expecting him to kick for touch for safety. But he didn't, did he? He just took off, beat the first three defenders and ran straight back at the Kiwis. He just couldn't resist it. I finished up on the halfway line applauding the try.'

If only representing England had been so fulfilling. When Duckham bumped into modern players, he would politely explain to them how things used to be. 'They say to me, "If you'd have played as many games as we do, you'd have had a squillion caps." To which I reply, "That would just have given me more opportunities to get dropped." That was our mentality then.'

England players also had to pay for their own shorts and the squad's nutrition and dietary advice was basic in the extreme. 'Micky Steele-Bodger was the first chairman of selectors I played under. We'd play these trial matches and he'd be shouting, "Who wants steak? Who wants fish? And who wants damn all?" We'd laugh and say, "We'll have damn all." What on earth is the point of eating a piece of steak for lunch before a Twickenham international. You've got no chance of digesting it.'

It was the same for contemporaries such as Alastair Hignell, so multitalented he played rugby for England at both scrum half and full back and scored a hundred for Gloucestershire against the West Indies. 'On the day of the game you could choose whatever lunch you wanted. The forwards would always have a dirty big steak – with chips of course. Bristol's Dave Rollitt would order raw egg and sherry. You wouldn't drink too much water. That would swill around inside your tummy, wouldn't it?'

The indefatigable Hignell, whose spirit in confronting multiple sclerosis continues to be an inspiration, also wonders how today's players would have coped with the prevailing conditions. 'In the mid-1970s it always seemed to be raining at Twickenham, the wind was constantly swirling and the grass was over your ankles. You practised with any old ball and then played with a shiny, light brown leather one. It was so new, it was slippery to touch. You didn't see it until just before the game when the captains would press it with their thumbs to gauge if it was pumped up enough.'

In retrospect it was remarkable the players strung together anything remotely half-decent. Players could only gather on the Thursday before, and Friday's priority was to park a car in central London to ensure a swift getaway on Sunday morning after the official post-match dinner. On Friday nights, as Hignell recalls, the squad would be driven into town to take in a show. 'It was around the time of the musical *Hair* and the Age of Aquarius. We saw something called *Let My People Come* which, as far as I can remember, was full of naked people. It didn't seem ideal preparation for playing rugby the next day.'

And when the young newcomer listened to his roommate Duckham – 'Whatever you do, don't make a mistake because they'll drop you if you do' – it was not always easy to feel upbeat about pulling on a white jersey. 'Coming from a world-class player, it was fairly dispiriting. You felt you were being analysed for what you didn't do rather than what you did.' Tactics were also on the rudimentary side of simple. 'Basically the line-out call was "West Stand" for Bill Beaumont and "East Stand" for Maurice Colclough or Nigel Horton,' recalls Hignell. 'There wasn't the time – or perhaps the will – to get on and become a tighter unit. We just accepted that that was the way it was.'

'It's a huge traffic jam, isn't it? The laws have gone a bit too far and there's so much physicality.'

On the day we met in the Midlands, though, Duckham also sounded unsure about several aspects of the modern game. 'It's a huge traffic jam, isn't it? The laws have gone a bit too far and there's so much physicality. It's the strongest guys putting their heads down and trying to burrow though and gain vital yardage. But that's not the way the game was designed to be played. The last thing Gerald Davies and I would do when we had the ball is try and get involved in a tackle. We'd try and beat the man, every time. Today's players, backs or forwards, just plough straight into them.'

Thankfully, there were some notable exceptions. Duckham particularly enjoyed, for example, watching Henry Slade play for Exeter and England. 'He's got style. I think of him as the Roger Federer of rugby.' He also used to wonder how he might have fared as a professional player himself. 'The one thing players of my generation fantasised about is how much better would we have been if we'd had the same access to technology and dietary advice that the players have now.'

In Duckham's case it all came to an abrupt end against Scotland at Murrayfield in 1976 when he sought to accelerate on to a pass from his England scrum half Mike Lampkowski. 'At the precise moment I caught the ball, two things happened. First I wrecked my hamstring and second the Scottish left wing David Shedden tackled me into the fifth row of the stand.' Over the subsequent summer he decided enough was enough. 'If I was honest, my heart wasn't really in it. I'd had a good run. I was the most capped England three-quarter in history at the time and I was proud of that.'

Duckham was also not remotely jealous of the money his modern successors now earn. He worked for Barclays bank during his own playing days and would occasionally be required to travel around the country visiting local branches. In Wigan one day two large gentlemen suddenly invited him to step outside. Around the corner was a parked car containing the then-chairman of Wigan Rugby League Club. A cheque book was brandished and, before he knew it, Duckham was being offered £15,000 to switch codes. He politely declined and spent the rest of his days living happily in Warwickshire instead.

But every now and again, at a hotel reception desk somewhere, people would still recognise the name. 'Is that David Duckham, the rugby player?' 'Awfully sorry, I'm afraid it is.' Sadly, there was no such recognition on this particular Tuesday lunchtime. 'Who was that guy?' asked the young barman as the departing red Audi passed the pub window. An all-time great, I told him, and perhaps his most prominent local celebrity. 'Really? Judi Dench's brother used to live in the village and the lead singer of Ocean Colour Scene drinks here sometimes . . .' Rugby really needs to cherish its surviving past masters while it still can. Rest in peace, Dai and Benny, and thanks for the indelible memories.

2

GREAT SOUTHERN LAND

There's a spirit in the Wallabies that words cannot describe.

To be a sports lover in the UK in the 1970s was to be a speck on an Antipodean horizon. 'Ashes to ashes, dust to dust,' as the old cricketing rhyme went, 'if Lillee don't get you, Thommo must.' A book called *How to Play Cricket Australian Style* had pride of place on my bedside bookshelf. The chapters were written by assorted legends of the baggy green cap – including the aforementioned Jeff Thomson and Dennis Lillee, Rod Marsh, the Chappells and Ross Edwards – and detailed the specific skills required to play cricket properly. Or, at least, better than the bloody Poms. I promised myself that, somehow, I would make it down under one day.

But how would I ever afford the flight? Fate intervened, when I was 16, in the form of a 25p scratch card purchased on the concourse behind the Tavern Stand at the Centenary Test at Lord's in 1980. If you scraped away the four red cricket balls and revealed four 6s, you scooped the jackpot. 'Er, I think I might have won.' Dad and I retraced our steps to the lady who had sold me the ticket. 'Wow, I've never seen one of these before!' she yelled, kissing me on both embarrassed teenage cheeks. The prize was £1,000 and the whole thing was beyond exciting. Well, it was until the bank rang to say the cheque had bounced.

Happily everything was sorted out eventually and I blew my entire windfall on a plane ticket. For an 18-year-old country bumpkin, Australia in January 1983 was a parallel universe. Arriving in Melbourne, I walked almost 8 km (5 miles) in boiling midday temperatures, idly wondering where all the buses were. I'd never seen a tram before. The locals saw me coming at the job centre as well. Any work going? 'Yeah, mate, ever done any fruit-picking?'

By the time I reached Sydney I felt sufficiently hardened to try my luck down the grades at the nearest rugby club. Northern Suburbs RFC – club motto: *Fortune Favours the Brave* – offered an immediate insight into the Australian sporting psyche. 'Yeah, mate, we'll pick ya, but only if you're any good.' Luckily the preseason trial game went okay. I was playing on the left wing when a scoring chance even arose from 10 metres out. Trying not to listen to the thunderous hooves of a trio of covering defenders, I dived for the corner. All three hit me simultaneously as if it were the last minute of a grand final. Welcome to Australian rugby, mate.

Even now the red and black hooped guernsey is still in the cupboard. A soft spot for dry Aussie humour also lingers. On one bus trip up the remote west coast, we reached the parched, iron ore town of Port Hedland. As we rounded a bend in the road, my eyes were drawn to a massive metal cage guarding a section of shoreline. 'What's that?' I asked the driver. His reply was classic old-school Aussie. 'Mate, that's to protect the sharks from the local kids.'

The Aussie male – young and free, girt by sea, surfboard in one hand, footy in the other – was pretty unreconstructed as well. Or, at least, that's how it felt to us. But as white, backpacking European kids, we didn't know the half of it. Up until 1967 indigenous people were not included in the census and did not have the right to vote. For a young Aborigine, one of 12 children, to grow up to be Australia's rugby union captain was to borrow someone else's fantasy.

Which is why it is so humbling to be standing in Forrest Place in Perth, talking to a man who redefined how rugby could be played, not just in Australia but worldwide. Mark Ella is edging towards his mid-60s now, but his eyes still twinkle and his handshake is warm. As with Phil Bennett, it is a reminder that meeting your heroes, contrary to received wisdom, can be thoroughly life-enhancing.

The respect that Australian sport still has for him can also be gauged by the fact that the Cook Cup, the trophy contested by Australia and England, has now been renamed the Ella-Mobbs Trophy. Not only that, it was designed by his niece Natalie Bateman, incorporating the mullet which Ella's fisherman father would catch to feed his large family. 'When you come from a family of 12, you don't really have a lot to argue when food is put in front of you,' says Ella now. 'We had mullet, baked mullet, skinned mullet, mullet soup . . . any way you could eat mullet was the way it was.'

Up until that 1967 referendum, Ella's father would have been allowed to have a beer only at the back of the pub rather than at the bar. The family was crammed into a three-bedroom home in La Perouse, one of the poorest parts of Sydney, and the kids would spend their summer days swimming or catching fish and crabs. As Ella once put it, 'Mum would say, "I'll see you at dinner time." We'd say, "What about breakfast and lunch?" She'd say, "What about it? You guys fend for yourselves."'

What an achievement it was, then, that four of the Ella clan went on to represent Australia. As well as himself, his twin Glen and Gary, who all played for the Wallabies, their sister Marcia was an international netball player. Even more extraordinarily, among their classmates from primary school and throughout Matraville Sports High School was none other than Eddie Jones, one of the game's best-known coaches. 'Tell him he'd be nowhere without us,' jokes Ella mischievously when we offer to pass on his best wishes at England's next media conference.

We agree to reconvene in Brisbane the following week when he has slightly more time. There is a huge Indian wedding under way and the foyer of his hotel is packed, but he is still instantly spotted by a rugby fan of a certain age. 'Could we possibly have a picture?' asks the man. 'My son is keen on rugby.' For a split second, as Ella gazes self-consciously down at my tape recorder and the stranger's camera phone, it is possible to understand why he walked away from rugby completely at 25.

But there is a good reason why so many of us still want to touch the hem of his garment. To say the Ellas and their schoolmate Lloyd Walker were special players is like calling the Sydney Opera House a vaguely prominent Australian landmark. As Ella once put it in an interview with the television station SBS, 'When my brothers and I were playing through school, it was like the circus had come to town. *Watch these Black kids play rugby.* In the early days we had a bit of racism, but once we started going up the hierarchy, getting selected in junior representative sides and senior representative sides, a lot of that racism quickly died away.'

All of them went on to be members of the undefeated 1977–78 'Invincibles' Australian Schoolboys side who cut such a swathe through Europe they are fondly remembered even now. Their coach, Geoff Mould, who also happened to be the Ellas' coach at Matraville Sports High, was a disciple of the creative playing theories from the 1920s and the likes of A.C. 'Johnnie' Wallace, Cyril Towers and Wally Meagher, all of whom believed that running rugby was winning rugby.

'We had a philosophy that we were going to enjoy the game, we weren't going to be too structured. When we started playing, we used to win by fighting.'

Mould decreed the ball had to be run at every opportunity and that players would be dropped if they kicked the ball unnecessarily. The result was that his team scored 110 tries – an average of just under seven per match – and conceded only six. Even the *Daily Telegraph*'s hard-to-please rugby correspondent, John Reason, wrote that 'the Australians play a style of football which has certainly not been seen in this country since the war, if ever. They make overlaps from close quarters as naturally as they breathe and undoubtedly the stars of the team are the three Ella brothers – Glen, Gary and Mark.'

The rugby league great Wally Lewis was also on the tour and subsequently described Ella as 'the best player I have seen in either rugby union or league'. The squad has since been credited with saving rugby union in Australia. The Australian Rugby Union was on the brink of insolvency in 1977 and unable to stage any Test matches; the significant interest generated by the Schoolboys was more than helpful. At the time, the only disappointment felt by the Ellas was the lack of any obvious mention in the sports section when they returned to Sydney. Their mother, May, gently told them to take a look at the newspaper's front page, over which their smiling faces were plastered.

Talk to Ella now, and you understand how much pleasure the tour and its impact brought. What did his parents reckon? 'They were very proud. We were Aboriginal kids from an Aboriginal mission.' And did their style find them or did they create it? 'I guess it suited us as indigenous kids: wanting to run the ball and not getting bogged down.

In those early years we didn't know anything different. We were just taught to play like that. We had a philosophy that we were going to enjoy the game, we weren't going to be too structured. When we started playing, we used to win by fighting.' After a couple of years, though, they decided that outclassing them on the scoreboard would be even more fun. 'It was more pleasurable, beating GPS schools by 20–30 points. It was unheard of. We were just this little public school opposite Long Bay gaol.'

Ella was captain of Australia at the age of 23, the first indigenous player to have the role. Anyone with eyes could appreciate the way he stretched the art of the possible – 'A lot of it was instinctive, but there was a lot of discipline' – with his flat-to-the-line running, deft hands, spatial awareness and outstanding support play. For the likes of Phil Kearns, starting out at Randwick where the Ella brothers had honed their attacking instincts, it was an instant education. 'It was rugby based on skill. I figured out very early on that if I followed Lloyd Walker or Glen Ella I was going to get the ball and score. They could just read a moment. All of a sudden the ball would be in my hands without me even thinking about it. It was hard to describe . . . there was just this feeling of *Wow*. I was in awe of those guys.'

At their best they made even the All Blacks seem drab and ordinary, with a young David Campese available to weave his own unique brand of magic. Skill, enjoyment and mischief, all wrapped in a golden Antipodean glow. Behind the exuberance, though, also lurked a steely desire among established players like Ella to make a point. 'A few of us had been to the UK four years earlier and we wanted revenge. I think we had a better all-round team in 1980–81 but we only won one of the four Tests. Bob Templeton was probably more structured and played the Queensland way, which wasn't a running game. This time we had a bit more say in how we played the game.'

Not that it was all plain sailing. Ella had a love-hate relationship with the new national coach Alan Jones, whose first act was to drop him as captain. This was to prove a masterstroke. 'I was a little bit blasé. I probably thought my shit didn't stink and that I was king. The best thing Alan Jones did was wake me up. There was a young guy called Michael Lynagh and if I didn't pull my finger out I'd probably lose my position.'

One thing, though, was not negotiable. 'I knocked on Jones' door after the Bledisloe Cup game and basically told him that that if we were going to be competitive on the Grand Slam tour I had to have control of the game. I said I didn't mind Slacky being captain but the no. 10 is like the quarterback, he's the one who'll dictate. To Alan's credit, he said yes. That gave me the inspiration to work a lot harder.'

Whatever the catalyst, the 1984 Wallabies proved to be one of the great touring sides, almost unrivalled in terms of their creative impact. They scored 12 tries in the four Test matches and conceded just one, scored by Wales' David Bishop in a 28–9 drubbing. On arrival at Heathrow, Jones had told every player to write down 'Business' in the box marked Purpose of Visit on their immigration forms 'because that's what we're here on'. Sure enough, they went on to become the first Wallaby side ever to complete a clean sweep over the home unions.

Ella was at the heart of it, achieving the equally unprecedented feat of a try in all four internationals. If you have never seen them, take a look on YouTube at the tries he scored against England and Ireland. At Twickenham it looks as if the home defence has been sliced through with a tin opener, so sharp is the edge and pace of Ella's line to the posts with Englishmen sprawled in his wake. In Dublin the Wallabies appear to be playing a different game to anyone else: backs surging on to the ball, straight and true, no thought of kicking, exuding the confidence of conjurers who know exactly when and where the rabbit will pop up. Passing the ball, rather than ceasing a player's contribution, is often just the start. And keep an eye on Ella who, having launched Michael Lynagh straight through the middle, runs diagonally towards the left corner flag to serve as an extra man for the jinking Campese. 'The passes went like lightning: bang, bang, bang. And then we'd be looping around,' recalls Ella, shyly sipping his coffee.

Which is why it feels such a pity that Ella never represented Australia again after that tour. He had already made his mind up to retire, although he had barely told anyone. 'I didn't want to play forever. I had a good job with Rothmans at the time, I wanted to get married. I just needed to change my life. Rugby was great, but I needed to move on. I would have moved on if we'd won or lost. I didn't tell too many people. Not many of the players knew at all.'

He even turned down a deal that would have made him perhaps the best-paid sportsman in Australia. Leading Sydney rugby league clubs wanted him and, as a 'leaguie' from way back whose uncle had played for Eastern Suburbs, he understood the game. In the end he phoned his good mate Wally Lewis. 'Wally and I talked a lot and he was captain of the Kangaroos and Queensland. I rang him up and said, "Wally, I can't do it."' Lewis was silent for a moment before asking how big the offer had been. Ella duly told him. This time Lewis's reply was instantaneous: 'You b— so and so. They'd be paying you more than me.'

Ella just laughed and, even now, has no regrets. 'It would have been easy for me to go to league because I'd played it for 12 or 13 years. But I just felt like I didn't need to prove anything. I was an amateur and it would have been nice to have that amount of money. But that wasn't what was driving me. It was playing the game that was more important. I just felt I didn't need to play league.'

'What I don't like about modern rugby is that they stand far too deep and run across the field rather than attacking the opposition the way you should.'

So back he flew to Sydney airport and made the announcement at the airport. 'There wasn't any thinking about it, I did it as soon as I got off the plane. There were probably a dozen journos there.' Four decades later his upfront honesty, particularly on the subject of the way the game is now played, has not changed at all. 'What I don't like about modern rugby is that they stand far too deep and run across the field rather than attacking the opposition the way you should. I couldn't play now. Unless you said to the coach, "Play it my way or I'm not playing." Which is not the right thing to do. I know the game has changed a little bit but I can't see any reason why they can't play like that. They don't even try.'

Time for one last question. Would the Ellas, for all their genius, have played union today? 'Probably not. You'd have to go to a private school. Rugby league and AFL are the dominant sports in Australia and they've got plenty of money.' He struggles to name even one current male indigenous professional player. 'Apart from Kurtley Beale, who was the last one? I can't tell you there's an indigenous player in the Super Rugby teams, let alone in the Wallabies. Considering the talent a lot of indigenous players have, both men and women, we should be making more of it. Acknowledging indigenous people is terrific, but we've got to take it a step further. What are we going to do from the playing perspective?' And with that he is away, weaving through the lobby full of Indian wedding guests with not a finger laid on him. Some things never change.

* * * * *

If anyone was well placed to appreciate Ella's strengths, he is now sitting across a table in Richmond-upon-Thames. There are good judges who will tell you that Michael Lynagh was an even better, more rounded fly half; he is also the most self-effacing and understated of men. He tells a particularly good story about standing on a school touchline in England, watching one of his sons play, when a nearby parent started complaining about the standard of the team's coaching. After a while Lynagh could take no more. 'Excuse me,' he said, 'but if you're such an expert, why don't you have a go?' At which point the parent turned to one of Australia's most distinguished sporting legends, snorted dismissively and delivered the immortal line, 'What the fuck would you know about rugby anyway?'

Hopefully that individual will read this book and clutch his head in shame. Lynagh won 72 caps for the Wallabies, captained his country and won a Rugby World Cup – and two of his sons are current professional players. Growing up in Brisbane, the son of a clinical psychologist, he was also a talented cricketer and only made his school's U13 B rugby team. Soon enough, though, he was being picked for an Australian Schoolboys tour and, aged 19, was chosen to go on his first Wallaby tour to Italy and France in 1983. New South Wales players had been dominating the national team, but times were changing. 'Suddenly Queensland were doing really well and that translated into the Australian team,' recalls Lynagh. 'All of a sudden, rather than NSW having 13 players on the Australian team, there was competition.'

By the time Lynagh made his international debut in 1984 – 'Michael Hawker was on his honeymoon, so I got to play a Test in Fiji' – there had also been a change of national coach. The voluble Alan Jones, who had won the Sydney Premiership with Manly, had taken over from the ousted Bob Dwyer and, characteristically, was determined to do things his way. 'Jones brought in this whole different approach about how we trained for rugby,' recalls Lynagh. 'In the past we'd be playing France and on the Friday we'd say, "Jeez, how are we going to defend against Serge Blanco?" I'm exaggerating a little bit but it was pretty amateurish in those days.

'Then, in 1984, Alan arrived. He used to watch videos of the opposition and analyse what they were good at and how we were going to play them. He'd say, "We're playing Scotland at the weekend, they're really good at toeing the ball forward and getting in the way, so we're going to practise diving on the ball and getting up."' Jones had also taken the decision to remove Mark Ella as skipper and install Slack. 'The first thing Alan did was get rid of Mark as captain. With the Ellas – and I mean this in the nicest way – it was a pretty relaxed environment, whereas Alan was very intense. We trained like we'd never trained before.'

The new training regime did not initially go down brilliantly. 'The Ellas were not the only ones who didn't like it, but it was all done at the start of the week. We'd work really hard from Monday to Wednesday but on Friday we wouldn't do anything. As a young kid, you'd go, "Well, we know what they're going to do, we know what we're going to do and we're rested. What can possibly go wrong?"'

Jones was also smart enough to know what he was presiding over. 'Jones didn't dictate to Mark Ella how to play the attack,' recalls Lynagh. 'He knew he was good at that, so he let him do it. What he did do was put in place an environment around him to help him do that. He had a really big strong forward pack with a good scrum and a good line-out and the backs did what they wanted.

'We also came with a different way of playing the game to what they were doing in the UK and Ireland. We felt we were more skilful with the ball. I also think there was a belief that we were fitter. That's not being arrogant. It wasn't because we ran around the ovals more often, it was because we were on tour and because of our climate back home. The England team used to get together on a Thursday afternoon. We were on tour and we knew each other better than the England team did.'

Coincidentally Lynagh now sees some stylistic similarities with the way Harlequins played when they won the 2021 Gallagher Premiership with his son Louis in the backline: the classic mix of a strong and stable set piece and backs prepared to have a go from almost anywhere. Back in the day, the flat attacking patterns and whirring sense of golden enterprise caught everyone's imagination, not least because of how much the Wallabies seemed to be enjoying themselves. They certainly weren't doing it for the money, with a daily tour allowance of £6, but Lynagh relished every second. 'I played around 12 games and was reserve for the rest, but you still went out, had a beer, played golf and had a pretty good time. We trained once a day from 9 a.m. to noon, had a lovely lunch and then the afternoon was yours. It was just the way rugby was back then. We weren't playing for contracts or anything like that. Playing for your country was the main motivating factor. It was about playing with your mates and not letting them down. I sort of hope that atmosphere still pervades rugby now.'

It could not last indefinitely. New Zealand may have won the inaugural 1987 World Cup, helped by Serge Blanco's late try in the semi-final which did for Australia, but players like Lynagh, Campese and Nick Farr-Jones exemplified the new breed of Wallaby coming through. If Australia were lucky to have excellent technical coaches – Dwyer, Templeton – and a clutch of world-class players, it was also underpinned by the dog-eat-dog personal rivalries of clubs such as Randwick. Kearns, famously, was plucked pretty much straight from the Randwick second team in 1989 to make his Test debut at hooker at the expense of the vastly more experienced Eddie Jones but still had to scrap his way to the top. 'It was totally competitive in training. We used to have games of touch football between first grade and second grade. Eddie was an absolute pain in the arse: very mouthy and would commentate on the whole game. But I always had enormous respect for him. For his size, to be able to do what he did on the field and get to the level he did is quite remarkable.'

And even after he had pulled on his Wallaby jersey, Kearns knew exactly what was coming. 'After my first Test in 1989 I went back and played club football the following week in second grade. Eddie was in first grade. It was as it should have been. I wasn't disappointed at all, it was what I expected. He deserved to have that respect shown to him for what he did for the club. He might say otherwise, but I think he and I always had a good, respectful relationship. What he has done in coaching has been phenomenal. I take my hat off to him.'

It was also clear Dwyer had some decent players at his disposal as the 1991 Rugby World Cup loomed on the horizon. By a happy coincidence I'd had a sneak peek in November 1989 when my new employers, Reuters, sent me to Strasbourg to cover the first Test of their French tour. It is a game enshrined into rugby lore as the first time Jason Little and Tim Horan shared a Test midfield together. The day before, I bumped into Dwyer, now back as Wallaby head coach, sightseeing outside Strasbourg Cathedral. He was friendly and courteous and looking forward to the game. I seem to remember him even cracking a joke about divine intervention. The following day Australia did not just beat France, they creamed them 32–15.

By the end of the following year Dwyer was quietly confident his team could do something special at the World Cup. He even phoned a number of his senior players 12 months out from the tournament and invited them to raise a glass of champagne that evening to toast their victory on the same day a year hence. The ensuing months were spent getting fit and organised and when the 1991 tournament did finally arrive, they were good and ready.

For those of us looking on from the press box, the Ireland v Australia quarter-final was as thrilling as any game in the tournament. To this day I cannot recall hearing a bigger Dublin roar than the one which accompanied an almost disbelieving Gordon Hamilton to the try line for the score that appeared, momentarily, to have knocked the Wallabies over. With four minutes left, Ireland led 18–15 but reckoned without Lynagh's cool, calm response. Rejecting a potential drop goal in favour of a backline move that had delivered success earlier in the game, the ball was moved towards

Campese on the right and then, when he was tackled, Lynagh picked the ball off his toes to score in the corner and silence the previously ecstatic crowd. 'It was one we escaped, I think. Only the other day I met an Irishman who said, "I was there in 1991." Along with the other three million!'

It teed up a semi-final against New Zealand, again at Lansdowne Road. The difference in demeanour between the two sides during the preceding days was stark. When us hacks popped out to a local bar for a quiet Guinness after a hard day's yakka, a sprinkling of Wallaby squad members was often already there. Lynagh also remembers it well. 'In Dublin that week you had these unsmiling All Blacks who wouldn't talk to anybody and then you had us, out on the streets selling T-shirts to fund our end-of-tour party. There was no curfew, no nothing. That's the best discipline, the one that comes from within.

'We had guys who weren't playing much and they'd go out and have a pretty big night. But there was almost an unwritten rule. After training the next day you'd do your extras. You might be able to smell the drink on a guy who'd been on a bender, but after training you'd still see him doing 30 minutes of training on his own.'

The semi-final could not possibly be as good, could it? How wrong we were. It is possible that Australia have never been as ruthlessly sharp as they were in the first half, pulling their opponents around as if the All Blacks were puppets on a string. At the centre of it all, inevitably, was Campese. If the sublime, no-look reverse pass over his right shoulder to Tim Horan was something else, the cuteness of the diagonal angle that had already taken him to the left corner without a finger being laid on him would have delighted any snooker player in the world.

New Zealand did come back harder in the second half from 13–0 down, but Australia were up to the challenge and came through 16–6. 'The second half was about holding on,' continues Lynagh. 'That was the great thing about the 1991 team. I still say it now: great teams have different ways of winning games. I remember Gary Whetton breaking clear down our right-hand side and I was the only one left. If I missed him, it was a try. You just close your eyes and do it.'

Which just left the final. Against England at Twickenham. Lynagh recalls Australia's players feeling the game was theirs to lose, having already beaten their opponents 40–15 in Sydney in July. 'We didn't want to stuff it up. We'd already beaten New Zealand who had beaten England in the pool stages. England didn't present anything we didn't know about.'

It proved to be an odd game. A grey, damp day with the wind swirling was not the obvious moment for England to deviate from their perceived strengths. For assorted reasons, however, they duly did so. 'The bit that surprised us a bit was the way they tried to play,' confirms Lynagh. 'Why would you change it? This is the game that's got them to where they are, why would you change it for the final?'

'Why would you change it? This is the game that's got them to where they are, why would you change it for the final?'

Not so long ago, he decided enough time had passed to discuss all this with the ultimate English competitor Brian Moore. 'I wrote to him and said, "I've read your book, I now understand you a bit more and we live close to each other. Let's get together because life's too short. I'll shout you lunch." We agreed to meet at a restaurant on the river near Richmond. I arrived on time and he was about half an hour late. By then I'd ordered a £50 bottle of Argentine Malbec because I knew he liked his wine. He sits down, apologises for being late and then says, "What's this shit? Let's go and get a decent one."'

And after a couple of bottles – and having established that Moore really had hurled his loser's medal into the River Thames – Lynagh decided it was time to address the elephant on the room. '"Okay," I said, "let's get this one out of the way: what happened in the 1991 World Cup final?"' Moore's reply was that the whole team had realised that playing the so-called English way risked a similar result to the summer. 'It was a fair enough argument, but if you haven't practised it and the whole team haven't bought into it?' asks Lynagh, rhetorically. 'Brian is very much of the *Why change it?* school.'

Back on 2 November, 1991 in the Wallaby dressing room, though, there was no such hand-wringing after their 12–6 victory. The players celebrated in the old-fashioned Twickenham bathtubs, the nagging fear of failure finally removed. Lynagh still feels a frisson, even now. 'There was just relief afterwards, a sense of *Thank God, we've taken that opportunity*. If we hadn't, I'd probably still be like Brian.'

Was the 1991 side better than the 1984 Grand Slam heroes? Lynagh, who played in both sides, reckons 1991 might just have shaded it but makes the obvious point that such simplistic comparisons are mostly invidious: 'It's like saying, "Is Bradman better than Chappell?". 'Was I better than Mark Ella? Yes and no, in different ways.' Australia, he reckons, actually hit their peak and played their best rugby in 1992 and 1993. 'Bob said to us, "We're world champions now. Everyone wants to beat us, so we've got to lift it to the next level."' For whatever reason, though, they were no longer quite the same force in 1995 when they lost to England in the quarter-finals.

And little did they realise, having lifted the Webb Ellis Cup again in 1999 and taken England to extra time in 2003, that the golden goose was about to stop laying. Why did Australian rugby union fall as far as it did? The steady rise of the AFL, an over-reliance on Sydney's private schools, Shane Warne . . . the reasons why the Wallabies lost their bounce extend well beyond the field of play.

Until now, that is. World Rugby has granted Australia the hosting rights to the 2027 and 2029 World Cups, for men and women respectively, a decision which will, hopes Lynagh, prove a major turning point. 'Australian rugby has a lot of issues, but I do see a bit of a light at the end of the tunnel. The 2027 World Cup and the British & Irish Lions in 2025 . . . all of a sudden those are bankable certainties. You can go and ask banks and World Rugby to lend more money. I can see rugby coming up again because of the interest that will create. That's the mistake we made in the last 20 years, in my view. All the money was put into the pro game, the idea being the gold dust would filter down on everything else. Which is a good idea in theory but it hasn't really worked.'

If the old bottom-up pyramid – school, junior club, state, Australia – can be restored, he believes the outlook could brighten rapidly. 'I think there are a lot of wealthy individuals who would support rugby as long as it was heading in the right direction and had a plan,' suggests Lynagh, thankfully recovered from the serious stroke he suffered in 2012. 'For the last 10 years they haven't been convinced.' Tellingly, he is not quite so sure about the English domestic system. 'I still don't understand the counties, the clubs, the Championship, National 1 and 2. It's a mess. That's been the big problem for England, I think. You've got all this structure underneath the Premiership which should be looked after. They leave it up to the academies to do it. But then the academies effectively get penalised for bringing players through. Those players should be off the salary cap. That would give the clubs the incentive to develop their own, which would help England rugby.'

Because nothing, ultimately, sells the game better than a successful national side. Kearns also highlights something else about the great Wallabies of old: the mateship and infectious larrikin spirit that bound the team to its public. 'There was a famous poem written by Peter Fenton called "The Spirit of the Wallabies". The opening lines sum it up: *There's a spirit in the Wallabies that words cannot describe. It's as if they are descended from a legendary tribe.*' By the time 2027 rolls around, reckons Kearns, a green-and-gold revival will be gaining genuine momentum.

3

SUNSHINE ON LEITH

I just feel fortunate to have played with so many good guys.

This is not just a book about people. In France they talk about *le terroir* and the almost mythical connection between the glass of local wine in your hand and the soil that created it. This sense of place, in turn, reinforces the importance of staying true to both your people and your roots. And forging the unshakeable bonds of loyalty which, it so happens, are also among rugby's foremost assets.

An empty ground, a set of silhouetted posts in winter sunshine, a sense of endless possibility. The old cavernous Murrayfield, with its wide open terraces, used to be particularly evocative. In the distance you could see the Pentland Hills, with the skirl of the pregame pipes offering a direct spiritual link to the glens and lochs further north. I was a country boy from the south of England, but I began to develop an affinity for the way Scotland played. Their forwards were white-kneed and seemingly fearless, their backs less constrained by orthodoxy than the English. Andy Irvine's first instinct was to attack and his teammates seemed on the same wavelength. At scrum half was Dougie Morgan, my other dark-blue favourite, who did virtually everything. When he wasn't bossing his forwards around, he was kicking the goals, with collar turned up for additional effect. Scotland fizzed with an underdog's energy and Bill McLaren's commentary further enriched the broth. 'They'll be dancing in the streets of Hawick tonight' may have sounded quaint to metropolitan ears, but for those of us from rural backgrounds it was exactly what we'd have done if one of our brawny local lads had done something special.

For years, in honour of Morgan, I would check Stewart's Melville FP's results and idly wonder if Goldenacre, home of Heriot's FP, had secretly

31

inspired Ian Fleming's James Bond novels. So when I enrolled as a student at Edinburgh University in the autumn of 1983, it felt weirdly like a homecoming. Sunshine on Leith? The air was certainly fresh and, on a clear day, you could stand above the New Town and look right across the Firth of Forth to Fife. I ended up dropping out after a year to become a trainee journalist, but I loved every second of my time in Auld Reekie.

Around that time, coincidentally, the national team were also on the up. Terrace tickets – costing £3.50 – would be stacked up beside the tills in John Menzies, and even impoverished students could afford to attend the games. In mid-November Scotland drew 25–25 with New Zealand thanks to an equalising try from Gosforth's Jim Pollock. Then, in early February, they beat England 18–6 before dismantling Ireland in Dublin 32–9 to clinch the Triple Crown. It set up a Grand Slam decider against France on 17 March, a big day on numerous fronts.

The expectation was that France, with the outstanding Jérôme Gallion at scrum half, would be too strong. As a penniless student, I jumped at the offer of a much-needed paid job selling commemorative Triple Crown brochures on the day of the game. The idea was that home fans, in the event of defeat, might fancy some consolatory reading. No one seemed to have factored in a potential tartan win, let alone a first Grand Slam since 1925. Which is how I came to be standing on the Clock Tower terrace at the final whistle with a teetering stack of 200 unsellable brochures at my feet.

At least the rest of the night was magnificent. A couple of the pubs on Rose Street – the popular drinking thoroughfare just up from the city's main Princes Street – ran dry by 9 p.m., with French and Scottish fans alike all up on the tables roaring out each other's anthems. It was a fabulous evening and, almost 40 years on, it feels similarly grand to be reminiscing about it with one of Scotland's conquering heroes. Adventurous, canny and a languidly brilliant runner, John Rutherford was as good as any fly half Scotland has ever produced. Happily, his view of 1984 also remains as rose-tinted as mine.

It turns out we share something else in common. Phil Bennett was also Rutherford's hero growing up, the Welsh wizard's sense of adventure rendering national borders irrelevant. 'Him and Barry John . . . they were just the greatest. You need role models and they were certainly mine.' Take a look back at that 1984 campaign and the deceptively languid Selkirk fly half is as beguiling to watch now as then. Up in the commentary box McLaren's hopeful, rising intonation – 'Laidlaw to Rutherrr-ford . . .' – reflected the delightful reality that anything could happen.

Ask Rutherford to pinpoint Scotland's collective secret, however, and he uses just two words: Jim Telfer. The previous year the master coach had come home from the Lions tour of New Zealand feeling it was time to step aside. 'Is there life after death?' he famously replied when asked about his post-tour future. Rutherford and other senior players, though, formed a delegation and asked him to stay on. 'Jim was going to pack it in after the Lions tour. It was tough. We lost 4–0 and were pretty beaten up by the end of it. A few of us got together . . . we just felt one more nudge with him at the helm would do it.'

There was no overnight success. Telfer was as sharp as he was shrewd, but this was still very much an amateur game. Perhaps the classic example came in 1982 when Keith Robertson was taken ill and the Gosforth winger Jim Pollock was called up at short notice to play in Cardiff. 'Jim arrived on the Saturday morning and nobody knew who he was,' recalls Rutherford. 'He was introduced to the squad and we just ran through a few things in the hotel garden. It just shows how amateur we were in those days. He turned out to be outstanding.'

When Rutherford looked around the dressing room at some of the more familiar faces, he could see a good team developing, too. 'It was a slow build, but by the time we got to the 1984 season we had all the pieces in place. We had a strong back row and a good front row, too. Iain Milne was maybe the best tighthead in the world at that time.' They also had Telfer. 'There were a lot of personalities in that team, but there's no question Jim Telfer drove the team to that Grand Slam. He was tough, there's no getting away from it. He could be tougher on some people than others, but he knew how to get a winning team.'

Part of that process was making sure his teams were fitter than the opposition, for the very good reason Scotland were among the smaller international sides. 'In Scotland we always had wee teams,' confirms Rutherford. 'We had to pride ourselves on our fitness and mobility. I was just over 11 stone when I got my first cap. I spoke at a dinner recently and looked up the difference in the average weights of back divisions then and now. It's two to three stone per man more than when I played. Jim Renwick, Ian McGeechan, Andy Irvine, Keith Robertson . . . we were all around the 12 stone mark. In a backline today

'There were a lot of personalities in that team, but there's no question Jim Telfer drove the team to that Grand Slam.'

you're looking at centres who are 15 or 16 stone and athletic. There are no fatties now.'

Rutherford, who had studied as a PE teacher, was ahead of his time in his appreciation of strength and conditioning. In the amateur era, though, this all had to be fitted in around the day job. 'I would come home for work and go straight out training. I knew that if I didn't, I'd have my tea and probably wouldn't be able to motivate myself. But that's what you had to do in the amateur days to keep fit.'

It helped that Telfer, in common with many of his squad, was also from the Borders. 'When you look through our team you had Jim Aitken, Colin Deans, Alan Tomes, Iain Paxton, David Leslie, myself, Roy Laidlaw, Keith Robertson and Peter Dods. We were also playing five or six times a year together for the South of Scotland district team as we did in those days.' Border folk didn't tend to get too carried away with themselves and neither did their mates back home. 'In between internationals we'd be back playing for Jed-Forest or Selkirk. It was quite good for keeping your feet on the ground. You could have played a blinder, but your teammates would only remember the one incident when you were crap.'

That year, though, the whole country began to sense something stirring. Iain Paxton's rampaging try against Wales, the humbling of the English in the 100th international match against the Auld Enemy . . . everything seemed to be going swimmingly. The Triple Crown was clinched in style in Dublin, although Laidlaw only lasted for 40 minutes. 'Roy was fantastic in the first half and scored two tries but he was concussed,' recalls Rutherford. 'At that time it was called athlete's migraine.

Nobody mentioned concussion. My Selkirk half-back partner, Gordon Hunter, came on and played a great game but running off the pitch at the end he collided with a spectator and fractured his cheekbone.'

This necessitated a hasty recall for Laidlaw – 'In those days they didn't have the protocols they have now. Roy felt much better and played the game' – for the title decider back at Murrayfield. If it was tense on the terraces, it was doubly so in the dressing room. 'It wasn't a good game. Both sides were too nervous; there was very little rugby played. It was almost a case of the first to blink.' Only after Jim Calder flopped on to an overthrown line-out to score Scotland's solitary try did the mood shift. 'We got the breakthrough and France started to make a lot of mistakes. We probably wouldn't have won that game a season or two earlier, but we had the maturity to hang on. They were the better side in the first half, but they couldn't get away from us. We just had that ability to hang in there.'

They also had one of the most accurate big occasion kickers in Scottish history. Even now Rutherford exhales softly at the memory. 'The player who never gets the credit he deserves is Peter Dods. He was absolutely outstanding and his kicking was world class. Along with David Leslie he was probably our best player that season. I don't know what his percentages were because they didn't really keep them at that time, but he must have been around 90 per cent.'

The aftermath of that 21–12 victory – later compared by Telfer to a history-making expedition reaching the South Pole – was as uproarious for the players as it was for the rest of us. Well, for all but one of them. 'It was always a tradition that we went to a pub in Rose Street and met up with our supporters after the game,' recalls Rutherford. 'Everyone was pretty knackered, but it was great.

'Then Jim Aitken organised for us all to get together on the Monday as well. There was a bit of phoning that had to be done to see if we could get the day off because obviously we were all working.' For Roy Laidlaw, an electrician, this was a particular problem. 'Roy's boss couldn't give him the day off. His job that day was to rewire the public conveniences in Jedburgh. We were all out on the lash while poor Roy was working in the loos down in Jed. He still remembers it fondly.'

So does Rutherford, now in his late sixties and happily in good shape following a bout of prostate cancer, the disease which killed his younger brother, Billy. While his old partner Laidlaw is now wrestling with Alzheimer's – 'He's a bit forgetful, but when you go back to the '70s and '80s he can remember everything' – the half-back duo still get together every week to play golf and reminisce with Robertson and Finlay Calder. 'We were fortunate. We were all amateur and there was no social media. You feel sorry for the boys now. They can hardly have a pint of beer without a photo being taken and posted. We were very friendly with the media. When we went on tour the journalists would travel with us and we'd go out for a beer with them. They really knew the players well. I know that can't happen now, but it's such a shame. I just feel so fortunate to have played with so many good guys – and to have had a bit of success as well.'

* * * * *

Track down some of the grand old stagers of Scotland's only other modern slam, in 1990, and the bonds remain similarly tight. John Jeffrey and Sean Lineen are godfathers to each other's children and Lineen is also godfather to David Sole's son, Chris. Lineen and Gavin Hastings go cold water swimming together most Fridays and Kenny Milne and Craig Chalmers sometimes join them. Over 30 years later, laughter still ripples around the room whenever they meet.

The old stories still hold up well. Like the time Lineen, the first of the so-called kilted Kiwis, went to Stornaway to meet his grandfather's brother. The former centre still rolls his eyes at the memory of his teammates persuading him – 'They told me they only spoke Gaelic up there' – that greeting the locals, including the mayor and the regional TV cameras, with the words *Pogue Mahone* would endear him to all and sundry . . .

Then there was the players' collective desire to share a post-match pint away from the post-match formalities. 'After the games at Murrayfield we'd go back to the Carlton Highland hotel and, naturally, want to spend a bit of time with each other. The wives and girlfriends would also want to say well done and share the moment. So we invented the 'President's drinks reception'. All the boys would tell their partners they had to go to this function. But there wasn't one. We'd just go around to The Mitre on the Royal Mile. The girls would eventually come and collect us, hammered, at around midnight and we'd all go off to Buster Brown's nightclub or wherever.'

Thirsty work, clearly. Back in 1986 Jeffrey had been banned for five months by the Scottish Rugby Union for a late night kickabout with the Calcutta Cup trophy which had also involved England's Dean Richards (who was banned for a week). It did not curtail his enthusiasm for a well-earned pint on a Wednesday night after Jim Telfer decided his forwards needed an extra session prior to the whole squad gathering on a Thursday lunchtime.

'We'd have the mother of all hangovers on a Thursday morning and turn up as shabby as anything for training.'

One or two out-of-towners were thus required to stay overnight in Edinburgh. Soon enough Wednesday nights became the new Saturday nights. As Jeffrey recalls, 'We'd end up in this piano bar called Fingers, just off George Street, singing Neil Diamond until 3 a.m. We'd have the mother of all hangovers on a Thursday morning and turn up as shabby as anything for training. But if it helped the bonding you needed to have, then fine.' The extra sessions became so popular that even those based in England started travelling up the night before to avoid missing out.

Occasionally, in the pre-mobile phone era, this also proved a surprisingly good way of unearthing the latest team news. 'I remember being in Buster Brown's one Wednesday night in 1988,' continues Jeffrey. 'At 3 a.m. we were walking back, hammered, up the steps to our hotel and through the old *Scotsman* building where they printed the paper when one of the guys working on the printing presses spotted me.

'Hey JJ, I see you're in the team.'

'No, I'm on the bench. I've been dropped.'

'Well, that's not what it says in here.'

At which point his informant plucked a paper off the rolling presses to settle the debate. 'There was a headline saying, "Jeffrey back in the team, Derek Turnbull injured". I only found out because I was leaving a nightclub at 3 a.m.'

The truth of it, though, was that Scotland had a team which was not just tightly bonded but also increasingly blessed with talent. Lineen had noticed immediately, having been around enough blocks to know a decent side when he saw one. As a youngster in New Zealand, he had played for Counties against both the 1983 British & Irish Lions – with Rutherford as his direct opponent – and France. A spell in the police force in New Zealand had also provided him with a crash course in reality. 'You learned how to do two things: how to run and how to fight. Working in South Auckland was crazy. There was a lot going on: breaking up parties and fights, a lot of domestic disputes. A lot of trauma and aggression. You had to learn how to control your emotions as well. Sometimes it was the mother beating the dad up. One of my very first memories was this idyllic Sunday afternoon about 5 p.m. when a guy comes running out of a house with a hammer in his head shouting: "She's trying to kill me!" Then this big Samoan woman comes out screaming: "Don't come back!" I was 18 years old and thinking: *What's going on here?*

Lineen, whose father Terry represented the All Blacks against the touring 1959 Lions, was also part of the police cordon around the field in Wellington during the 1981 'flour bomb' Test – 'It really divided the country' – against South Africa, and life was almost as lively when he pitched up in Wales in 1985. 'What struck me was they were even more passionate about rugby than the Kiwis. Ray Prosser, Bobby Windsor, Eddie Butler, Dai 'Bish' Bishop. We played twice a week, so it was brutal. It was rugby 24/7, even more so than New Zealand.' Living in Usk they also crossed paths with some unlikely new friends. 'One Christmas I met Robert Plant in a bar and had a drinking session with him and his cronies. Paul Young had a recording studio in Usk . . . it was just mad. We got into a lot of trouble with a small "t". I had a fantastic time there.'

Once he fetched up at Boroughmuir in October 1988, however, his life changed almost instantly. He met his wife Lynne at an aerobics class within a few weeks and when people realised that his mother's maiden name was MacDonald his promotion to the Scottish national squad was swift. 'I was picked to play for Edinburgh against Australia at Myreside in

November. That was also my first taste of port. They had a band on that night and I remember me and Scott Hastings taking over on stage. And me trying to play the guitar – which I can't play.' He formed an instant bond with Hastings, who subsequently became his best man.

By the time he made his debut against Wales the following February, he felt among kindred souls. 'I think people underestimate how important team spirit is. How that dynamic works. Without realising it, we were pretty much all leaders. There were a lot of strong characters who talked and listened and pushed each other. We weren't afraid to criticise each other but we also enjoyed each other's company. I think that was really important. Teams have to work at that now, but we had it in spades.'

There were certain other factors in Scotland's rise. Both their 1984 and 1990 Grand Slams came directly off the back of British & Irish Lions tours. 'After 1989 we came back saying, "We're as good as our opposite numbers,"' recalls Jeffrey now. 'There was nothing to fear. We had the mentality that anything was achievable.'

Rugby in the Borders was also still strong, with top-notch players like Gary Armstrong coming through. 'We were kicking shit out of each other for Kelso, Melrose, Hawick or Gala,' recalls Jeffrey, whose blond hair, pale complexion and predatory playing style helped to popularise his long-time nickname, The Great White Shark. 'For some bizarre reason it made you stronger when you came together for the South of Scotland and stronger again when you came back. There were an awful lot of strong characters who probably captained their own club teams. They knew a bit about leadership . . . any number of them could probably have been captain.' Lineen recalls a correspondingly healthy media interest in club rugby. 'There was *Rugby Special* on terrestrial TV and and more coverage in the papers. Norman Mair in the *Scotsman*, Bill Lothian in the *Pink Un* on a Saturday night. The oxygen of publicity is less now.'

And, ladled on top of everything else, was the still-thriving coaching double act of Telfer and McGeechan. Even Kiwi-raised incomers like Lineen were impressed by their tactical and psychological expertise. 'The level of detail really opened my eyes. And how smart Jim and Geech were in terms of identifying what our strengths were. Our back row was probably our strength, along with Gary Armstrong. They always say you need five or six world-class players to be a winning side, and we had that. It was also the way they trained us. Geech would say to us, "Let's get as fit as any team." Whether we were or not, it gave us the sense we were. I think that was really important. Whether they inflated the fitness testing results, I don't know, but that was the message: *You're as fit as any other team*. We weren't going to lose out to anyone in the last 10 minutes.'

Jeffrey, Finlay Calder and Derek White, however, had worked out that Telfer would often single them out for special attention, conscious of their talismanic importance to Scotland's marauding game. As Jeffrey recalls, 'He was savage on us. Brutal. You couldn't get away with it in the modern world. Finlay, Derek and myself worked out that if we sat together we were an easy target. So we'd go and sit in separate parts of the room so he couldn't target us. He'd go mental. "Where are you, Jeffrey? Where are you, Calder?"'

The mischief extended to White's penchant for a wee dram the night before a game. 'Derek would always bring in a bottle of whisky. So on the Friday night before the team meeting he, Fin and I would have a couple of drams. I'm not a whisky drinker – I think the last time I drank whisky I got banned for five months – but one night we even got Geech in for a couple of drams. Geech then did the team talk full of whisky, which wasn't like him.'

White, though, was to be at the heart of Scotland's opening success against Ireland in 1990, scoring two tries in a 13–10 win in Dublin now infamous for the post-match team address by the then-Scotland president Jimmy McNeil. 'We hadn't played that well but we'd won,' remembers Lineen. 'We were sitting in the changing room when Jimmy McNeil came in and said, "Hard luck boys, better luck next time." He thought we'd lost.'

The second game against France at Murrayfield produced a stunning 21–0 scoreline, significantly helped by the sending-off of Alain Carminati for stamping on Jeffrey. From the latter's perspective it was a surreal day all round. 'We'd decided to play with the wind in the first half, but the wind changed at half time. We were saying, "We're going to get our arses kicked here." Instead, having lost Carminati, it was France who were blown away.'

Wales were subsequently beaten 13–9 in Cardiff, after which Jeffrey and the senior players laid down the law. 'We said, "Right, the only people who are going to speak to the media are Finlay, Soley, JJ and Gav. And we'll just major on how good England are." Everyone was building England up, ourselves included, because they had played fantastic rugby during that championship. They had basically spanked everyone, but I always preferred to play a team who had won the week before rather than lost. I always thought teams played a lot harder the second week because they'd be fighting for their survival.'

Unbeknown to anyone else, Jeffrey also had another hurdle to surmount prior to the England game. 'I'd been shooting on a neighbour's farm and he'd said to me, "You need to start riding horses and go hunting with me." Now I'd never

'I always preferred to play a team who had won the week before rather than lost.'

ridden but this chap had lost a kid to cot death and was raising funds for a cot-death charity. Of course, I said yes, only to discover the date he wanted me to get on a horse for the first time in my life was the Wednesday after the Wales game. Unknown to the SRU I had to go and do it. I could very easily have fallen off that horse, injured myself and been out of the Grand Slam game. It's bonkers to think about it now: on this muckle [big] horse jumping fences, probably helped by a couple of very strong stirrup cups.'

For the rest of the team, the preparations that week were stern-faced. The rest is rugby legend: Scotland's slow, deliberate walk out on to the field, English overconfidence, the haunting strains of 'Flower of Scotland', Tony Stanger's try (did he touch the ball down cleanly, your honour?), the 13–7 scoreline, the grandest of slams. Perhaps most telling of all is that Scotland have not managed another one since. 'We've only ever won three, so to win two within six years of each other with completely different teams is mind-blowing,' says Jeffrey, now World Rugby's vice-chairman. 'When I'm watching Scotland play now, I just want them to still be within a score with 20 minutes left. I'd settle for winning a championship first before winning a Grand Slam. We've got a good cohort of players but we've got to get our strongest team on the pitch every week.'

Lineen, on a benign summer Saturday in Edinburgh, feels likewise. 'At the time it was a big deal, but I didn't realise how big a deal it was. And as time goes on, it gets bigger. That's why we're all going: "Come on, guys!"

41

We'd love someone else to do it.' So, could it still happen? 'Yeah. It needs to happen at some stage but it's getting harder and harder. We're a small rugby-playing country. We haven't got many players who take it seriously, we haven't got many players who understand the sacrifice it takes. People also don't understand that it's always been cyclical. What right have we got? It's going to take a number of things to come together.'

History also records that Scotland came very close to beating the All Blacks on tour in New Zealand that same summer. And the squad, reckons Lineen, were sporting trailblazers in another lesser-known respect. 'Everyone's now belting out "Sweet Caroline", but do you know where it started? It was Fin Calder's tour song on our team bus in 1990. We thought, *This is the best song ever!* He was a man ahead of his time.'

What a diamond of a team they were, now and then. These days Murrayfield is encircled by higher, more enclosed stands and there is less opportunity to recite the opening line of Psalm 121 and lift up mine eyes unto the hills. But the second verse of 'Flower of Scotland', sung loud and unaccompanied, still prickles the hairs on your neck and the game day expectancy on a big weekend north of the border is, for me, unsurpassed. The only thing missing is another of those elusive Grand Slams.

4

TAKE ME TO THE RIVER

We played beautiful rugby – and rugby 10 years
ahead of its time.

One of the strengths of rugby in Britain – and sometimes its Achilles heel – is its huge regional contrasts. We often talk about English rugby as if it were some easily identifiable, homogenous pile of blazers just off the A316 in Twickenham. It is a stereotype that's hard to shift. As the biggest (and wealthiest) union in the world, England is often the least loved. The only characteristic upon which their neighbours agree is their alleged arrogance. Which, for the most part, is complete tripe. If you head to Cornwall or Gloucestershire or Leicester or Northumberland, you will encounter down-to-earth rugby diehards who are a million miles removed from the entitled stereotype.

Part of the equation is football's all-encompassing profile. The national sport increasingly swamps all else, and media coverage these days is as skewed towards the round ball as it has ever been. This can cause occasional misunderstandings. When I first arrived in old Fleet Street as a trainee coffee boy at Hayters Sports Agency in 1984, I soon learned two unwritten rules. One was to make the coffee badly, otherwise you might be handled the kettle permanently and never escape the office. The other was that people in London spoke a different language. In those days rugby results would be phoned in, usually by a half-pissed club secretary from a crackling payphone, for inclusion in the following day's papers. One weekend someone called to inform us of the final scoreline in the big Cornish derby between Camborne and Redruth. Next day a team called Red Roof made the nationals.

With no fax machine to take the strain (not yet part of the office furniture), we would be required to type up the day's minor league football scores – complete with sheets of carbon paper – and then run them around every Fleet Street newspaper office by hand. I am currently staring at a black and white photo from the mid-1980s, another relic from a bygone era. It shows a cheerful youth (with hair, remarkably) sitting at an absurdly bulky manual typewriter.

It was a tough school, but you learned swiftly enough from your mistakes. The rugby environment, meanwhile, remained resolutely amateur. Even at some of the bigger clubs, spectators still stood on pitchside duckboards, clutching battered hip flasks. England played international matches in front of wooden stands and, as Hignell had discovered, the Twickenham grass was so long and thick you could virtually hide a schoolboy scrum half in it. The phone number of the Rugby Football Union was ex-directory and 'mobile' was a word sometimes applied to open-side flankers.

Amateurism was still in its pomp. Tweed remained the press box's fabric of choice and Hospitals Cup matches still merited full reports in the broadsheets. I was handed the young, thrusting title of Old Boys' Rugby Correspondent for the *Daily Telegraph*, which basically involved phoning random clubhouses and asking if something interesting had happened. One club in south-west London advised me that their half backs had been excellent and had scored all their points. I asked for their names. 'Sure. They're called Steve Kick and Paul Chase . . .' Hmmm. In went the story and on we went.

Otherwise my typical mid-1980s beat would involve trips to a sparsely populated London Welsh, Richmond or Harlequins on a Saturday afternoon. If a Welsh club were involved, there would normally be at least two or three Welsh papers requiring bespoke copy. This would require me to scribble frantically into a notebook before tearing off the barely decipherable pages and giving them to my invaluable 'phonist' Hugh Godwin, now the esteemed correspondent of the *i* newspaper, who would then gallantly dictate the words to a splendidly bored copytaker. Regular radio updates might be required as well, which was a problem at London Welsh because the payphone in the groundsman's shed under the stand was out of sight of the pitch.

'What's the latest score?'

'Um, still nine-all, I think.'

Looking back, it was a miracle anything appeared in the papers, particularly at the more convivial venues. Most Christmases I would volunteer to go to London Irish's old home at Sunbury, ostensibly to cover their annual festive fixture against Old Millhillians. It was lovely and cosy in the old upstairs bar with few patrons paying close attention to the actual game. By the second half pretty much the only way to keep abreast of on-field developments was to rub the occasional hole in the condensation on the windows. 'Dear boy, have you any idea who scored the try?' was the soundtrack to my professional youth.

And what characters roamed the inky-fingered sports pages! I well remember sitting in the East India Club listening to the then-chairman of the International Rugby Board seeking to advise the *Daily Mail*'s highly experienced correspondent what line he might take the following day. The outraged, thunderous response – 'You are the lawmakers. We are the phrase-makers!' – should be etched on every press room wall.

Slowly but surely, though, times changed. Computers and chunky mobile phones materialised, the tweed quotient diminished and it became harder to spend one's whole working day down the pub entertaining 'contacts'. The problem, in the end, was of a practical nature: dictating lucid copy after four or five pints is still feasible (with a bit of practice) but typing accurately on a computer when drunk is not.

I also well remember doing a double take the first time I saw a well-known player – Rob Andrew – drinking something other than an alcoholic drink after a club game. Press officers would frequently offer a warming brandy at half time, and if you phoned a club player up at their place of work for an interview they tended to assume it was a wind-up. Once, in early 1985, I was invited at the last minute to stand in for my boss at the post-match dinner after England's game against Romania at Twickenham. I found myself seated next to Austin Sheppard, the Bristol prop who had been an unused replacement. Aware I would shortly be required to phone a Bristol player to preview their upcoming John Player Cup tie, I asked Austin if he would mind giving me his number. 'Why do you want to talk to me?' he asked, not unreasonably. What I didn't know was that, in real life, he was an undertaker. Let's just say it wasn't ideal timing when I rang him in the chapel of rest a few days later.

The annual national knock-out Cup, though, was my favourite competition. Not only did it possess an FA Cup-type resonance, but David still had a faint chance of upsetting Goliath. It seems crazy now, but as recently as the 1986–87 season Old Reigatians emerged victorious against Exeter and Saracens before going to Kingsholm and giving Gloucester a genuine contest in the last 16.

Being the Old Boys' Rugby Correspondent at the time, it was my good fortune to cover both those Saracens and Gloucester games. The story was almost too good to be true. Before the Saracens encounter, the Old Reigatians pack had been invited to practise on a neighbouring club's scrummaging machine but, in freezing weather, had been unable to adjust the settings. As a result they ended up scrummaging lower than normal, took the opposition by surprise and ended up winning 12–10. Afterwards the Saracens skipper treated us to his party trick which involved bashing a metal-rimmed drinks tray on his head until it was entirely flat. Different times, and all that.

Nowadays the plucky amateurs would be annihilated, but Gloucester beat them 18–6 at Kingsholm in a closer game than the scoreline suggests. The dawn of professionalism, though, shifted the goalposts. Perhaps the last hurrah came in 1999 when Saracens, Francois Pienaar and all, travelled down to Lydney's Regentsholme ground. While the Fancy Dans won 40–0, it was not a cosy experience. One local spectator even seized the Irish international lock Paddy Johns from behind and tried to drag him into the crowd. The magic of the Cup meant something else in the Forest of Dean where, to quote the *Independent*'s Chris Hewett, visitors from the big smoke rarely went home entirely unscathed. 'London sides, in particular, were considered fair game by the hill people of the West Country, who licked their lips with cannibalistic intent whenever they caught sight of a pampered Wasp or a mollycoddled Harlequin . . .'

* * * * *

From the mid-1980s onwards, though, the real power in the land were Bath. Among my assignments on wintry Mondays was to gather material for the tournament's weekly press releases. This would involve phoning anyone with a pulse to gather a few quotes about that week's upcoming ties. Luckily the most easily contactable skipper in the country was Bath's Roger Spurrell, who ran a nightclub out of a converted city centre public convenience on what the locals affectionately call Bog Island. As long as you didn't ring him too early, the hard-edged Spurrell was more than happy to chat rugby.

His club had won the Cup for the first time in 1984, courtesy of a missed late penalty by Stuart Barnes – then of Bristol – and were clearly a talented side on their way up. Simon Halliday and John Palmer were quality international centres and the skilful half backs Richard Hill and John Horton both toured South Africa with England that summer. Up front, at Spurrell's elbow, were the heavy-duty likes of Gareth Chilcott, John Hall and Nigel Redman, all England internationals as well. To nobody's surprise they won the Cup again in 1985, this time at London Welsh's expense. If you wanted flowing rugby with a hard edge, it was to be found on the banks of the River Avon.

Ask Halliday now and he still insists the foundations of the most compelling team in English club rugby history – they won 10 domestic cups and 6 league titles in 13 years between 1984 and 1996 – did not involve Barnes, the brilliant Jeremy Guscott, the future England head coach Andy Robinson or many of the other household names who subsequently joined the party. 'Even then we realised we had something. We put 60 points on Neath in November 1983, for example. If you look through the results over that period, they were quite unbelievable. People talk about Barnes or Robinson being touchpapers. That was actually after it started.'

Another crucial catalyst was Tom Hudson, who had been Llanelli's fitness coach when they famously beat the All Blacks in 1972. 'He was ex-SAS, an ex-Olympic modern pentathlete and the director of sport at the University of Bath. His opening line to us was, "I've been watching you play for the last 12 months and none of you are fit enough." We all went, "Um, okay. This guy doesn't even know who we are."'

Constructive criticism, though, was rarely an issue in the ever-competitive Bath environment. Hudson's message hit home soon enough. 'He was right,' recalls Halliday. 'So on a Thursday at the end of training we would replicate the last 20 minutes of a match. By the end of it we'd be hanging, it was so tough.' Every now and again Hudson would sidle up to a wheezing player, bent double with hands on knees, and murmur, "This is what will define you." And sure enough it did. 'We'd beat sides by 30 points and they'd say, "Where did that come from?"' remembers Halliday. 'It was because we'd gone up another gear. No one could live with us.'

'[Hudson's] opening line to us was, "I've been watching you play for the last 12 months and none of you are fit enough."'

He remembers the team being similarly committed even without the ball. 'One of our best defensive performances came when we were 35 points up and Spurrell just said, "They're not going to score a try." It mattered to us because we'd decided we were going to send them away with a nil. We had a really hard edge in terms of how we wanted teams to think about us. I never lost a game at the Rec in eight years. That doesn't just happen.'

The mix of different characters in the dressing room, few of them short of an opinion, poured further fuel on the fire. The fast-emerging Guscott was local, but no one was more committed to the cause than the fiendishly competitive hooker Graham Dawe, who drove hundreds of miles up from the Cornwall–Devon border every week to train and play. Hill arrived from Salisbury, Barnes from Bristol and some of the arguments were epic. As Halliday puts it, 'You had all these different people who only barely tolerated each other from time to time, particularly on the field. There was lots of arguing.

'We had violent disagreements, for example, about whether we should go up the short side or kick a high ball. And all the time I'd have Jerry Guscott next to me saying, "This is so boring, when are we going to get

48

the ball?" We had 15 leaders on the pitch . . . everyone wanted to be captain. We had to be told to shut up on a number of occasions. But we never argued to the point where we diminished our own performances. We were trying to get the best out of each other.'

* * * * *

Tempted out on a midweek lunchtime to one of his local pubs in Wiltshire – literary inspiration does not necessarily flow from mineral water alone – Barnes needs little invitation to play devil's advocate. In retrospect, he reckons this chapter should be about Leicester. Or maybe it is Saracens' modern European crusaders who deserve to be hailed as the best English club side of all time. 'We won a lot more trophies than everyone else put together but we never did back-to-back doubles. I think we were great with a small "g". We needed to win back-to-back doubles to be great with a capital "G". To me the greatest club team of my lifetime has been Dean Richards' Leicester. Followed by Saracens, because they kept winning Europe. We would have won Europe, but it didn't exist, so we couldn't.'

He might have a point. Comparisons between eras can be horribly subjective. But let there be no doubt about the central premise: Bath, in the era of their tall, idiosyncratic coaching guru Jack Rowell, were miles ahead of the curve. 'Bath wouldn't be a Premiership side now without Jack,' insists Barnes, whose 'Judas' switch from Bristol to Bath was made at Rowell's behest in 1985. 'When I first joined the club, we'd sometimes train at the Rec and afterwards we'd go and have a cup of tea or half a pint in the committee bar. I remember looking up at the mementos of Bath's glory years. One of them involved an unbeaten tour with wins over Weston-super-Mare, Taunton and maybe Bridgwater. I'd played against Bath as an 18-year-old for Newport and a fat bloke called Chilcott gave me a few problems. But we essentially fielded two-thirds of a second team. If we'd been playing Gloucester or Bristol we wouldn't have done that. Bath were next to nothing until Rowell arrived from the north-east. Everything starts with Rowell.'

I liked Rowell, too, for journalistic reasons. The *Telegraph*'s rugby correspondent, John Mason, was unavailable one Friday and the call went out for someone – anyone – to deputise. I remember sitting nervously in John's seat in the *Telegraph* office on Fleet Street and staring at his typewriter, which was attached to a central column by a metal chain to stop anyone stealing it. As well as working out how to use this unfamiliar piece of equipment, I desperately needed someone to talk to about the following day's rugby. When Jack phoned me back, I could have hugged him.

Barnes, who was as close to Rowell as anyone, reels off a lengthy list of attributes, starting with the business acumen that also set him apart off the field. 'He wasn't the most professional manager around in those early days, he was the only one. He took his corporate ability as a managing director and applied it to rugby. I asked him about it once and he said, "I always look two years ahead, that's the key." Nobody else was doing that. He was looking at players we hadn't even heard of. The plan was for them to come in and eventually take our places, to keep the pressure on us. Jack also understood man-management like no one else. Again it was a corporate skill. Chilcott was playing for Old Redcliffians in Bristol: it was quite a good standard but rough rugby. No one other than Jack would have got him. Bath already had Roger Spurrell, who was an aggressive catalyst, but he wanted a horrible little psycho.'

Tactically, Rowell also knew precisely what was needed. 'Jack saw a team as a spine. It was the spine which did the dirty deeds and made the big decisions. Throughout his career at Bath, Jack knew who he needed to maintain the balance. He knew how to press players' buttons. He'd be nice to me – "We need you, Stuart" – and horrible to my mate Richard Hill. Hilly would come in after a game and go, "That'll show the bugger." With me it was always, "You're the man." I'm sure I wasn't the only one, but he always said it because that's what brought the best out of me in a Bath shirt. I think Jack saw a kindred spirit . . . he knew what made me tick, that what I was best at was managing a game. Jack allowed me to take tactical control."

Underpinning the brains, though, was a collectively hard physical and mental edge which Rowell actively encouraged. 'Jack would say, "In the nicest possible way, so-and-so has to be off the pitch." I would then reiterate, in a very cold-blooded way, that the only reason we were there was to win. We weren't there to play rugby or entertain. We were there to win the game, the league or the cup. Ultimately that preoccupation with winning held us back, but it was our driving motivation.' Bath's hard nuts always knew precisely what was expected of them.

'I'd go away with the backs to talk about one or two technical things and hear eight blokes on the other side of the changing room screaming. Well, either screaming or so silent you thought there was going to be an assassination. There was always that duality of responsibility: tactical and physical.'

> **'The biggest regret of my career is that we became so obsessed with winning that we wouldn't take risks.'**

And sitting there, with the pub's front window behind him, a more urgent tone enters Barnes' voice. Suddenly all the intervening years – the Sky studios, the *Times* columns, the Bob Dylan albums – melt away and he is back where he found true fulfilment. 'We were no different to any great team. The first thing you want to do is win. All these years on, I wish we hadn't been quite so obsessed about having to win every game. But to be a great team you've got to extend your ambitions to and beyond the boundaries. The biggest regret of my career is that we became so obsessed with winning that we wouldn't take risks. But I wouldn't have been me – and we wouldn't have been us – had that not been the case.'

For Barnes it was almost a physical affliction. 'When I got home from work on a Friday before a Saturday game, my wife couldn't speak to me because of my tension. I felt sick with fear. I'd lie in the bath on a Friday night and think through the game, from the other team kicking off to Nigel Redman catching it and where we'd go next. I'm regarded as a fairly relaxed bloke, but I'd be absolutely wound up. No one would say a word in the house if we'd lost. It very rarely happened but when it did it was terrible. When we won there was very little joy. Just massive relief.'

Significant defeats – and there were a few notable ones to Moseley, Leicester and Waterloo in the Cup – would essentially send the entire club into crisis mode. Barnes did not play in the 4–3 quarter-final loss to Moseley in February 1988 because he was coming back from a broken cheekbone, but every detail of the inquest is still fresh. 'I can remember the devastation. I'd played for the second team that afternoon and remember saying, "We've got to get back to the Rec now." We had to address the pain and channel it. It felt like a council of war. I can remember spending ages talking to Jack. I think he was probably blaming me for having a broken cheekbone.' He did not play against Waterloo, either, having accepted an invitation to play for the Barbarians instead.

It was a slightly different story when Leicester came down to the Rec in the Pilkington Cup third round in 1990 and won 12–0. The Recreation Ground in midwinter was notoriously heavy and neutered Bath's attacking prowess, narrowing their focus significantly. 'In the Leicester game we got tactically done. The Rec was a bog and Brian Smith kicked every ball he got in behind us. Dean Richards had the most monumental game and imposed himself against Jon Hall. He took us and Hally on and, on our own patch, beat us at our game. I remember getting back into the changing room afterwards and it was like someone had died. For two years I'd been wearing a pair of lucky red socks. I never lost when I wore them. That evening I walked outside to the weir and threw them as far into the river as I could.'

* * * * *

On other days, though, Bath were so good they almost startled themselves. Particularly on the dry, firm grounds of early autumn and spring, they could be unstoppable. Those present still marvel at the September day in 1988 when, in the opening game of Barnes' first season as captain, they travelled over to mighty Pontypool and beat them 50–9. 'Pooler', who had lost just two games the previous season and were the Welsh Merit Table champions, were simply run off the park.

Even now Barnes reckons it was Bath's finest hour and 20 minutes. 'I don't think we ever played a better game. I stood at fly half and looked great because I was throwing flat passes at this young kid called Guscott.

But none of that works if you can't confront teams like Pontypool. Most English clubs couldn't physically handle them . . . they were miners, they were steel workers, they were hard working men. English rugby, essentially, was very middle class. Jack changed that by getting in a Cornish fisherman who had been a paratrooper and a rough diamond like Chilcott. The worse it got in Wales, the more they liked it. That made life an awful lot easier for the rest of us because it meant we could play on the front foot.'

Bath went unbeaten for 30 matches that season, not losing until mid-February. They had great individuals but, as Barnes says, the real power was collective. 'Playing for Bath you were very rarely seen as a great player. You were part of a great team. Jerry Guscott used to get the shit ripped out of him because he'd become a superstar. There weren't superstars at Bath, no matter how well you'd played. You were part of Jack's package. We were very good at learning from our errors. People don't remember the ugly wins, but we still tend to remember the ones when we weren't that good and nicked it.'

There was a touch of the theatrical, even so, woven into the blue, black and white tapestry. Bath were the only high-performing sports club in the country where fully laden trays of gin and tonic would be borne aloft through the Bath clubhouse by current international players after matches. And when it came to gamesmanship, Barnes and co would happily oblige. 'When I was captain and we played Gloucester away, I made it policy that we wore blazers and bow ties and walked over to The Shed. Some of the things said to us wound up our boys so much that Gloucester didn't have a hope of beating us. Jack would giggle away because he knew exactly what we were doing.'

To ratchet things up further, Rowell then invited in the enlightened Brian Ashton, teaching nearby in Bruton, to help sharpen Bath's attacking game. It took half a season before things really started to hum, but Ashton insisted Barnes had to play flat to the advantage line to maximise the benefit of Hill's pass, the longest and quickest in the land. 'Brian changed our back play. We had fast men, skilful men and, suddenly, we were threatening on the gain line. I found myself able to see where the space was and the Bath backline was absolutely transformed. We played beautiful rugby – and rugby 10 years ahead of its time.'

Which, of course, begs the old question of whether the England team of that vintage should also have spread their wings a little more. Instead Rob Andrew was largely preferred at 10. Barnes, the 'people's choice', had to be content with the occasional cameo, notably the break from deep inside his own half against Scotland in 1993 which caused an entire nation to purr in appreciation. What a shame it was that he played just one further game for England.

'As I got older, you realise selection isn't about being better or worse. It's about what suits.'

The passage of time, though, has encouraged a greater degree of acceptance and understanding. 'If I'd have been trusted and in charge and been playing the Bath way, maybe I'd have liked England a lot more. I was just never comfortable for England. They were controlled by the pack and I didn't need 30 caps to start being me. At the time I was really resentful because I thought I was better than Rob Andrew. But as I got older, you realise selection isn't about being better or worse. It's about what suits. Rob suited an England team that had a great big line-out, a big scrum and big ball carriers.'

And given his chance again, Barnes also accepts he could have been more diplomatic, rather than pointedly making himself unavailable for national selection. 'Maybe I should have just kept my head down or practised my kicking more. And in retrospect I used the fact I didn't have any patriotic bones in my body to cover the fact I had a disappointing [Test] career. Maybe it was sour grapes. I made errors but it was easy for me to make the errors I made because of the structure, ferocity and ambition at Bath.'

It is equally fair to say that umpteen Bath teams have tried – and failed – to rekindle those glory days over the last quarter of a century. In truth, they have had an impossible act to follow, even if Barnes and his old friends would never say as much. 'It feels immodest to say I was part of a great team. I always fear the old-farty "In my day . . ." thing. It was a bit easier then because there weren't as many dangerous opponents. But when Leicester fans talk about our rivalry in those days I say, "What rivalry?" When I was playing for Bath, you won one league and one Cup. We won five leagues and seven Cups.'

'I also remember someone saying, after we beat Harlequins in extra time to win the 1992 Cup final, that we should have shared the trophy. I said to them, "You don't understand Bath, we don't share things." To draw with Harlequins – and they'd been the better team that day – would have been a psychological defeat of such epic proportions that 10 of us would probably have thrown ourselves on to the fast lane of the M4. We couldn't have taken it.' Which, for younger readers, is precisely the reason the legends of Bath endure to this day.

5

ALL ABOARD THE CHARIOT

I've never been a comic-book hero, I've never been an arrogant bastard. I'm somewhere in-between.

It is a Wednesday afternoon in London's Mayfair. If you're visiting from out of town, it feels like another planet. There is even a chauffeur-driven Rolls-Royce idling on the side of New Bond Street, waiting for its elegant passenger to re-emerge from one of the reassuringly expensive fashion houses. Dior, Givenchy . . . if I keep walking, they might fail to spot my crumpled trousers. Into Albemarle Street, and the front window of Tiffany's sparkles seductively. The only thing missing is Hugh Grant, flashing a rakish grin and ushering a glamorous companion across the road to Brown's Hotel for a drink.

In the foyer of Brown's, as it happens, I bump into a blonde South African woman of a certain age who advises me to head straight for the bar and enjoy one of their bespoke cocktails. 'The guy who makes them is famous,' she pronounces, just as the most recognisable British rugby player of his era strides into the building behind her. Not as well known as this bloke, I think, even a quarter of a century after he retired.

Will Carling has proposed the venue and, until the bill turns up, it feels just right. If anyone ended up elevating English rugby from the cellar to the penthouse, on and off the field, it was the man once affectionally known as Bum-Chin. He was the face of the sweet chariot, a regular on the front and back pages. He captained his country for eight years and monochrome moments were few. To certain people he epitomised pretty much everything they loved to hate about the English.

Which is what makes him intriguing company now, as the nearby pianist tinkles her way through 'A Nightingale Sang in Berkeley

Square'. Carling was 22 when Geoff Cooke, the national team manager, made him captain in 1988. England were underachieving and had already been through four other skippers in a little over a year. When Cooke called him, Carling assumed he was ringing to tell him he was dropped.

Sworn to secrecy about his surprise new appointment, he stood uneasily at the bar at Harlequins listening to his teammates discussing who would be the next national skipper. His name was not even mentioned. 'I remember saying to them, "Well, I think it might be me!"' His colleagues snorted derisively and resumed their debate, blissfully unaware what was about to unfold. 'When Geoff announced it to the squad in the Petersham Hotel, there was just this silence. Years later I spoke to Peter Winterbottom about it. He said they all wandered off to the bar and said, "Two games, four max."'

Right there and then, though, Carling felt himself being cast away to someone else's island. 'When you put the phone down, it feels fairly life-changing. And it was for me. Good and bad.' An Army scholarship to attend university had also meant receiving some officer training, so he had a veneer of confidence, but inside he was panic-stricken. 'There's this view that you must be this supremely confident guy because you captained England at 22. Well, I wasn't. You look back and think, *How on earth did I stand up?* In the end it was because I hated losing in that shirt more than I was petrified.'

His first Test as skipper, against Australia in November 1988, was momentous. An England captain even younger than we were? Still a student at Durham Uni? It felt a big deal even to those of us backpacking around Oz at the time. I'd assumed, naively, that the rugby would be showing in every bar in the southern hemisphere. Brian, an electrician with a golden ear stud who was also staying in our hostel in Perth, was less confident. 'AFL's the game, mate,' he drawled, blowing the froth off another gaseous lager in a deserted pub in Fremantle. Just up the street we discovered another sawdust-strewn dive where a local heavy metal band were busy tuning up. In the back bar, though, we found a tiny television stuck high on the wall. Using the thick end of a pool cue we could just about reach the power button. Alleluia! There was Twickers, in all its wintry, splintery glory.

Carling, rather closer to the action, still cannot quite believe how everything panned out. A dry, sunny afternoon proved to be an auspicious one as England finally cast off their shackles and played the kind of rugby their supporters had been craving. Two sharp second-half tries for the flying Rory Underwood on the wing, a charge-down finish by the scrum half Dewi Morris on his debut and, late on, a try for Simon Halliday with Carling smashed in the act of giving the scoring pass. The final score was 28–19 and the new captain's early nerves – 'You're shitting yourself, but I was just focusing so hard on what I needed to do' – were replaced by overwhelming relief. 'The greatest thing for me, bizarrely, was the fact I got knocked out near the end and had three minutes in the changing room before the rest of the team came back in.' It was only then that the whole magnitude of his appointment finally hit him. 'The truth is I just sat there and cried. I was just so relieved it hadn't been a disaster. I remember wiping my face so that no one would see the tears.'

> **'Everyone has this image of Will Carling. But I've never understood who that bloke is meant to be.'**

Almost 25 years later, this might seem hard to believe. Amateur era or not, a winning England captain with a rueful smile and a muscular charm was very definitely box office. Carling, though, now says he was impersonating someone else right from the outset. 'Everyone has this image of Will Carling. But I've never understood who that bloke is meant to be. I can understand where it comes from. I didn't help it because I never opened up to anyone media-wise. How was anyone meant to know that person is not really similar to how you really are? I've never been a comic-book hero, I've never been an arrogant bastard. I'm somewhere in-between. With the same amount of flaws as anyone else but riddled with insecurity as well.'

The problem was that most people could not see beyond the public persona. 'On the pitch you're England captain and you want to transmit a bit of confidence to you and your players. We're good and we're going to win this. There's a massive difference between what you're trying to portray at that moment and who you are. But that's the thing with sport. You can watch someone on the pitch and think, *Arrogant bastard*. But that's them performing. They're trying to win. You're a completely different person out there.'

There is no getting away from the fact, though, that Carling was the poster boy for English rugby for nine years. Think of the early Carling years and you are transported back to a different age, when Margaret Thatcher has just been re-elected as prime minister for a third term. In 1988 George Michael, Michael Jackson, Phil Collins and Bobby McFerrin all topped the charts and the biggest sporting story was Ben Johnson's disqualification in the 100 metres final at the Seoul Olympics. Tellingly, perhaps, the Premier League did not commence until 1992. It was an ideal moment for rugby to nudge its way into the spotlight.

Or to put it another way, from Carling's perspective, there was no escape. 'I'm sure someone like Simon Halliday must have thought, *It could have been me*. I had been watching all those guys on TV. They were my heroes. Even being in the same team as them was quite mind-blowing. There's a part of me that wishes I'd had more time just to be a player. I think I could have been quite different and made more of a mark. I went up to see Geoff with my wife Lisa five or six years ago. Lisa's mum lives near him, so I said, "We'll go and have lunch with Geoff." And I asked him why he made me captain. He just replied, "It was the last roll of the dice really." But he had a slight smile on his lips, as if to say, "I'm not going to blow smoke up your arse." So he's never really told me exactly why.'

The record books insist it was an inspired decision. Carling played 72 times for his country and captained them 59 times, leading England to victory on 44 occasions. Under him England won three Five Nations Grand Slams in 1991, 1992 and 1995 and reached the 1991 World Cup final. Aside from the 2003 World Cup winning squad, no English rugby team has enjoyed such high levels of public recognition before or since.

Would it all have happened had Cooke anointed someone else? Probably. But what if Carling had stayed one of the boys rather than being thrust on to such a pedestal? Or if the captains, as now, had been slightly less of a figurehead than their coaches? It is an interesting topic and, you suspect, one that Carling has contemplated more than once. 'I'm the type of guy who, if I walk in a room, prefers to stand in the corner and have a look. You can do that if you're Joe Bloggs. If you are England captain and you're young you're meant to walk in and go, "I'm here!" I fucking hate that. That's never been me. So it swiftly becomes a case of, "You're arrogant. You're aloof."'

That was certainly the prevailing view in Scotland. Rarely has any nation enjoyed a win more than the Scots did in 1990, having won a Grand Slam themselves and simultaneously denied the favourites England the same prize with a fabled 13–7 win at Murrayfield. It took a good while for Carling to get over it. 'I hated losing. I still do, even in the garden at home. I was obsessed by it and it consumed me for those eight to ten years. That 1990 disappointment lasted us five or six years; it drove us. Not because of the result, necessarily, but all the mistakes we made. People say, "You lost to Scotland." I say, "No, we were beaten by Scotland." There's a difference. They out-thought us and outplayed us. That's the bit that hurts. As captain I made loads of mistakes: in preparation, in the game.'

It was only subsequently, though, that he properly snapped. 'I remember doing an interview with a Scottish journalist in the Café Royal in Edinburgh. He goes, "Right, last question, Will. How do you feel about the fact that the whole of Scotland hates you?" I remember leaning forward and replying: "That's fine. Because I fucking hate you a damn sight more than you hate me." I remember he dropped his pen. He picked it up and said, "You can't say that." I said to him, "That's what really pisses me off. You're allowed to say you hate us, but we can't hate you back." Luckily he didn't put it in his article. But I wanted us to be as passionate about playing for England and you're not allowed to be.

'It's history, isn't it? If England try to be passionate, they're accused of being arrogant. When the Welsh or the Scots are passionate, we go: "That's nice." But we're not allowed to be like that. Even the English seem to like one-off wins more than consistent success. It's not something we're brought up to aspire to. It's almost like not English. It's only when you look back that you appreciate it. We won three Grand Slams in five years. And we've only had two since. People talk to me now and go: "Those times were great." But, if you remember, at the time we were always being told we were boring. It's funny how it changes.'

* * * * *

For another perspective I've invited myself down to Paul Ackford's kitchen in north Cornwall. If anyone knew Carling well in those early years it was his Harlequins and England teammate who made his Test debut, aged 30, in that same 1988 game against Australia. 'Ackers' also possesses one of the sport's more striking CVs. Imagine being an inspector in the Metropolitan Police at the same time as playing lock forward for England – and then turning to journalism afterwards. Could it be that he enjoys confrontation?

He was also the first sportsperson, to my knowledge, to knock out Sunday newspaper columns on games in which he'd just played. 'I just used to write it in longhand on the bus, sitting in the corner of the back seat. The guys used to take the piss unreservedly. Then, once we'd driven up to the Hilton where the post-match dinners were held, I'd phone it through to copy from our room while my wife, Suzie, was getting ready. I remember when we lost that Grand Slam game at Murrayfield in 1990. The sports editor of the *Observer* was gobsmacked the copy still arrived.'

It was truly a remarkable effort, although these days he usually only gets asked about the day in 1990 when he was knocked out by a punch from the 18-year-old Argentine Federico Méndez at Twickenham. 'Twenty-two England caps, three Lions Tests, a World Cup final appearance and all I'm remembered for is being the victim of a punch by an 18-year-old schoolboy.' On top of all that, though, he also helped Carling write his autobiography and was the colleague to whom the young England captain turned when he was trying to get a grip on the captaincy role. 'I lived in

Wandsworth and he was in Clapham. What he wanted was a sounding board. He didn't want to go to the older players because I don't think he wanted to be beholden to them.

'We used to go out and have curries during the week and he'd ask my opinion about how things were going. But it only lasted for as long as it took him to get his feet under the table. By then he'd worked out what he needed to do and he'd got his confidence up. He was mentally quite tough right from the start – and he also had a plan.'

In Ackford's opinion, Cooke's quiet, unselfish guidance should also not be underestimated while the freakish strength of England forwards such as Wade Dooley, Mike Teague and Dean Richards was another key ingredient in England's success. Most of the time they were unshakeable, save for occasional days like the Murrayfield Grand Slam decider when Ackford acknowledges overconfidence was part of their undoing.

'Twenty-two England caps, three Lions Tests, a World Cup final appearance and all I'm remembered for is being the victim of a punch by an 18-year-old schoolboy.'

'About 15 minutes into that Murrayfield game I gave away a breakdown penalty, which I wouldn't ordinarily have done. It was down to the pressure of the occasion and I remember thinking, *We're in trouble here*. We just couldn't get the pressure and dominance we were used to.

'It was such a momentous defeat and you felt the visceral disappointment of it. But afterwards I remember Wade Dooley and I saying, "Right, we're not going to hide away, we're going to take this on the chin." So we went into a pub on the Royal Mile for a couple of pints before the post-match dinner. As we walked in the whole place fell silent. People didn't quite know how to react. In the end, though, they were all saying, "Well done for coming out" . . . It was just sport.'

Like everyone else, though, Ackford reminisces fondly about an era when players lived a life that could stray beyond the tramlines of their sport. He remembers, for example, being contacted by Teague who had decided to take up riding but couldn't find a horse large enough to support his sizeable frame. 'He said, "Ackers, I can't find a horse that's big enough for me." So I rang up the Met Police stables and managed to find him a retired old police horse.'

The passing years, though, have loosened a few of the brotherly bonds. Ackford retired after the 1991 World Cup final – 'I didn't want to be dropped basically . . . I was arrogant enough to think I wanted to call it a day myself' – and is wary of excessive, treacle-coated nostalgia. 'They are funny relationships, those team friendships. Everyone thinks you're best mates and, for a time, you are. Partly it's proximity, partly it's frequency and partly the shared objective. But when you get dropped or retire you move on to different things.'

Either way, he remains convinced the loss to Scotland was the catalyst for all the success that followed. 'It's a cliché but it's true. Defeat fuels you more than victory. The memory of 1990 fuelled the whole thing, really. You don't get many chances to achieve those sorts of things.'

* * * * *

Back in Mayfair there is still some tea in the pot and Carling sounds suitably reflective. If that 1991 World Cup final defeat to the Wallabies still eats away at him, he hides it very well. 'I hate to say it, but they were a better side than we were. If we'd played them 10 times, they'd have beaten us six or seven times. Yes, we could have won that final, but we got beaten 40–15 by them in Sydney earlier that year. We got whacked, so we were thinking, *Shit, we've got to change something*.

'The biggest mistake – mine, us – was during the game when we were far more dominant up front than we thought we were going to be. So we should have tightened up. We didn't react well enough in the game. Yeah, my fault. But we didn't get lured into changing tactics. If we had played the same way we had in the summer, we might have got whacked again. People go, "You got conned." No, not really. It doesn't eat me because we lost to a very good side. They dismantled the All Blacks in the semi-final. We'd already lost to the All Blacks in the first game. I don't think we could honestly claim to be the best side in the world that year. I think they could.'

Significantly happier are his memories of games in Paris, not just the staggeringly physical World Cup quarter-final but the 1992 Five Nations game when France had two of their forwards sent off in one of the most volatile contests of them all. 'Christ alive, those games were pretty brutal. I remember lining up for the anthems in 1992. We'd sung ours and I looked across at the French captain Philippe Sella. Alongside him were the French front row. They were all sobbing and they hadn't even sung *La Marseillaise* yet. Rob Andrew was next to me, so I nudged him and said, "Look at that." He leant forward, looked across and just went, "Oh shit". That's when you realised, *This is going to go mad*. And it did.

'At the Parc des Princes you used to come out of the changing room and walk down a very thin corridor before waiting in the main corridor to go out on to the pitch. They always used to put their forwards at the front and some of them were already bleeding. They were just staring at me. You're basically trying to show absolutely no expression but your mind is whirring. *What the hell has been going on in their changing room?* You could just tell they were absolutely on the edge. But that's the challenge. If you can get through that, be composed and get back in having won, that's the moment when you think, *That was special*. That's what it's all about. The harder you push, the more special it becomes.'

No wonder Carling reckons the 1992 side were as good as any team in which he played. With the exception of France in the late 1990s, no one has won back-to-back Grand Slams since. Watching them you were struck by their forward power but also their sense of certainty. It all felt so reassuringly strong and familiar that when stalwarts like Teague, Dooley and the outstanding blond-haired flanker Peter Winterbottom retired, Carling found it hard to deal with. 'During the Lions tour of New Zealand in 1993 I was a mess. I was thinking I would finish as well. I didn't know if I wanted to carry on if those guys weren't playing. I was only 26, but they meant so much.' Not everyone was impressed by his attitude on that tour, but the trip was not entirely fruitless.

'Weirdly the best thing that happened was getting dropped. It was the only time in my career since I was a schoolboy that I hadn't been picked. Once I'd put my bottom lip back in, it was a case of asking, "Do you really want to retire? Um, maybe I don't." It was a useful experience in that sense.'

It was just as well for the scriptwriters that he decided to hang around. Rugby effectively went professional after the 1995 Rugby World Cup, but Carling had been at the epicentre of the whole vexed debate for years. 'In 1994 England toured South Africa. In the first game in Durban one of their players scored a try against us and up on the big screen flashed the details of his bonus for scoring. I remember saying to Ian Beer, the RFU president, "And you're still trying to tell us this is an amateur game?" There was this real friction. We were just saying, "Guys, it's got to be one or the other. At the moment, this is just a shambles."

'They were fighting for the old amateur world, but we were saying, "It's gone. You can't ignore it any more. We want to beat these people, but you can't do it with one arm tied behind your back." They couldn't really carry on denying it.' Then, when the game did go pro, the English authorities fatally delayed for a year and uncertainty ruled. 'That's the sadness of it. They should have thought about it more. Only a tiny part of the game needed to go professional. Letting the whole thing go as they did is still causing issues today. The relationship between the clubs and the RFU is still not where it needs to be. All we were trying to say to them was: "This is where it's going."'

There was still just enough time left in the amateur era, though, for him to be temporarily sacked as England captain after referring, off camera, to the Rugby Football Union committee as '57 old farts' following an interview with Greg Dyke for a Channel 4 documentary. 'I was stitched up by a guy who went on to be in charge of the BBC. He got his story, but I'm not convinced it's the way you go about it. I'd love to bump into him again and say, "Really? Did the ends justify the means?" I shouldn't have said it within earshot of a microphone, but it was meant to be just a laugh. When you look back on it, it was quite surreal. I remember turning up at the pretournament lunch at the 1995 World Cup and the Aussie committee turned up in baseball caps with "Old Farts" written on them. It didn't go down well with our lot.'

And then there was Jonah Lomu. England had squeezed past Australia in the quarter-final in Cape Town, but in the same stadium against the All Blacks the following week it was carnage. Those of us who were there will never forget Lomu rampaging down the touchline in front of us, like a human monster truck. He scored four tries on his own and New Zealand ran out 45–29 winners. 'To be that size, that fast, that balanced . . . it was unbelievable. We tried to treat him as just another player, which didn't work. He wasn't a normal player. After that game I remember thinking, *You can't stop that.*

'Guys, this is down to us now. It's pride. We either just give up or we fight with everything we've got.'

'As captain I always thought I was pretty prepared for most things that would happen on the pitch, but I never contemplated standing under our posts 20 minutes into a game having conceded four tries and the game being over. What do you say? You just go: "Guys, this is down to us now. It's pride. We either just give up or we fight with everything we've got."

'In the final the South Africans looked at it and decided they'd treat it like lions against a buffalo. One guy would jump on him and the rest would follow.' He reckons Lomu would have been just as much of a handful in today's game. 'I remember sitting with him at the 2015 World Cup when he came over to be an ambassador for Heineken. The massive Nemani Nadalo was playing for Fiji against England and I felt a nudge in my ribs. "Will, mate, he's still not as big as me." That's how far ahead he was.'

Hence why Eddie Jones, during his England tenure, recruited Carling to offer some big-game advice to his players. Carling played his final Test in 1997 in Cardiff but believes many of the lessons he had to learn the hard way are still applicable. 'It's really about understanding how you behave before a game in terms of preparation; how you make sure you are as prepared as possible for everything they might throw at you. And also what systems you have in place for dealing with things during a game.

That's the key bit. Who's watching what's happening, how is that being fed back, how are people reacting to it? That's a key part of a successful team. You don't want to be waiting for the coaches to feed on the messages, you've got to work it out yourselves.

'It's about getting yourself organised and appointing the right people to talk about the right stuff. It's also about understanding the whole emotional wave. In terms of tournaments, you've got to get up to the right pitch and then allow players to come down afterwards. In a tournament that's hard . . . coaches want to get on, but guys have to recover before you can get them back up again. Having the confidence to allow that . . . it's a question of balance, of coaches and players being in synch. You don't want to miss the chance to be really well prepared, but you don't want to overdo it so guys just become knackered. It's a tough one.'

And whenever anyone asks his advice, he will insist tough times can be the making of players. 'I don't want to talk massively about the current squad, but there's a generation who don't like to spend time on stuff which is painful and makes them feel uncomfortable. Sometimes you have to really learn the lessons.' How does he find the modern player? 'They're brilliant rugby players but they are human as well: nervous, worried and insecure. People go "No." But they are. They work out a way of dealing with pressure, but don't ever think they are supremely confident people. They're not. I don't think any group of people are.'

People can say what they like about Carling – and often do – but he is fascinating to listen to. Not to mention a more relaxed figure these days than was the case when, at the height of the tabloid frenzy surrounding his friendship with Princess Diana, he took a flat in Covent Garden for a year and 'never opened the curtains or blinds in case anyone looked in'. He says it all feels like another universe now. 'I'm very lucky and very happy with where I am. Life, family . . . I wouldn't change any of it. You get all that smoke blown up your arse when you're England captain. Then you get a lot of things wrong in your life, get a real kicking and it does you a bit of good. It brings you down to earth and makes you reassess everything. There's ups and downs, but overall I've been very lucky. There's nothing for me to really whinge about. There were certain experiences with certain areas of the media which weren't particularly pleasant, but there's far worse things in life.

'I never dreamed of being famous. You just wanted to play rugby. I talk to a lot of ex-players who say, "Do you miss running out in front of all those people? I do." And I go, "No." For me that wasn't what it was about. Those people don't know who you are but your teammates do. I miss that bit sometimes – the changing rooms, lying there afterwards and just smiling across at a mate. They know you. All the rest of it is not real. Fame is just bizarre.'

6

THE GREAT DIVIDE

*We were lifting in the line-outs like we were trying
to lift a dead giraffe.*

Close your eyes and think of Welsh rugby. What instantly springs to
mind? The red jersey. The *hwyl*. The passion. For me, the individual who
epitomised it best was the late, great Ray Gravell of Llanelli, Wales and the
British & Irish Lions. He also happened to be the first big-name player I
ever approached for a post-match quote. 'Write this down,' Grav told me,
his eyes twinkling, after I'd plucked up the courage to ask why his beloved
Scarlets had been disappointingly beaten at London Welsh. 'We're like a
fine wine, we don't travel well.'

Bless you, Grav. Until his death in 2007 aged 56, he represented all the
best qualities of both rugby and life: humour, toughness, empathy,
fellowship. And Wales, for a long time, was also the place where rugby
transcended all else. I used to enjoy heading to Aberavon or Maesteg for
the crackle of collective local anticipation as much as the actual games.
There was a tight-knit communal atmosphere and warm humour in a
packed Welsh clubhouse that few of their English counterparts could
match. My all-time favourite was the day at Aberavon when I walked in
and found everyone glued to the Boat Race on television. 'C'mon, Oxford'
and 'Go on, Cambridge!' were not what I had expected to hear in Port
Talbot. There must have been a few quid on it.

The loudest cries of anguish across the land, though, were reserved for
the most unthinkable of sins: the departure of high-profile Welsh
internationals to rugby league. When the national captain Jonathan
Davies signed a contract to switch to the 'other' code and join Widnes in
early 1989 for a fee of £230,000 it was as if the sky had fallen in,

Asterix-style. 'By Toutatis! Jiffy's gone north!' It took another six years for the sport to become fully professional but, for some, the world stopped turning that grey January day.

At that time Jiffy was very much The Man. Even those of us not reared in Llanelli or Neath loved his impudence, his skill and the razor-like sharpness of his instincts. Every now and again *Rugby Special* would wrap up its worthy county championship coverage from the Vale of Lune and broadcast some Welsh highlights. It was a glimpse into a parallel universe. Welsh club rugby in the 1980s was still spectacularly intense and the rise of Neath was among its more compelling storylines.

With his black collar cheekily turned up, the endlessly watchable Davies seemed to treat most of his opponents as pawns in a game largely of his own creation. It was not so much what he did with the ball – or his penchant for drop goals from all angles – as the endless sense of possibility. When he began strutting his stuff at no. 10 for Wales, he turned decent international players into immobile statues as well.

Track him down to the Gower Peninsula these days and, like Grav back in the day, there is still a glint in his eye. Vision is what sets the best fly halves apart and Davies' ability to look one step ahead has stayed with him in later life. In addition to the commentary and punditry (in two languages), Davies has been president for over a decade of the charity fundraising for Velindre Hospital. At the last count, he had helped them raise over £40 million. Having lost both his father Len and his first wife Karen to cancer – he was just 14 when his dad died – he has always been driven to try and help others in need.

Few, too, have a keener sense of exactly how it feels to walk away from his people and exile himself in completely alien surroundings. When he headed north, he knew the score. Rugby's amateur regulations meant he was taking a one-way ticket away from almost everything he had ever cherished. All he had wanted to do as a kid was play for Wales. Now, in the eyes of some, he was turning his back on his country.

Wales, ironically, had not taken much interest in him as a schoolboy. Llanelli initially rejected him, and it was only when Phil Bennett, his hero, recommended him to Neath that his life changed. 'I got a phone call on a

Sunday after a few pints and played on the Tuesday, not having met any players and never having been to The Gnoll.' Thirty-five club games later he was chosen for Wales, being named man of the match on his debut against England in 1985. It was Neath, however, who supplied that stairway to heaven. 'On a Saturday afternoon when you drove up to the ground the place was absolutely rammed. The whole town was buzzing, because of the way we played and certain individuals who played there. I just wanted to go out there, perform and enjoy it.'

Coincidentally, he had also fallen under the spell of Gravell, his fellow West Walian, when the pair shared lifts to training. 'I'd just sit there next to this massive ginger bloke, larger than life, playing Irish rebellion songs and singing his head off.' Gravell also regularly used to bump into Davies' mother Diana shopping in Kidwelly on a Thursday. 'I once played against him for Neath against the Scarlets and went for an outside break. He smashed me in the face, then picked me up, dusted me off, turned towards the stand and screamed, "Sorry, Diana!"'

'We knew straightaway it wasn't a level playing field. The whole World Cup was geared up to a New Zealand v Australia final.'

The wider world of rugby, though, was changing rapidly. When Davies travelled with Wales to the 1987 Rugby World Cup in New Zealand and Australia, the gap between the hemispheres was conspicuous. 'We knew straightaway it wasn't a level playing field. The whole World Cup was geared up to a New Zealand v Australia final. I remember seeing John Kirwan on the TV advertising facial cream or something and then Andy Dalton was doing the same with quad bikes. You knew straight away something wasn't quite fair.'

Davies, in relative terms, felt fortunate. 'I was a contracts manager for a painting company in Cardiff. I had two great people in my life who understood sport and people. One was Brian Thomas, who gave me the opportunity at Neath. And the other was Neil O'Halloran, who played centre-forward for Cardiff City and scored a hat-trick on his debut against Charlton in 1955. He was a hell of a character. Terry Holmes and I both worked for him and he allowed me to train in the afternoons. He'd say,

"Go and do your sprints, whatever you need to do, but if I need you for a meeting you're there. You're going to be the next Welsh outside half and I want you in that meeting."'

Winning the Triple Crown in 1988 also encouraged Davies, who switched from Neath to Llanelli that year, to believe a potentially bright future awaited the national team. 'We lost to France by one point on the final weekend and on a sunny day I still think we'd have beaten them. Although they had a great side, we were on a roll and we had players who could do things. We thought we were quite close.' They were wrong, as it turned out. On the now-infamous summer tour to New Zealand that year, everything unravelled again. 'It was just different gravy. The level of their provincial rugby was so strong and everything in the game there was aligned. The Tests were just a different world and they were different specimens. When I came back I realised the northern hemisphere weren't going to win anything – aside from France, on their day – for years. And I was right until 2003.'

But when Davies and Rob Norster wrote to the Welsh Rugby Union asking for something to change to close the gap, there was scant official appetite. As Davies later told Ross Harries, author of *Behind the Dragon: Playing Rugby for Wales*, he could scarcely have been treated with more contempt 'if I'd suggested planting potatoes at Cardiff Arms Park.' Even now he shakes his head wearily. 'We weren't advocating getting paid to play. We just wanted the same preparation time to have a chance on the field. Bringing sponsors in to reimburse companies for allowing players time off, for example. The commercial department should have stepped in, but in those days it was slightly archaic and very amateur. They couldn't really foresee what was going to happen in 1995.'

Losing the über-talented David Bishop, who headed north in October to join Hull KR from Pontypool, should have been another flashing warning sign. Instead a 15–9 home defeat to Romania in December was the final straw for Davies, among others. 'What you needed, as captain, was the backing of the union and I didn't feel I had that. I really enjoyed my club rugby – Neath and Llanelli were brilliant clubs and I put my heart and soul into it. But I think I needed more at international level. I loved the Five Nations, but it was always a case of whether we could compete against the bigger packs of England and France. Not having the opportunity to perform on a global stage and to show your talents because we weren't good enough was a disappointment for me.'

Also niggling away was a desire for personal fulfilment. 'I was playing the best rugby of my life for the Scarlets. In my last-but-one game we beat Gloucester by 60 points. We were a very good side. But from a Wales perspective I still felt that maybe I was the next one on the chopping block.' So when Widnes came calling, Davies listened. 'Fair play, Dougie Laughton and Jim Mills came down and they did a great sales job on me. I gave them my word that if they actually came up with the deal they were promising I'd come back tomorrow and sign. They phoned me back at midnight and I went and signed the following afternoon. And then the whole world went crazy.'

The footage of him arriving in Widnes is almost uncomfortable to watch now. How pale, even in January, can a new signing possibly be? 'You sign that form and think, *Jesus, what have I done?* You're taking your family away and moving to a totally different game and environment. Unless you've been through it, I don't think anyone can imagine what it was like. I always had the self-belief that I was good enough and tough enough to do it. But it was the exposure that frightened me a little bit.' He knew enough about the media, even then, to understand how potentially newsworthy his debut would be. 'You even had the columnists there. If I break my leg or jaw, it's suddenly a great story . . . the southern softie, heading back with his tail between his legs. And another kick in the teeth for rugby union.'

Burning away inside him, though, was a desire to send a specific message to a number of different people. 'Was the challenge greater than playing in my first game for Wales? Not really because I'd achieved my boyhood dream. It was my pride that drove me. My main goal was to show people – league or union – how good a rugby player I was. I wanted to show them I could play. And I wanted to show the union boys what they might have missed had I gone on the 1989 Lions tour. That's what drove me.'

To his credit, his leap into the unknown paid off handsomely. Not only did he thrive for Widnes, Warrington and Great Britain but he also enjoyed some productive years in the NRL (National Rugby League) in Australia. While missing out on the 1989 Lions tour remains an itch he cannot scratch, his performances in the rival code – 'I think rugby league saw the best of me' – were eye-catching by any standards. 'I missed the Five Nations but instead you had those big Wembley days for Great Britain against Australia or New Zealand.'

'It was my pride that drove me. My main goal was to show people – league or union – how good a rugby player I was.'

And if he was edging past his prime when he finally returned to union in 1995, following his wife Karen's cancer diagnosis, his passion for the 15-man code remains as strong as ever. In 2022 he was sharply critical of the 'lack of leadership' within the WRU (Welsh Rugby Union) and makes no apology for having done so. 'I just had a sense of frustration, watching the Welsh age-group sides and the regions losing. The Dragons went to South Africa and lost 51–3 and it's treated as if it's acceptable. This is professional sport. I think if you're professional you should reach a certain standard.

'I got really fed up and said what I thought. There was no agenda. I just thought that things needed to be shaken up. There were too many yes-men and the standard of coaching in Wales isn't good enough at the lower levels. The lives of academy lads now are also too easy. There are a lot of average things going on in Welsh rugby and it's not good enough.' Wales may have been rocked to its foundations when Jiffy headed north to league but, in his heart of hearts, he never really left.

* * * * *

The most special rugby moments are often in the eye of the beholder. You should have been been there in 1977 when our school's Junior Sevens tournament reached its climax. Entering the final 30 seconds of the final, our team of plucky underdogs were still level with an opposing team spearheaded by our super-talented mate Colin. Sensing space out wide, I moved the ball right towards my other great friend Rich. Now, Rich knew the Latin name of every British plant and bird and bowled crafty off-spinners, but contact rugby was not his thing. He also still had 15 metres to cover, with Colin charging diagonally across the field to make a corner-flagging tackle. It is perhaps the only case in rugby history of a trophy-clinching try-scorer sobbing tears of pure fear as he neared the line. He just made it, but it is a more poignant memory now. Colin died suddenly in 2009, aged only 43, not long before his wife Victoria gave birth to their first child, a beautiful daughter named Leonora. We miss you massively, big man.

Most people, though, remember great deeds from more high-profile days. Perhaps the most gloriously striking professional try I've seen live was scored in the third minute of the first Test between the British & Irish Lions and Australia in 2001. The Gabba in Brisbane was a heaving sea of red jerseys and the Wallabies were understandably braced for a full-frontal collision. They were not expecting the ball to be moved quickly left to Jason Robinson, who expertly skinned the home full back Chris Latham as if his bigger opponent were stuck in a vat of treacle. Billy Whizz, as they called Robinson, had struck again.

Anyone keen to understand the true extent of Robinson's talent can either study his prolific try-scoring stats in two different codes of rugby or simply listen to England's World Cup-winning defence coach Phil Larder. The vastly experienced Larder rated him as 'the greatest footballer in the world' and always sought to give him the licence to play. 'I like using Jason as a free spirit,' said Larder back in the early noughties. 'Then, as his old Wigan coach John Monie used to say, you just sit in the stand and say a little prayer he's wearing your jersey and not playing against you.'

Not many other mere mortals, certainly, would have represented England within three months of switching to a new sport and then toured with the Lions four months after that. 'I don't think people realise how quick the rise was,' says Robinson, in pensive mood on a damp Friday morning in January. 'I was as raw as anyone rugby union has probably ever seen in terms of how I played. I didn't know anything about union when I made the switch. I didn't know the technicalities and made no secret of that.'

There were those, he still reckons, who were keen for him to fail, if only to bolster their own union egos. 'While there were a lot of people who wanted to see me succeed, for those already in the game there would be nothing better than making me look a fool and not good enough.' Initially he wondered if he had made the right decision. 'My first game was against Coventry in the Tetley's Bitter Cup and one of the guys I was playing against painted his hair pink and shaved his number into it. There were 1,500 people at Heywood Road and I'm thinking, *What on earth is going on here?*

The sceptics underestimated him. High on his list of qualities was his conviction that attack was the best form of defence. 'I'm sure initially it was a case of them thinking, *Just kick it to Robinson. He can't kick and we'll catch him out.* There were times when that happened, but the key thing was I backed myself. I was learning on the job but I still had the conviction to stick to who I was as a player. While they tried to catch me out, I caught them out more.'

Opponents regularly found themselves grasping at thin air, vainly trying to catch a human grasshopper who was never where they expected him to be. Among Robinson's many gifts to the game was his habit of jumping in the air directly in front of an opponent, giving defenders no idea which direction he would dart in when he landed. 'I'd learned the game differently to how a conventional rugby player would learn it. While I was new to rugby union I was very confident in my ability and had a lot of knowledge of performing under pressure. I had played day in, day out at Wigan with Shaun Edwards, Andy Farrell and Martin Offiah. We were winning trophies back to back to back. We were expected to perform; if you didn't you were out.

'While I was quite raw, I had more knowledge than people gave me credit for. Over the subsequent months and years people started to think, *This guy is better than we thought.*' Robinson pauses momentarily. He is wary of sounding too big-headed, but there is no ducking the truth: 'I helped transform the game in certain ways. I made other teams change the way they played because of how I played. When I went on to the pitch, I had a completely different mindset to everybody else. Mine was *Attack, attack. Do what you're good at.*'

By the time he had helped England win the 2003 Rugby World Cup, complete with famous fist-punching celebration after scoring his side's only try in the final, everyone was aware of his genius. Which makes it all the stranger, he suggests, that England have seldom trusted players of his ilk since, nor asked for his opinion on how they might proceed from an attacking perspective. 'Sometimes it's bizarre for me. Look at the England team. One of the fundamental things wrong with the English game has been their attack. I don't want to speak out of turn or blow my own trumpet, but I don't think England have had a better attacker since I finished. I don't think anyone has had the confidence. New Zealand and South Africa have got people who can turn a game and get you up on your feet. England haven't had it – and I hope this is coming across in the right way – for a long time.'

Robinson, like Davies before him, believes it is partly down to entrenched attitudes on either side of rugby's great divide. Not unlike another sporting Yorkshireman, Geoff Boycott, he also thinks it is time people heard a few home truths. 'There's been a mindset for too long that you've got to be this size or that. A load of nonsense. Everyone thinks that because I'm small I wasn't good in the air, but I'd love to compare my stats of taking high balls with anyone in world rugby. I think my stats would be up there. It was very rare I dropped a ball. There's this mindset that you have to be 6ft 5in [1.95 m] to play full back now. No, you don't. You just need to be able to catch a ball.'

By now he really is warming to his theme, with blinkered rugby thinking top of his hit list. 'People used to say to me, "You can't kick." I didn't have to kick back in league because that wasn't the game I played. But when I came to rugby union I thought, *Why kick away the ball?* Over the years I realised the easiest thing to do in rugby union is to collect the ball, run forward, kick it up in the air and compete. The reason so many people do that is they haven't got the confidence to take it back. I was high risk, high reward. But those risks come down when your teammates know what you're going to do. Richard Hill, Lawrence Dallaglio . . . they give you a bailout. It was a case of *Wherever he goes, look after him*. That gave me more confidence. If I thought it was on, I would go.'

He also thinks modern players and coaches are becoming depressingly risk-averse. 'How many times do people do quick throw-ins now? I used to do them all the time. It's that mindset – and I see a lot of it – of fear.' It is certainly doubtful whether Wigan and Bath would risk coming together nowadays as they did for their two cross-code challenge matches in May 1996, with the first played under league rules at Maine Road followed by a union fixture at Twickenham. 'There was a lot of hype around it. "Our game's better than yours". "The posh kids against the council estate kids".' Wigan duly tore Bath apart 82–6 in the league game, only for the northern club to receive an equally stark lesson about the technicalities of union in the rematch. 'We didn't have a clue. It was like the *Cool Runnings* of rugby union. We were lifting in the line-outs like we were trying to lift a dead giraffe. We were so poor, it was ridiculous.'

'How many rugby league players and coaches receive honours? How many Sirs are there in rugby league?'

The final margin was 44–19 but, as Robinson freely admits, it could have been considerably wider. 'If Bath had played as they easily could have done, they'd have beaten us by 80 points. It would just have been scrums, line-outs and rolling mauls. If Bath had scrummaged properly, they'd have broken everybody's necks. The games are completely different, but a mutual respect came out of it.'

With Farrell and Edwards now excelling in the union coaching world, Robinson also wonders when league will finally receive the wider praise and recognition he feels it has long since deserved. 'Rugby league has never got the credit in many circles. Look at someone like Ellery Hanley. Or Martin Offiah. They don't get the credit they deserve. I'm not sure why. The credit I get is often based on what I've done in rugby union. How many rugby league players and coaches receive honours? How many Sirs are there in rugby league? For some reason it's not seen in the same light. But look at Shaun Edwards. Or Andy Farrell with Ireland now. There are so many people like him in league that don't get the credit until they move to rugby union.'

The impassioned testimony from Robinson that resonates most strongly, though, is triggered by my question about how he feels in retrospect about becoming England's first Black captain back in 2004. He appreciates the achievement even more now he understands just what a quantum leap it was from his tough upbringing in Leeds. 'I never knew my father, my mum was a cleaner, my brother was a heroin addict. There were just so many challenges growing up. Now I've retired I look back and think *Wow*. To have come from where I did, to become captain of the England rugby team was a huge honour.

'That's why I'm so passionate now about going back into deprived areas to inspire kids. If I've been able to do what I've done, surely there have to be more kids in there who could potentially be something? There's a talent pool the game is missing out on. And it's not changing because people don't understand the areas, the kids, the challenges. One day I was helping one sponsor and it just seemed all they wanted was their logo on the shirt and a few pictures. I realised they didn't get it. They didn't get the barriers that a lot of kids face. I was one of those kids. You haven't got a car, so you can't get to places. You can't afford the training gear and everything else. So, I thought, *Instead of being told to do things by people who don't have a clue, why don't you just set up your own programme up?*'

It makes you wonder afresh why Robinson is not more cherished by a grateful nation than he presently is. His JR Sports Stars programme aims to help the kind of young people who most need a motivational hand, and he also speaks out powerfully against racism. Just over two years ago, he found another striking example when he went online to gather some information for use in Black History Month. 'I was doing some research and looking at Black captains and my name didn't come up. It wasn't even on Google.' It chimed with some of his personal experiences in the sport. 'I know as a Black player that I've had to work so much harder than my white mates. It's as simple as that.

'It's always hard saying it, but I'm not saying it because I need any praise or anything. I'm very comfortable in my own skin. But people don't see you in your true light because you don't get the full credit for the stuff you've done. If I was to put everything I've done on to a piece of paper, there's very few in the game who could ever come close to it. I played 550 games. Now it's massive if people have played 300. In the season I switched over to rugby union, I played 60 games. The last seven were on a Lions tour which was absolutely brutal. But I can look back now and see the impact I've had. I can see that I've been true to myself in the way I played despite people saying, "He can't do this or that." I knew what I was good at. That in itself is a huge achievement.'

Still nagging away is a desire to persuade more people that rugby can be a key vehicle for promoting social change. 'I believe England should do a lot more in terms of going into areas where the game is not played. If it wasn't for my schoolteacher, I wouldn't have got into rugby. You can't just let your circumstances and what's happened to you dictate the rest of your life or define what you become. For me it was all about taking some of those situations and using all the frustration and anger in a really positive way.

'While the game might be grateful for the impact I had, I'm so grateful to have played rugby league and union for the discipline and opportunities it has given me. And for giving me a story that will hopefully resonate with people. Particularly those who have been told "You can't do it" or "You're too small". People get put off by that, but I can say to them, "Hang on a minute, I didn't have much. I had the cheapest boots on, I was the smallest. If I can do it, why can't you?"' Rugby, he fervently believes, has a rare ability to unite people. 'There aren't many games where you can bring so many diverse people – shape, size, background – together, stick them in a team and it works.' What a player, what an inspiring example.

7

QUEENS OF THE STONE AGE

*Women's rugby is just as hard. We just don't
have a macho problem.*

For every male rugby player who thinks he has had it tough, there is a woman who has endured far worse. Gill Burns, one of the all-time great trailblazers for the women's game, tells some grim stories on the subject. Not least the time she attended an all-male dinner at the East India Club as the token woman. 'We were all standing around afterwards when a senior RFU member said, "Well, it's been lovely having you here. And hopefully, one day, there'll be enough of you to be able to have your own 'do' somewhere else."'

That same evening Burns had already politely declined the offer of a pinch of snuff – 'That's not my style' – and had consented, through gritted teeth, to using the club's back door rather than the front. Dinosaurs still roamed rugby's corridors of power and misogynistic attitudes were depressingly common. 'I just laughed,' says Burns, shaking her head even now. 'I remember saying to the group I was with, "Don't worry, ideas like that will die out." You'd hope his grandchildren will have a more positive outlook when they're his age.'

Such was the landscape for the pioneering queens of modern women's rugby. Nowadays there are professional women's players and leagues and genuine respect. Let's just say the new breed owe a seriously big debt to their predecessors, particularly the game-changing efforts of, among others, England's Burns and Carol Isherwood and Wales' Liza Burgess. In the kitchen of her home in Prescott near St Helens, Burns lays out some of her carefully curated scrapbooks. They feel like genuine historical artefacts, albeit without the medieval Latin text.

The bare statistics will tell you Burns represented her country 73 times during a 14-year international career. She also played in four World Cups and was part of the victorious English squad who won the 1994 tournament, beating the USA 38–23 in the final to secure their first world title. Strong and fast, she was a prodigious all-round athlete, representing British colleges at hockey, basketball, swimming and athletics as well as earning diplomas in tap, ballet and modern dance.

'Rugby just had everything for me. I knew at the first training session.'

The most staggering thing about Burns, though, is her inexhaustible stamina – and, when it comes to getting a job done, her strength of will. She has needed every ounce of the latter at times, having spent a lifetime banging on doors that are only just starting to open. 'A lot of the negativity around women playing rugby would get you down if you let it,' she says, recalling some of the hurtful barbs thrown at her over the years. 'Criticism when you're in the gym, people saying women shouldn't be playing. People saying things like, "What are you? A man or a woman? Or are you just pretending?"'

Burns' response, for the most part, was to turn the other cheek. 'I'm not going to fight a losing battle with people. It really wasn't worth getting upset by it. I made a conscious decision to be the bigger person and to feel pity for them. There's no point trying to make an ignorant person understand.' She also understood that major societal shifts take time. 'I'm not sure there was an appetite for it before the 1980s. Post-war all the women's sports were closed down when the boys came back from the battlefields. It was almost like "We're back now, you carry on doing what women do."'

What the bigots failed to grasp was that Burns did not just want to play rugby for the sake of it. From the moment she took up the sport in her late teens, it became her passion. 'I loved the whole physicality of it. I'd been quite a good netballer, but you had to stop at the line and couldn't touch anybody. Rugby just had everything for me. I knew at the first training session. There were 12 of us training in the dead-ball area. Even then I was thinking, *This is brilliant.*'

In her very first game, playing for Liverpool Polytechnic at York University, she also sensed there might be a role for her as a marauding no. 8. 'I'd been watching the men for a few weeks and we had a scrum on the halfway line. I thought, *This is it. I'm going to pick it up and run.* I probably went 20–30 metres and got into the 22 before I was tackled.' It was a life-changing moment of revelation. The daughter of a musician and a dance teacher, her youthful dance training – 'I'm convinced that's why people bounced off me, because my core was strong' – and energy made her a serious proposition. 'I probably wasn't the most skilful player in the world but because I was powerful I did well.'

And yet there were still those at her club Waterloo – where she helped launch a women's team and for whom she played until 2013 – who believed women did not belong on a rugby field. 'My favourite official at Waterloo is 80-something now, but we thought he was ancient 30 years ago. He and his pal used to say, "I don't know why you play. You girls shouldn't be playing rugby." Two-beat pause. "But I thought that back-row move on the right was great." We just used to laugh. They couldn't get their head around the fact we were girls and wanted to play rugby. And the fact we were quite good. It emasculates some fellows who are insecure, for whatever reason.' Until now, that is. 'One of them rang me up after an England game last year. "Hiya, flower, saw you on the telly. Brilliant. I love watching the women's game. It's better than the men's."'

Back in the late 1980s, though, such nationwide platforms were non-existent. Burns and her friends organised the first county games in the north, having initially met at Birch Services on the M62 to discuss the logistics. Even gathering players together for training sessions was an adventure. 'We'd meet in Leeds for the weekend, stay in the cheapest hotel, have two days of rugby skills and then enjoy fantastic socials. The Women's Rugby Football Union existed, but there was no one officially in the north.'

Which is how, as a junior England squad member, Burns came to organise the first rugby international ever staged in the north. 'We weren't pioneers really, we were selfish. We wanted to do something, so we sorted it for ourselves. I didn't expect for a minute I'd be playing. Then the team was announced and I was picked in the second row. I'd never played there in my life.'

No matter. Soon enough Burns was playing in World Cups and turning England into a force to be reckoned with. Woe betide anyone, a man in particular, who tried to argue women's rugby was softer than the men's game. 'I've always said women's rugby is just as hard, we just don't have a macho problem,' retorts Burns, who never had any issues in standing up for herself. 'There's the occasional fight, but I can put my hand on my heart and say I never struck anyone. I hit people bloody hard in tackles, though. And if anybody did anything to me, I made sure they were hurt after I'd done the next legal thing to them. When people did try to hit me or stamp on me, I'd say to them, "What was that? Was that making up for lack of talent?" Which would wind them up even more. The rest of the girls used to love it.'

Regrets? Burns, now in her late 50s, has one or two, mostly surrounding the 2002 World Cup final defeat to New Zealand, her final Test appearance. 'I loved playing for England and I wanted it to last as long as it could. The fact I wasn't picked to start my final game was a kick in the teeth. I knew I should have been playing. I was bitterly disappointed on the day because we could have won that game.' And while fitness was never a problem –'I was genuinely fitter than I'd ever been at that last World Cup when I was 36 or 37' – she does occasionally ponder how it might have been to be a full-time player, rather than juggling her sport with her day job as a teacher. 'To play in the back row now, between Alex Matthews and Marlie Packer, would have been incredible. I would have been really interested to see the athlete I could have become.'

Burns, even so, is adamant that standards in her era were loads better than some like to suggest. 'I find it quite funny. Everyone goes, "Oh, 30 years ago it was rubbish." I say to them, "It wasn't actually." We had very strict fitness regimes. You were out of the squad if you didn't reach certain levels. Our fitness tests were almost as competitive as the rugby. The difference was that, in those days, you'd have four or five world-class players in each team. Now the whole squads are world class.'

Her lifetime in rugby – she was made an MBE in 2005 and became the RFU's first female Privileged Member in 2012 – has also taught her the key to nationwide acceptance. As England's football Lionesses have proved, it lies in improving the product and marketing it properly rather than worrying about the bitter and twisted naysayers. 'Getting sceptics to change their mind was something we tried to do. But I made a conscious decision not to argue too hard or to complain because that's no way to open doors.

'I know that now it's all about demanding things and saying, "We deserve this or that." But if I'd been like that, I wouldn't be around in rugby now. The negativity would have got me down. There's no point banging a drum in front of somebody who's not listening or is not open to seeing what's happening in the women's game.'

Which is why her parting message to the players of today and tomorrow is to dream even bigger and to pick their battles with care. 'I'd say to the current players, "You've got to play your part in making this even bigger and better. Don't complain, build it. Share the love of rugby, not the negativity. Don't just say, "Why haven't we got women's kit or why aren't we paid as much as the men?" Focus on the positives, do your best and make things better for the people who follow you. That's better than earning a few extra quid."'

* * * * *

If anyone can identify with the tiresome sexist hoops through which Burns had to jump, it is Liza Burgess, her old friend and international rival. Like any other kid growing up in Newport in the 1970s, she was reared on heartfelt stories of Wales' rugby prowess and, after a while, decided she would quite like to have a go herself.

'Why can't I play rugby?'

'Girls don't play rugby.'

'Why not? It looks a great game.'

'Oh, it's not ladylike. It's not something you should do.'

'That's ridiculous. Why can't women play? Why not?'

It was a similar story when Burgess went to school. 'I said I wanted to do carpentry, but they said I had to do home economics. Then I wanted to go into the Marines because I wanted to go on Arctic explorations. They said, 'You'll have to go next door to the Army. Women don't belong to the Marines.' It was really hard to get my head around those things. Rugby was exciting. I was Welsh. The whole street would stop to watch the internationals. I wanted to be part of that.'

'We didn't think then we were creating history, we were just doing something we loved.'

It was not until she showed up at Loughborough University in 1983, carrying her hockey stick, that an opportunity to play rugby finally materialised. The great Jim Greenwood helped to nurture the coaching careers of, among others, Clive Woodward and Andy Robinson, and Burgess swiftly became another disciple. 'He remains the most inspirational coach I've ever had and way ahead of his time. We just wanted to be the best athletes we could. We were passionate about it and decided it was something we wanted to pursue. We didn't think then we were creating history, we were just doing something we loved. Nothing was going to get in our way.'

As a good all-round athlete who had also been a keen swimmer, Burgess – known to all in the women's game as 'Bird' – already possessed the athleticism and talent. Her most vital attribute, though, was her absolute refusal to take no for an answer. 'There were loads of obstacles. God, how long have you got! At Saracens we had to train on Friday nights and play on Sundays because that was the only time we could access the pitch. We even had to go to court to change an old by-law which prohibited whistles being blown on a Sunday.' For both club and country there were also plenty of unglamorous chores. 'Picking up dog poo before we trained on Sophia Gardens was normal. It was the same at Saracens. You also paid for your kit, you paid your subs, you paid for everything. That was just what you did back then.'

Everyday discrimination was also rife. 'When we set up Saracens in 1989, it was difficult initially. They would say, "Can you run the shop, help with the programmes, help behind the bar and work in the kitchen?"

Yes, we said, we'll do all that.' When Christmas came around, the ever-willing rugby girls even found themselves asked to wait on the men at the club's festive lunch. They agreed to do so but, 12 months later, quietly made sure the roles were reversed. 'They waited on us at the next year's Christmas dinner. It became a family club when we were at Bramley Road and Saracens did embrace us. We also made it through the Championship and reached the Premiership. They obviously thought we meant business.'

She and her fellow players also had to pay their dues when they represented Great Britain for the first time in 1986. 'When we played for Great Britain, we stayed in youth hostels. We were sleeping on the floor and doing jobs before we played the games. Before we played France, I had to clean out the toilets before we went off to play.'

Even more evocative, perhaps, are the stories attached to Wales' first women's international, played against England at Pontypool Park on 5 April, 1987. Burgess was the natural choice as captain, but the players' first requirement was to set up the dressing rooms before the crowd turned up. 'It was a novelty. People were like, "Oh, it's women playing rugby." The support wasn't there. The understanding about what you needed to become an athlete wasn't there. The pool of players wasn't there. But there was this great drive: that nothing whatever was going to stop them.'

While the actual game was eventually lost 22–4, the aftermath proved even more memorable. With no other accommodation available, 12 players ended up sleeping on the living room floor of Liza's parents after a convivial sing-song at a local pub run by the Wales international prop Graham Price. As Burgess puts it, 'I remember phoning my Mum and saying, "Can one or two people stay over?"'

Burgess has multiple claims to rugby fame. In total she won 92 caps – 87 for Wales and six for Great Britain – and played in four Women's World Cups, including the first in 1991. She captained Wales 62 times and played her last Test at the age of 42 before graduating into coaching. She was assistant coach for the inaugural female Barbarians team in 2017, and she played a role in sparking the career of England's Maggie Alphonsi, whom she first encountered as a PE teacher in Edmonton. 'She was just a phenomenal athlete. I remember her picking up a discus and breaking the borough record with one throw.'

Crucially, though, it was Burgess who suggested to the young Alphonsi that rugby was a sport worth considering. 'I came in one day with a big black eye and I remember her saying, "How did you get that, Miss?" I told her it was from playing rugby. She was like, "I really want to play rugby."' Fast forward to 2014 when England beat Canada 21–9 in the final to secure the World Cup. 'The day she won the World Cup she sent me a message saying, "I couldn't have done this without you. Thank you." As a teacher it's quite emotional when you think about how kids have grown and developed.'

In her quieter moments Burgess also wonders what sort of player she could have become had she been able to train full-time. 'I do think about how good I could have been in terms of athletic potential. Yes, I was good because I was athletic, but I never had access to a full strength and conditioning programme, nutrition, diet, recovery or injury management. It was a case of fingers being pulled back in, strapping you up and on you go.'

In her current role in charge of the Welsh Rugby Union's female Age Grade pathway, though, she makes a point of not boring today's young players with her old war stories. 'I don't tell them about myself, but I am passionate about making sure the culture and environment is right. That people respect that environment and leave it as they find it. If there's something on the floor, you need to pick it up. We'll provide everything for them, but they've got to put the effort and work in. Instilling that culture is really important. You will carry your bags on to the bus. It's about making sure they don't take things for granted. And if they do, picking them up on it.'

There is no magic wand available, but she does believe the women's game in Wales is now making some headway. "There's a great appetite for women's rugby in Wales . . . I think the right people are there to drive it forward. This year we had 114 girls put their hand up for U20 trials, including athletes from other sports. The exiles are another untapped area because we don't know what's out there. We're starting to talk to parents in New Zealand and Australia who are Welsh-qualified. There are lots of areas to develop.'

Money, inevitably, is another major factor, but the sight of the England Lionesses being celebrated far and wide after winning football's EURO 2022 has given Burgess, and others, hope that old-fashioned attitudes towards women's sport are finally disappearing. 'It is very emotional as a female to see that. It's right and it's proper and it should have happened a long time ago. I'm proud women are now getting the rightful recognition they should have had.' Thanks, in no small part, to the unsung heroines who blazed a trail.

8

THE LION KINGS

I've always likened it to being selected for the Special Forces.

Touring has traditionally been among rugby's major trump cards. The challenge of heading to the opposite side of the world to take on distant, forbidding giants in their own backyards is hardwired into the sport's psyche. And of all the touring teams ever to have boarded a long-haul flight, there are still none with the fabled resonance of the British & Irish Lions.

To be a Lion, the cream of four countries, out in a foreign land, under relentless pressure . . . surely there could be no higher calling? For those of us reared on the legends of Willie John McBride, Carwyn James, Bill Beaumont *et al.*, it transcended all else. John Hopkins' familiar line from 1977 – 'A major rugby tour by the British Isles to New Zealand is a cross between a medieval crusade and a prep school outing' – captured its unique essence perfectly.

Ask Lawrence Dallaglio for his opinion and, for a moment, he slips into old-school geezer mode. The jawline hardens, a nostril twitches and there is a theatrical sniff, like a nightclub doorman about to tell it like it is, son. In this instance, though, the words are genuinely emotional and heartfelt. 'It changed the course of my life,' murmurs the big man. 'I've come back a better player and person from all my Lions tours.'

Behind him the view is properly spectacular. Dallaglio is working as a pundit for BT Sport and from the top of the BT Tower in central London you can see for miles and miles. Right now, though, the former England no. 8's eyes are staring unblinkingly into the middle distance. Suddenly it is 1997: he is 24 years old again and embarking on his first British & Irish

Lions tour. Even the passing of a quarter of a century has not diluted the thrill.

Thousands, if not millions, of other rugby fans around the world feel likewise. That 1997 Lions tour to South Africa has been immortalised in numerous books and endless after-dinner speeches. And, above all, people remember the video. Every sport is now familiar with fly-on-the-wall documentaries, but *Living With Lions* took it to a whole different level.

You must have seen it? John Bentley's infectious sense of fun, Rob Howley's injury anguish, Doddie Weir's tour-ending despair, the 'court' sessions, the man management of Ian McGeechan and Jim Telfer. Even people who have never played rugby can recite every word of the latter's 'Everest' speech and talk you through Jeremy Guscott's series-winning drop goal through those distinctive black-and-white uprights in Durban. Crucially it still holds up wonderfully because of the characters involved. If we were to try to identify Peak Rugby in terms of public interest, this is the tour millions would pick.

Which, in some ways, has hung like an albatross around the necks of every subsequent Lions adventure. Even when the Lions have returned home as winners – and it doesn't happen often – their deeds have not resonated quite so strongly with the public. If ever there was a classic example of how to sell rugby to a wider audience, *Living With Lions* was it.

Dallaglio even rates his Lions tours above anything else – World Cups, Grand Slams, European titles, the lot – that he subsequently achieved. 'I can only say that I regard my selection and involvement with the Lions, on and off the rugby field, as the greatest experiences I've had in my life.' It is a massive call, but the big man remains adamant. 'Winning a World Cup is special. I'm glad England won it in 2003. But the two biggest challenges in rugby – and not a lot has changed – have always been winning in New Zealand and winning in South Africa. When you've done those two things, you can really feel you've got to the top in rugby.'

Unsurprisingly his view was shaped by the 1997 trip. Not only was it his first Lions tour but it was also the first of the professional era. The amateur days were supposedly over, but a sense of fun had not quite been eradicated. 'When we filled in the media questionnaire for the 1997 tour,

I seem to remember being asked, "Where do the Lions rank?" I hadn't won a World Cup at that point but, for me, it was the pinnacle. I played rugby for another 11 years and that remains the case. I've played in World Cup finals, but I just found that whole experience special.'

The jaw flexes again, this time as a reflection of distant pride. 'One of the great things about rugby is touring, and one of the great things about the Lions is that they only ever tour. So if you take the best players in your country, put them together with the best players from three others and take them away to the southern hemisphere, surely that's the ultimate? Playing for your country can never be taken away from you. Winning your first caps and subsequent caps is very special. But once you've done that, the next step is to play for the Lions. And once you're a Lion, the next step is to win.'

'Once you're a Lion, the next step is to win.'

What a feat it was, then, for McGeechan and Telfer and the manager Fran Cotton to weave together a 1997 touring squad that became more than the sum of its already impressive component parts. The captain Martin Johnson as the unsmiling totem, front-rowers Keith Wood and Jason Leonard riding shotgun, Scott Gibbs and Jeremy Guscott adding midfield class, Alan Tait and Bentley bringing some rugby league edge. And even a raw Will Greenwood, not yet capped by England, in the mix as well. 'The selection was phenomenal when you think about it,' confirmed Johnson in the excellent retrospective book *This Is Your Everest* by Tom English and Peter Burns.

From the moment Dallaglio met his new colleagues, he felt likewise. 'If you're going a long way from home and going up against some of the best teams in the world, you've got to pick the right people. Things will happen on tour that go with you and against you. You've got to stick together, and the selection of that group of players in 1997 was unbelievable. I've always likened it to being selected for the Special Forces. You try and come together for one week before heading down to the southern hemisphere. It's the best of the best.

'I was 24 and had only been playing international rugby for about a year-and-a-half. For me it was just an incredible journey of discovery. I quickly realised that if we were going to be successful, everything I'd learned as a player and a person needed to be shared. It's not easy to create that environment where you're basically giving away all your intellectual property and everything you've learned. But you do it because you're going to get a lot back.'

The record books now show the Lions won the series 2–1, the first winning Lions series in South Africa since 1974. What they don't necessarily capture is the classy nature of some of the midweek rugby the Lions played, nor the heroic efforts of some of their previously lesser-known forwards, not least Tom Smith and Paul Wallace in the front row. Smith died young in April 2022 at the age of 50, a victim of cancer, but his place in Lions folklore is assured.

For someone like Dallaglio, the whole trip served as an epiphany. 'To have come away with a winning series under your belt as a Lion at the age of 24? What's not possible after that? Rugby is such a hard game physically and emotionally. The most important thing is believing you can win. Everywhere I went after that, you had that experience to lean back on. *If I can do it there, I can do it anywhere*. And I made friends for life. It makes you respect people in a different way and made me think differently about the relationships we had with other countries.

'There aren't many victorious Lions tours and that's what makes it even better. In the immortal words of Jim Telfer, "Getting picked is the easy bit. The greatest thing you can achieve is to be part of a winning Lions series." That was something I never forgot. You can be a Lion, but to be a legend you've got to win. I'm sure it's the same for New Zealand. You can be an All Black but you've got to be part of a winning All Blacks team.'

The same esprit de corps was still there in 2022 when the squad met up for a 25th anniversary reunion. Dallaglio's only concern was that the famously hard-edged Telfer might interrupt the occasion to call another of his infamously brutal training sessions. 'I thought he might have brought his rucking net and his broomstick along. I was having nightmares about that.' He also recalled what McGeechan used to say back in 1997: that a Lions player, even 30 years hence, would be able to bump into a teammate and not have to say a word because of their mutual, unbreakable bond.

'He got it wrong by five years, but the sentiment was right,' smiles Dallaglio. 'He got up and made a very similar speech at the reunion and nearly had us all in floods of tears again.

'We all look a bit different, some are in good shape, some have let themselves go a bit, there's been a bit of tragedy there as well. But he was right. What he said back then in Cape Town is true. It was just a look. And when you have those kind of experiences with people, it shapes your life forever. If the Lions do that for you, why would you not want it to carry on?'

Welcome to the bull elephant in the room. The recurring problem with Lions tours is that the bad ones cause everyone to query their existence. On recent tours, too, the reluctance of club administrators to make any kind of fixture list concessions to assist the Lions' preparations has threatened to undermine the whole concept. On the 2017 tour to New Zealand, players were still so jetlagged they were falling asleep on the team bus up to the opening game in Whangārei. 'Everything about the Lions is set up to fail,' nods Dallaglio. 'You're pulling four teams together who don't really like each other. That's unique. You fly to the other side of the world to play one of the best teams in the world. And – until recently – with their referees in charge. Plus their fans. You don't even know who's going to be in the team until the last minute.'

There is a difference, though, between the odds being stacked against you and the entire experience leaving people so deflated they fall out of love with the whole idea. Dallaglio also toured with the Lions in 2001 and 2005 and was invalided out of both expeditions prematurely with significant knee and ankle injuries respectively. Neither of those grim personal experiences, though, left him as empty as the sight of the 2021 Lions contesting a series in South Africa behind closed doors, courtesy of COVID-19. 'What happened in that last series was a tragedy. Playing in front of empty stadiums is not the way it should be done. It needs to be reinvigorated.'

Dallaglio, to be clear, remains the ultimate Lions supporter. 'If I was going to go on a rugby tour purely as a fan, I'd go on a Lions tour, no doubt.' But with South African provincial sides now playing in Europe, for example, the special feel of a Lions tour is potentially further diluted. If even their biggest fan can scent existential trouble ahead, where does that leave us?

* * * * *

The uncomfortable truth is that the Lions concept is at a significant crossroads. The world has moved on and the Lions, in some respects, now belong to another age. A bunch of barely acquainted individuals trying to be competitive in a sport which grows more professionally intricate by the day? Thousands of UK and Irish fans flying to the far side of the world for a boozy jolly as the climate catastrophe intensifies? Amid increasing pressure for independence in Scotland and Wales and a shifting political situation on the island of Ireland? The question marks are multiplying by the year.

At the heart of it all, too, is another crucial assumption: the desire of the modern player to continue to buy into the Lions ethos. 'They'll always be interested in the money' is the perennial cry. Not necessarily, not if the global calendar is reformed and different types of inter-hemisphere fixtures – both club and international – start to become commonplace. If you are already playing in South Africa once or twice per year in the United Rugby Championship, heading back out for another six weeks suddenly becomes less of a novelty.

We are still sitting high up above central London and the lunchtime view remains sensational. A sharp change of mood is coming, though. Austin Healey, one of Dallaglio's colleagues at BT Sport, has a very different perspective on the time-honoured Lions concept. Healey was on the 1997 tour as well, but he flew out as an instinctive sceptic even then. 'Everyone says the Lions is the pinnacle, but it just wasn't for me,' he explains, as searingly direct as ever.

'I wasn't particularly a rugby fan as a kid. I was a football fan. I grew up in Birkenhead. There really wasn't any major rugby clubs to look at. I could tell you who was playing at 15 for Birkenhead Park, but I couldn't tell you who was playing 15 for England at the time. So I didn't really watch the Lions growing up. It made no sense to me; I always wanted to play for England. You were deemed to be one of the best players from the home unions and Ireland – which is nice – and you get reasonable stash, but I wasn't overly bothered. I didn't have the same emotional connection with the Lions as I did with England.

'People say, "That's disrespectful, you're not respecting the history." But what's the history got to do with me? I sat there in the first meeting in 1997 and they kept harking on about 1974. After the coaches left, we said to each other, "Can we just set our own history? This is about us, it's not about them. How does 1974 reflect anything we're going to do in the next eight weeks? It doesn't affect us at all." Some people absolutely love it. But if you ask me how much I love England compared to how much I love the Lions, it's a completely different scenario. I think the Lions is put on a pedestal and a lot of that is from the *Living With Lions* video in 1997. We're talking now about bringing more eyeballs to rugby and how we do that. That tour was like a Pandora's Box . . . everyone was let in.'

But surely the camaraderie of 1997 counted for something? Only up to a point, apparently. 'The reason it was such a good tour was because it enabled players like me who weren't emotionally engaged in the Lions to become so. The connectivity, the people, some of the injuries – the Doddie Weir injury, in particular – and the negative press you get on a Lions tour particularly galvanise you.' Well, that and the fact that Matt Dawson was picked at scrum half ahead of him. 'In 1997 I was England's first-choice scrum half and I'd fought my way to that position. I go on the Lions tour and my first game is in a monsoon, basically like playing in a swimming pool. We played some great high-tempo rugby in those midweek games – Transvaal, Free State – but I still didn't get a look-in in the Tests. It just annoyed me, so I thought, *What's the point?*

Good old Austin. Even now he reckons the entire 1997 series probably turned when he fell on a loose ball close to the Lions' line at a key juncture in the second Test. 'No one ever mentions that. They all talk about Jerry's drop goal, not the fact Neil Jenkins dropped the ball 5 metres out and someone dived on it quickly. Jerry's nice little drop goal in front of the posts? I could have back-heeled that over in my sleep.'

It is probably worth noting, at this point, that Healey has since become one of the UK's sharpest broadcast analysts, never afraid to tell it like it is. It is a trait which did not always thrill every coach he played under, not least Graham Henry on the 2001 Lions tour to Australia. As a member of the midweek team – the self-titled 'Driftwood' – Healey credits Wales' Dai Young as the man who papered over the cracks that, for assorted reasons, had begun to open up.

'The only time we really got galvanised was when the Australian press got stuck into us.'

'He held that tour together. If he hadn't been there, I think the tour would have split. Henry had lost a large bunch of that midweek side, they weren't turning up for training, particularly in the in-between weeks between the Tests.

'Although 2001 was still an enjoyable tour it was led by a rugby relic whose style of coaching was closer to a school bully than a coach. At no point on that tour did he develop me as a player and for that reason I have little respect for him. The only time we really got galvanised was when the Australian press got stuck into us. It's like when a teacher tells you you'll never make anything of your life. You want to show them. That was the trigger for me.'

In his quieter moments, though, Healey does have the occasional pang of regret about never starting a Lions Test. 'On both tours I didn't feel I was given a fair shot . . . maybe that's because I'm a gobby little shit.' John Bentley grew so exasperated with him in South Africa in 1997 that he would stop talking to the Leicester man from 4 p.m. each day. Which explains why Healey cannot resist the occasional jibe even now. 'In 1997 we had two or three video cameras inside the camp. Bentos stole all of them and filmed himself.' Four years later the film-making novelty had slightly worn off. 'In 2001 they gave everyone a camera and I think most of the guys sold them before they went on the tour.'

When they write the modern history of the Lions, though, Healey's name will forever be associated with the lead-up to the third and final Test of the 2001 series against the Wallabies in Sydney. 'I suppose I'll be remembered not for being part of some of the best midweek performances we've ever seen in 1997 but for Eddie Butler writing my column while I was in hospital,' he sighs, reflecting on the infamous 'plank' and 'plod' remarks directed at the Australian lock Justin Harrison that were printed under his name in the *Guardian* on the day of the game.

The punchline was that Harrison soared to steal the crucial line-out, effectively clinching a series victory, and the Australian media seized gleefully on Healey's words as the catalyst. The truth was rather more mundane. 'I was in hospital having an X-ray on my back when Eddie phoned me. I just told him to write whatever he wanted. So he did. In hindsight that was a mistake. On that tour it had been decided everyone would shut up shop in case it offended the opposition and they played better. But ask Justin Harrison if he caught that line-out because he'd read the column on the morning of the game. I don't think he'd say that was his motivation. Well, he might say it for a laugh, but I don't think he believes it. Although, in fairness, it has made him a lot more famous than his rugby ever could.'

Nor did the affair end there. After Healey had returned from a family holiday in Hawaii with his friend Martin Johnson, he was summoned to a disciplinary hearing in a Dublin airport hotel. It did not go well.

'You know why you're here?'

'Yes. For a column I didn't write.'

'The charge is that you've brought the Lions into disrepute.'

'Okay, fair enough. Have you read the contract?'

'Yes.'

'Can you tell me the end date of the contract?'

'No.'

'What does it say?'

'Um, it says 16 July.'

'What date did you write to summon me to this hearing?'

'Er, 17 July.'

'The contract's over, guys. You've got no jurisdiction. Thanks very much and good luck for the rest of the season.'

'Sit down.'

'No. Unless you want to get a lawyer in here who tells me you have got jurisdiction, in which case I'll sit back down.'

'Well, okay. But . . .'

In the end, though, Healey's club director of rugby Dean Richards advised him the best option would simply be to get it done and to move on. Healey was fined £2,000 but is still upset to have been made a scapegoat. 'I've not spoken to Graham since the disciplinary committee in Dublin when I told him to shove it up his arse.' Convinced that, legally, he was in the right, he declined to pay the fine. 'For about the next two years they sent me legal letters and were trying to sue me. I'd just send them back with a one-line reply, "Take me to court."'

There was, however, to be a sting in the tail. Prior to the 2003 World Cup, Healey had just come back from America where he had been receiving rehab for his injured knee when Clive Woodward phoned him.

'I'm naming the training squad this week, but I can't pick you until you've paid your Lions fine. Bill Beaumont has phoned me and said it is still outstanding.'

'Tell them to sue me, Clive. Legally, I don't owe them a penny.

'They want their money.'

'Are you joking?'

'No. Pay the money and I'll pick you.'

Healey thought about it and eventually decided he had no real option. 'So I paid the money and he still didn't fucking pick me! It was the final nail in my Lions coffin. That's why, if I was asked to play for the Lions next week, my answer would be: "No".'

Personal grievances aside, it is Healey's firm belief that the Lions model either needs to be stripped back commercially or reinvented, regardless of the fact that the 2021 tour made a profit despite the global pandemic. 'They took 70 backroom staff and spent millions of pounds. It reeked of wastage for me. On the next tour don't take 70 backroom staff. Don't put a whole load of corporate responsibilities in place for the players. Don't pay the players. Ask the players to donate their fee to their local rugby club where they started. Then see who still goes. That's when you'll find out if it's the pinnacle or whether it's just another decimal point in a bank account.'

Either way, argues Healey, the player experience nowadays is a far cry from the happy-go-lucky expeditions of old, with the 2005 tour to New

Zealand under Woodward a prime example. 'Clive effectively took two teams in 2005 and separated them. Why? Because a scientist tells you an extra day in bed might see your performance go up? The Lions is about travelling, camaraderie and experiencing the local environments – not going on driving days with sponsors and their high-paying guests. I don't like the fact people fly in for the Tests now. They get there Thursday and bugger off on Sunday. That's not what a real fan looks like, it's what the corporate fan looks like. It's turned into a big corporate engine. They want it to be the utopia of rugby, but to get to that you've got to spend a lot of money. I don't necessarily like that. I think it's lost its ethos but I'm obviously in a minority.'

Okay then. Does he reckon, in his heart of hearts, that the Lions have a long-term future? 'If they're still making money. And if they can fit it into the season. Player welfare seems to drive everything at the moment until you get to the Lions, at which point everyone says, "Let's kick it out of the window." Will it still exist in 20 years? I hope so if it's in the right format.

'The 1997 tour changed the Lions into a franchise you could monetise in a way you couldn't do with any other rugby team around the world. Even the All Blacks. Fair play to them, they keep making a load of money. Good luck to their sponsors. But they've lost the essence of what the Lions is about.'

Behind him, appropriately, a few clouds are bubbling up on the London horizon. The Lions have been the greatest touring team in rugby's history. The *Living With Lions* video is still wonderful viewing. But all good things come to an end eventually. In a changing world, even the Lions are not entirely safe. And if they were to disappear, how on earth would rugby union ever replace them?

9

SILVER FERNS AND GOLDEN ERAS

Playing for the All Blacks was the most important thing in my life.

New Zealand can be spectacularly beautiful. To take the road from, say, Queenstown to Wanaka or Te Anau to Milford Sound is to lapse into slack-jawed silence. The South Island is not just gorgeous but fabulously empty. The snapper, the Central Otago pinot noir and the flat whites are equally memorable. There is just one fly in the ubiquitous pumpkin soup: the occasionally unhealthy national obsession with rugby. The Kiwi author Lloyd Jones summed it up neatly. 'We do sort of put all our eggs in one basket when it comes to national morale. We're bloody good at farming, but there are no Olympics for farming. It's not on any visible stage out there in the world, but rugby is.'

In 2011, when New Zealand last hosted the Rugby World Cup, it genuinely felt as if the entire nation was preparing to sit for some kind of life-defining exam. Shops in the main street of Dunedin were offering 50 per cent off all clothing with one proviso: the garments had to be black. On domestic flights the in-flight safety video featured All Black players adopting the textbook position in the event of a crash. The aforementioned coach Graham Henry could also be heard issuing mock-stern warnings to every passenger: 'If you choose to smoke on this flight, consider yourself dropped from the team.' The previous month had even seen the hasty withdrawal of a wince-inducing promotional campaign, fronted by Sean Fitzpatrick, suggesting New Zealanders should abstain from sex for the duration of the tournament. Let's just say Kiwis can get carried away on the oval-ball front.

Some of us had been introduced to this phenomenon several years previously. One night, on a backpacking adventure around the South Island in the late 1980s, our retro bus pulled over in a one-pony town halfway up the west coast. It was still early enough for a drink, so we popped across the main street from our hostel for a beer at the local working men's club. Above the bar was a television set relaying the era-defining events taking place that same day on Tiananmen Square.

I happened to be standing behind two locals, perched on their stools at the bar, gazing silently up at the screen at the symbolic image of a lone protester confronting the tanks. After a contemplative second or two, one of them nudged the other. 'Eh, mate,' he said, eyes still glued to the dramatic footage, 'How d'ya reckon the All Blacks will go on Saturday?' Say what you like about Kiwis of a certain vintage, but they know their priorities.

Sometimes you wonder if players and fans alike might not be better off persuading each other it is only a game and should not be taken quite so seriously. Then again, when Steve Hansen tried to suggest as much before the 2019 World Cup semi-final between the All Blacks and England, it felt strangely off-key. 'Let's hope the game can live up to the hype,' he told his audience. 'Because, if it does, we will be sending a message around the world – "Wow, what a wonderful game" – to rugby lovers and people seeing it for the first time. There's an important side outcome but, ultimately, it won't define the All Blacks and I'm sure it won't define England either.'

We knew what he was trying to say. That family is more important, that the sun would still rise in Yokohama the next morning. But, ultimately, it is the desire to outdo the rest of the world that has propelled New Zealand's rugby to such rarified heights. 'We are the most dominant team in the history of the world,' read the famous message on a whiteboard in their London hotel, accidentally discovered by a UK sports journalist when he popped his head around the wrong door in 2014. Why bother underplaying the truth?

It goes some way towards explaining why New Zealanders can instantly switch from being the planet's most hospitable, mellow people to the most forbidding, depending on which side of a white line they happen to be. I once spent an instructive evening in a Dublin pub the night before Ireland played England in March 1991 listening to Wayne 'Buck' Shelford discuss his upbringing. His father was born on the bare floor of a mud hut and instilled a formidable work ethic into his children. As a young naval recruit, Shelford would run eight miles to work, cycle home, cycle back to work the following morning before running all the way home again. On the eve of his All Black debut, someone asked if he was willing to shed blood for the cause. 'I thought to myself, *Well, I'm in the military. I am prepared to go to war and die. Of course I am prepared to bleed for the jersey.*'

Few have ever put their bodies on the line like 'Buck' did during the infamous Battle of Nantes against France in late 1986 when he eventually came off with concussion, several missing teeth and a torn scrotum that required 18 stitches. He still sounded pretty damn tough even perched on that Dublin bar stool. 'Isn't his cruciate ligament the only thing keeping his two ears attached to his head?' he rasped at one point, delivering a blunt verdict on a new squad member who, following a knee injury, needed to sharpen up to become a great All Black. It was a telling snapshot into the mindset required to wear the silver fern on a consistent basis. Traditionally the English rugby psyche, cluttered with class-based, geographical and historical baggage, tends to be less clearcut. In New Zealand, with its cradle-to-grave oval-shaped fixation, there is no such confusion.

* * * * *

Exactly what it means to be an All Black is reinforced when you track down Sean Fitzpatrick. Sitting in the offices of the Laureus Foundation just down from Fulham Broadway in London, the great man looks trim in a dark blue shirt and jeans. Only a discernible limp hints at his seriously hardcore sporting past. This is a man who, by his own admission, refused to acknowledge when he was beaten.

The stats are almost otherworldly. Fitzpatrick played 92 Tests for the All Blacks and started 91 of them. The only time he was picked on the bench was for the last of them, against Wales at Wembley in 1997. Warren Gatland sat on the bench behind him for years and never won a full cap. 'Poor old Gats,' says Fitzy now, not looking totally remorseful. 'I always say to him, "Look at the money you're making now, that's purely because you sat on the bench watching how the game was played. I turned you into a great coach."'

'I had 11 years at the top playing for the All Blacks and it takes everything out of you. You're sacrificing everything.'

Maybe, but the lengths to which Fitzpatrick used to go to retain his place were something else. 'I used to watch Gats go off for a run in the morning and think, *Where's he off to?* So I'd follow him down the road. It was the same if he was practising his line-out throwing. *Fuck, I'd better get out there.*' The modern concept of rotation was unthinkable. 'In the All Blacks in those days we had a Wednesday team and a Saturday team. Gats was in the Wednesday team and I was in the Saturday side making sure he stayed where he was. He made me a better player without question.'

There have been precious few other sporting organisations anywhere, suggests Fitzpatrick, in the same obsessive league as the All Blacks in their pomp. Among them, for a while, was the Mercedes Formula One team and their champion driver Lewis Hamilton. 'Mercedes are one of our partners and I've been up to Brackley a few times. I said to Toto Wolff – and Lewis was there, too – that it was the closest thing I'd seen to the All Blacks. Just the whole pursuit of excellence, the single-mindedness. You see it in Lewis. And Tiger Woods.'

It did not always translate into victory, but at no stage did they ever contemplate settling for second place. Fitzpatrick's eyes narrow ever so slightly. 'The best way to explain it is when people say to me, "Do you miss playing?" And I say "No." I had 11 years at the top playing for the All Blacks and it takes everything out of you. You're sacrificing everything. When I speak to companies now, I say there are two key ingredients to success. The first is preparation. The best prepared people will win. And the second ingredient? Sacrifice. When I was playing for the All Blacks it was the most important thing in my life.'

The same ethos still exists, he believes, even if the current All Blacks generation are no longer as invincible. 'I spend quite a bit of time with them and the guys are exactly the same. It's still the same attitude.' Weakness is for lesser mortals. 'In my day in New Zealand some guys would play one Test and we'd know. *Jeez, you're not the right person.* Now those sorts of people don't even get to first base.'

He also cites Australia's head coach Eddie Jones as another good example. 'He's driven. He's like us.' Fitzpatrick, though, wonders aloud if Jones' efforts to transfer that mindset to England was ever going to work long term. 'They can do it for one or two years but then they start to think, *Jesus, we've got to do it again?* That's why, at one stage, Eddie opted to say, "See you later" to the fat and lazy ones and the ones who'd been to three World Cups.'

If anyone should know what it means to represent the silver fern, it is Fitzpatrick. His father Brian played 22 games, including three Tests, for the All Blacks in the early 1950s but there was no such thing as a preordained passage into the national squad. 'I had three years sitting on the bench at Auckland. John Hart wouldn't pick me because I couldn't throw the ball in. He'd say, "Until you can throw the ball in and sort your discipline out, I'm not going to play you."'

It was only courtesy of Bruce Hemara popping a rib in a scrummaging session on the eve of the All Blacks' first Test against France in 1986 that Fitzpatrick was selected for the 'Baby Blacks' side, with most of the starting regulars still suspended having taken part in the NZ Cavaliers tour of South Africa. 'The only reason they picked me was because Brian Lochore had coached me in the U21s and believed there was something there. Someone recently asked me if I had imposter syndrome. I didn't know what that was back then, but you do feel that way.' Arguing the toss with the senior voices in the All Black dressing room, the Andy Hadens and Murray Mexteds, was out of the question. 'Those guys taught us a lot in terms of the whole ethos. You didn't talk, you learned. But once you earned their respect, they brought you into the inner sanctum. It taught me a lot about leadership, both good and bad.'

He learned a bit, too, in the same infamous Battle of Nantes where, along with Shelford, he was part of an All Black pack beaten 16–3 by their legendarily pumped-up hosts. 'That exposed some of our leadership and exposed that some of the players were past it. We went away and said, "That's never, ever going to happen again."'

It was to serve as a crucial launchpad to the first ever World Cup, staged in Australia and New Zealand in 1987, a defining tournament in more ways than one. The Cavaliers tour of South Africa, where apartheid was still very much in place, had caused huge controversy and large swathes of the Kiwi public had been alienated. 'You've got to remember that in 1987, because of the Cavaliers, rugby wasn't liked in New Zealand,' recalls Fitzpatrick. 'Brian Lochore said, "Right, we've got to win the nation back." That's when we went to Wairarapa, got billeted and trained at schools. For the opening game of the World Cup there were 13,500 people at Eden Park. People didn't like the All Blacks.' Nor were they favourites to lift the trophy. 'I don't think we were expected to win that World Cup. I remember Ian McGeechan saying that, four weeks before the World Cup started, Scotland didn't even know if they were going. Australia were odds on to win it . . . they'd already beaten us the year before, but luckily for us the French beat them.'

New Zealand duly went on to blitz the French in the final, but it was a different story in Britain and Ireland four years later. The All Blacks still had an aura about them but, as Fitzpatrick now acknowledges, some of the players had begun to believe their own publicity. 'We'd talk about needing to be arrogant to be successful but leaving it on the field. By that stage, though, we'd taken it off the field. We never analysed the opposition, we never analysed our own performance. We'd win three games and think, *We're much better than them*. I never thought Phil Kearns was any good, for example, but he was much better than me at that stage. And whereas previously we used to do 100 scrums in training, we started doing 25.'

Everything came to a head when the All Blacks were well beaten by Australia – and David Campese – in that remarkable semi-final in Dublin. 'The game was over at half time. They smashed us. I remember walking back down the tunnel and saying to Alan Whetton, "Mate, I'm out of petrol." "So am I," he replied. We both said, "Let's retire." I was 27 years old.'

Back home he was still toying with that idea when, flicking through the paper one day, he spotted a picture of Kearns. 'He'd been out grinding on a big yacht somewhere and was holding the Americas Cup in one hand and the Rugby World Cup in the other. The headline was, "The world's best hooker becomes the world's best sailor." I looked at it and went, "No, I'm the best hooker in the world." At which point my wife turned to me and said, "No, you're a fat bastard."'

The rugby landscape, though, was changing. South Africa were about to be readmitted to the international game, potentially reigniting one of the sport's greatest rivalries. Even Bronwyn Fitzpatrick – 'You can't retire, you've got to get back in there' – felt he should give it another go. In the early months of 1992, Fitzpatrick also took a phone call from the new national coach, Laurie Mains. There was no cosy repartee.

'Do you want to be an All Black?'

'I'd love to.'

'Well, you're probably not going to be. Because at the moment you're fat, lazy and arrogant. You're taking your position for granted and you've lost respect for the All Black jersey.'

It was a pivotal moment, not just for the hooker but for the All Blacks as a whole. 'Laurie was the one who changed things and pushed the idea that great people make great teams. He sacrificed some great talent. Some of the best All Blacks I ever played with were thrown out.' The Whetton twins, Gary and Alan, were among the casualties but Fitzpatrick, Zinzan Brooke, Richard Loe and Michael Jones were all still around when the 1995 Rugby World Cup in South Africa rolled around. 'Everyone thinks we were favourites going into that tournament, but we were about number five in the world. We'd lost in Australia in 1992. In 1993 we were lucky to beat the Lions but lost to England that November. In 1994 we lost 2–0 at home to the French. We took a lot of pain and got rid of a lot of kids. We didn't find Andrew Mehrtens until we played Canada in 1995. We didn't find Josh Kronfeld until that game. Then, in 1995, Jonah Lomu was thrown out of a training camp for not being fit enough when no one knew he had a kidney disorder.'

Perceptions had changed somewhat by the time the mighty Lomu was running over England in the World Cup semi-final in Cape Town. The press box at Newlands happened to be relatively low down and we had a perfect view of Lomu trampling over Mike Catt for the defining score. Catt almost had caterpillar tracks imprinted on his white jersey when he regained his feet: it remains the most destructive half of Test rugby this author has ever seen. 'We were as fit as we'd ever been and we were going to play this high-tempo game,' recalls Fitzpatrick now. 'The game hadn't seen that pace of game before. And by doing that we ultimately created the space for Jonah.'

The All Blacks had also not forgotten their 15–9 defeat at Twickenham some 18 months previously. 'England were a bloody good team, but what happened in 1993 had really hurt us in terms of the way we got beaten, the aftermath and the way they were towards us. I remember Olo Brown saying that the fans were all giving the All Black bus the finger as they drove out of the car park.' The Kiwi view, as famously expressed by Mehrtens, was that England's players were 'pricks to lose to' on the rare occasions it actually happened. 'At the post-match dinner at the Guildhall, they were horrible and they know that,' confirms Fitzpatrick. 'They were also having a reunion for the 1983 and 1973 teams who had beaten the All Blacks. We just said, "This is never going to happen again." In that 1995 World Cup semi-final week our call was "Remember 1993."'

So dominant were the All Blacks and Lomu that it seemed nothing could stop them. Until prefinal illness famously swept the camp, with Fitzpatrick among the lucky few to avoid its effects. 'I was fine, but 16 of the 21-strong match day squad had food poisoning. They couldn't get out of bed on the Friday. Even Colin Meads was out on his feet and we couldn't have a team run. We just went to Ellis Park and had a walk around.'

Combined with the emotional resonance of seeing Nelson Mandela wearing a Springbok jersey and the special nature of the occasion, Fitzpatrick knew his side would have to dig deep. 'On game day it was unbelievable. When we played England in Cape Town in the semi-final, it was like the Blacks and Cape Coloureds were all supporting us. It was like a home World Cup. Everywhere we went, they loved us. And then, all of a sudden, when Nelson Mandela embraced that "One Team One Country" theme, everything changed. The atmosphere in the stadium . . . it probably was meant to be, but we could so easily have won that game. I still tease Mehrts even now, "How the fuck did you miss that drop goal with a minute to go in normal time?"

As it happened, though, New Zealand took a measure of revenge the following year. Again Fitzpatrick had been pondering his future, assuming the 1995 final would be his international swansong. 'I remember saying to my friend Ric Salizzo, "This is my last game for the All Blacks, no matter what happens. Win or lose." But after the

> 'I still tease Mehrts even now, "How the fuck did you miss that drop goal with a minute to go in normal time?"'

game I met another mate in the pub. He said to me, "You've got to come back here next year and be captain of the team that beats the Springboks in South Africa."'

That ambition was still lurking in the back of his mind in the early weeks of 1996 when he was building a house and received a visit from Hart, now back as New Zealand's head coach.

'Do you want to be an All Black again?'

'Look, I don't know. I've got a few reservations.'

'Well, if you'd like to be an All Black, I'd like you to be my All Black captain.'

Hart and Fitzpatrick went back far enough to trust each other implicitly and, with the world game having just officially turned pro, it did not feel like an ideal moment to walk away. 'Laurie had built the team and Harty just took it to another level in terms of professionalising it.'

And so commenced one of the great feats of modern rugby endurance which saw the All Blacks embark on a crazy schedule involving 10 Tests in the space of 12 weeks. Having won the first seven – a win over Western Samoa followed by two wins apiece against Scotland, Australia and the Springboks – their attention turned to a three-Test series in South Africa. Leaving aside their one-off win in 1992, no All Black side had ever won a series there and here was a golden chance if they started well at King's Park. 'It was the first tour where we'd taken 36 players . . . the whole aim was to win the series. We said, "If we don't win in Durban, we've got no chance of winning the two up at altitude." They duly won 23–19 and followed it up with a 33–26 success in Pretoria – 'The quality of the rugby was just phenomenal' – to seal a historic triumph. After the final whistle Fitzpatrick was greeted in the tunnel by the ex-All Black full back, Don Clarke, who had emigrated to South Africa. The latter had tears running down his face and thanked Fitzpatrick on behalf of every gnarled old All Black who had previously fallen short.

* * * * *

Back home they call them The Incomparables and it still feels about right. Lomu, Fitzpatrick, Christian Cullen, Jeff Wilson, Michael Jones, Zinzan Brooke, Josh Kronfeld, Frank Bunce . . . has any single nation ever had a richer pool of talent at any one time? Admittedly professionalism had just arrived and the All Blacks were miles ahead of their European brethren in terms of ruthless preparation, but they were box office in every respect. Which makes you wonder what might have happened had the World Rugby Corporation breakaway, in which Fitzpatrick and others were prime movers, actually come to pass.

In 1995, the day before the World Cup final, Rupert Murdoch's News Corporation announced a 10-year US$555 million television deal involving the SANZAR nations. It was notionally still an amateur sport, but every single one of us present at the press conference at Ellis Park knew the playing field had tilted irrevocably.

For the players, it was finally a chance to contemplate a markedly different future. 'We had two options on the table,' recalls Fitzpatrick. 'Rupert Murdoch or Kerry Packer. We loved the All Black jersey, but we had Murdoch on one side who had done a deal with the unions and hadn't even consulted or spoken to us and Packer on the other.' In the 48 hours after the World Cup final, the Packer hard sell intensified, with Fitzpatrick and Mike Brewer the chief negotiators for the All Blacks. 'We had Packer's son, James, telling us what his dad was going to do. It was exactly the same money involved: NZ$350,000 per year. They were going to have conferences; it was exactly the same discussions that are still happening now. We said, "Right, we'll work our way through this but we're not going to split. There's not going to be two competitions. As soon as we split, that's the end of it."'

In the end it never happened, with the unions desperate to avoid the unthinkable and public opinion starting to shift in their favour. 'The media machine was working against us and suddenly the whole nation turned against us,' recalls Fitzpatrick. 'We were like, "Oh my God, what's happened?" The board weaselled their way in and got Jeff Wilson and Josh Kronfeld and that was basically it.'

Over a quarter of a century later, the same traditional unions still hold the whip hand but football, basketball, gridiron, golf, tennis and assorted other sports have left rugby union choking in their financial dust. Fitzpatrick senses the game, in New Zealand and elsewhere, has reached a crossroads. 'Even now the money the players earn is not enough for them to retire. They're either going to have to get a job in the media or do something else. That's the case with everyone. The Beauden Barretts of the world are going to have to get a job. Even Dan Carter's got to get a job now.'

For that to change he reckons rugby needs a reboot in terms of what it offers the floating fan. "We need a product that people want to watch. You and I are happy to consume sport the way we did 10 years ago, but the kids of today . . . look what's happened to Formula 1 and the extra numbers watching purely because of *Drive To Survive*. They've attracted a whole different audience of girls and 18-year-olds generally . . . which is exactly what we need.'

That requires everyone, New Zealanders included, to think more broadly and more collectively. 'The All Blacks have close on a billion fans globally, but we've only got 800,000 registered fans. There is so much scope there and, in my opinion, that's what Silverlake will bring. That's their expertise. Fan engagement. We've got such good products: the Six Nations, England, Ireland, the All Blacks, the British & Irish Lions, World

Cups, the Rugby Championship, a club window . . . everyone has just got to give a bit.'

Times, in other words, are changing. When Ireland can travel south and win a series in New Zealand, as they did in 2022, it is obvious the north are fighting back hard. Fitzpatrick has been suitably impressed by some of the rugby he has seen in England and France – 'Super Rugby is becoming stodgy. It used to be the other way around' – and also reckons that COVID-19 affected New Zealand rugby more than some appreciated. 'I don't think people realise New Zealand has probably been more affected by the pandemic than anyone else . . . we've just been playing against ourselves and getting into bad habits. We're probably six months behind at the moment in terms of the style of rugby they're playing up here.'

Woe betide, even so, the northern hemisphere know-it-all who thinks New Zealand will never again be as all-conquering as they were in their golden eras. Decades ago, at Blackheath's Rectory Field, I asked Graham Henry, then involved with Auckland, to share the secret of successful rugby coaching with me. 'Get over the advantage line from first phase' was the gist of his terse reply, and Fitzpatrick still reckons there is an innate rugby knowledge in New Zealand rugby that few other nations can match.

It is further boosted by the perpetual Kiwi willingness to travel overseas to further their knowledge. 'We're quite prepared to go offshore and learn. That's the problem up here. Try and get someone out of Wales and take a cut in salary to go somewhere else.' A curious coach or player, though, will always benefit from a change of scene. 'Ronan O'Gara is a great example,' suggests Fitzpatrick. 'He's coached in New Zealand and France and he's already the better for it.' True enough. But are we really saying New Zealand rugby cannot rise again? That an obsessive rugby nation will collectively start to shrug its shoulders and switch over to the badminton instead? Surely not. Because the day the All Blacks cease to capture the global imagination is the day the entire sport of rugby fades to grey.

10

BOKKE, BOKKE!

It wasn't just about a team, it was about a nation.

There has still never been a sports story laden with as much political symbolism. President Nelson Mandela, clad in a green Springbok jersey, handing over the golden Webb Ellis Cup to a white South African captain, the ultimate example of Rainbow Nation reconciliation. The 1995 Rugby World Cup final remains the most extraordinary occasion upon which many of us will ever report, even before you factor in trifling details such as the actual rugby. No wonder they made a Hollywood film, *Invictus*, about it. Even those of us who had not grown up in South Africa in the apartheid era felt history's hand upon our shoulder.

Working for Reuters at the time, I sat in our cold little office inside Ellis Park, staring at my laptop and contemplating how on earth to sum up what we had just seen. There was so much to take in that, for a while, nothing came out. Afterwards, having attempted to do vague justice to a truly special day, some of us headed to the Radium Beerhall, one of Johannesburg's more convivial institutions. Before too long we were toasting the greatest of African sporting days with celebratory pints of *catemba*, a head-shredding blend of red wine and cola. Then, as one, everyone in the bar conga-ed out into the street, all races and backgrounds in shared communion, swaying to the same pulsating groove. You don't tend to see that on Twickenham High Street.

The 1995 Rugby World Cup was an eventful tournament from the outset. We still laugh in our house about the pretournament incident at Heathrow when, after saying farewell to my beloved wife and walking away through the departure gates, I heard 'Good luck, Rob!' being shouted behind me. I turned for one last tearful wave, only to find Mrs K trying to attract the attention of Rob Andrew, her favourite rugby player at the time.

On arrival in Cape Town we were billeted in the Holiday Inn on Eastern Boulevard. I was allocated to a room in which, to judge from the smell, someone had either just died or spent a very unpleasant few days. Table Mountain was covered in smog-thickened cloud and all I could see out of the window was the nearby expressway. It did not immediately feel like a life-enhancing assignment.

The tournament welcome lunch at Groot Constantia, the oldest wine estate in Cape Town, was also interesting. With all the squads in attendance, it started raining so hard that water began to pour through the roof of the marquee. Amid the chaos the Ivory Coast squad were busy selling T-shirts at 30 rand each to try to raise much-needed funds. It was just my second time in South Africa, following a brief initial trip three years earlier to cover the Springboks' readmission to Test rugby after years of apartheid exile. There was no real sense of the host nation being on the verge of anything life-changing. South Africa's women also seemed fairly disillusioned at the time, to judge from the knowing joke whispered in my ear by a female friend of a Reuters colleague. 'What's the difference between Ellis Park and an erogenous zone? Most South African men know where Ellis Park is . . .'

When another visiting agency colleague tried to deposit some cash in the hotel safe in Johannesburg, the manager asked if he would like to store his gun there, too. We were advised that 50 per cent of people in Joburg carried a firearm; true or not, it focused the mind. As did the trip to Gugulethu township on the outskirts of Cape Town for a community rugby session. On the way back to the main highway, we saw a sight that lives with me still: a local man driving a horse and trap with a battered old car strapped on top of the cart. As a symbol of South Africa's societal and economic divisions and its relationship with the modern world it was crazily perfect.

Amid the relentless madness, though, a country and its rugby team were stirring. It is certainly instructive, a quarter of a century later, to

The great Phil Bennett, kicking for touch during the British & Irish Lions Test series in New Zealand in 1977.

Adrian Murrell

Gareth. The Welsh rugby stars of the 1970s were such legends they did not require surnames.

Paul Wright

The wizards of Oz. The brilliant Ella brothers transformed perceptions of Australian rugby.

David Cannon

School of ruck. Scotland's 1990 Grand Slam champions before their defining 13–7 win over England at Murrayfield.

Carry him home. Will Carling rides a human wave back to the dressing rooms after captaining England to 1991 Grand Slam glory.

David Campese has always been his own man. Here he is studiously ignoring New Zealand's haka prior to the 1991 Rugby World Cup semi-final in Dublin.

Vintage England. Brian Moore gets the party started to celebrate England's 1991 Grand Slam triumph. They completed another 'Slam' the following year.

The way we were. Pontypool's Eddie Butler takes on Saracens at a snow-covered Bramley Road in February 1983.

Adam Pretty

The trail-blazing Gill Burns on the charge against Australia in Sydney in 2001. Nothing ever held her back for long.

Vincent Amalvy

South Africa's momentous 1995 World Cup triumph at Ellis Park. No wonder they made a movie about it.

Alex Livesey

The greatest tour? The 1997 British & Irish Lions expedition to South Africa, involving Lawrence Dallaglio (top) and Jerry Guscott (bottom) among others, is still fondly remembered.

Jonah Lomu performing the haka at Twickenham in November 2002, the final month of his Test career. He scored two tries but England defeated the All Blacks 31–28.

David Rogers

David Rogers

All Black magic. Captain Sean Fitzpatrick and coach John Hart savour their side's series-clinching victory against the Springboks in Pretoria in August 1996.

Odd Andersen

On top of the world. Clive Woodward (above) and Jonny Wilkinson (left) on English rugby's night of nights in Sydney in November 2003.

Damien Meyer

Shamrock 'n' roll. Brian O'Driscoll celebrates his hat-trick of tries against France in 2000, which secured Ireland's first victory in Paris for 28 years.

David Rogers

Peter Muhly

Happy days. Ronan O'Gara scores for Munster against arch-rivals Leinster in the semi-final of the 2006 Heineken Cup.

Chris Lee

A battered Jacques Burger puts his body on the line – again – for Namibia against New Zealand at the 2015 Rugby World Cup.

David Davies, Alamy

Twin peaks. Wales and Namibia contest a line-out during their 2011 Rugby World Cup pool game in New Plymouth.

Christopher Lee

David Davies, Alamy

Raging against the dying of the light. Sandy Park, Exeter, 2015.

Few England players have overcome more barriers to reach the top than Maggie Alphonsi.

William West

Rugby's worst nightmare. The former All Black prop Carl Hayman, pictured here in 2007, is now suffering from the game's physical effects.

Mark Kolbe

We Shall Overcome. Fiji's sevens team and coach Ben Ryan give thanks after winning the country's first ever Olympic gold medal at the 2016 Games in Rio de Janeiro.

Siya Kolisi and Tendai 'Beast' Mtawarira belt out the national anthem before the Rugby World Cup final against England in Yokohama in 2019.

David Rogers

Master and commander. Eddie Jones keeps a close eye on his forwards before England's 2020 Six Nations game against Italy in Rome.

Chris Ricco

Tom Jenkins

They shall not pass. Michael Leitch and Fumiaki Tanaka try to catch South Africa's Handre Pollard during Japan's sensational 'Brighton Miracle' win at the 2015 Rugby World Cup.

David Rogers

Little big man. Argentina's Gus Pichot after his side's 30-15 pool win over Ireland in Paris at the 2007 Rugby World Cup.

Anton Want

Philippe Saint-André, an ex-captain and coach of *Les Bleus*, understands the contrasting worlds of English and French rugby better than most. Here he is duelling with Scotland's Kenny Logan at Murrayfield in 1994.

A greener planet. Ireland celebrate their 2023 Six Nations grand slam at the Aviva Stadium.

David Rogers

The 2023 World Cup promises to be the most competitive tournament the sport has ever known. The host nation France (wearing white here) are hoping to hoist the Webb Ellis Cup for the first time.

Paul Devlin

listen to someone who enjoyed a prominent ringside seat through the whole tumultuous period. When we first met, Edward Griffiths was an ambitious young journalist and editor, Zimbabwean-born but schooled in England and looking to make his mark in South Africa. Along with the rest of us, he still vividly recalls the August day in 1992 when the Boks met New Zealand at Ellis Park in their first official Test since 1984.

Not only was the occasion historic but it was also politically highly charged. The referendum to end apartheid had taken place just months earlier. The African National Congress was supporting the game on three conditions: the old South African flag was not flown officially; *Die Stem*, then the national anthem, would not be played; and a minute's silence would be held to remember the victims of South Africa's township violence.

But on the day, as Griffiths recalls, an altogether different vibe was discernible. 'There was all this talk beforehand that the national anthem *Die Stem* was not going to be played. I remember looking along from the press box at Ellis Park to the corporate boxes and people were putting up speakers to play the national anthem themselves. It was a highly politicised moment. It was a time in the country when everyone was nervous about the future. There was no certainty at all of a Rainbow Nation and everyone living happily ever after. It felt like a really dangerous moment. Emotions were very high.'

With kick-off a mere 90 minutes away, Griffiths, the sports editor of the local *Sunday Times*, decided it might be wise to visit the presidential suite, one level up, and check the situation with SARFU's then-president Louis Luyt.

'What do you think?' Luyt asked him.

'I think you have to play the anthem. Because, whatever happens, it's going to be played. At least if you play it, it'll look normal. If you don't, and there are all these people playing their own sound systems, it's going to look like a mess.'

Luyt needed no second invitation. After *God Defend New Zealand* and before the haka, the old South Africa let forth one last defiant roar. 'It was like a rally,' remembers Griffiths. 'Scary stuff. From the outside it looked like white South Africa was saying, "Whatever happens in this country, we're not moving. This is our stadium, the Springboks are our team, we're back in international sport and we're still here."

'There's a scene in *Cabaret* when Michael York's character goes to a Bavarian beer garden. A blond boy sings "Tomorrow Belongs to Me" and the whole thing goes from a gentle Bavarian ballad to a full Nazi rally. It wasn't far off that. It was very, very emotional. It wasn't just about a team, it was about a nation. It was about an identity which they felt was threatened. It was about so much more than just a game of rugby.'

'It was about an identity which they felt was threatened. It was about so much more than just a game of rugby.'

New Zealand still emerged victorious, more comfortable winners than the 27–24 final scoreline suggested, and the following week, at a damp Newlands, Australia also registered a 26–3 success over the Boks. It was clear the home team had post-isolation ground to make up on the rest of the world. The national squad was often split along provincial lines and was almost exclusively white. In 1994, shortly after Mandela had been elected as South Africa's first Black president, a touring England side led the Springboks 20–0 after just 16 minutes at Loftus Versfeld. At which point Mandela, who was present at the game, apparently turned to Luyt beside him and said, 'What are you going to do about this team?'

By the time Transvaal's Kitch Christie was appointed national coach in succession to the sacked Ian McIntosh in October 1994, such questions were growing louder. 'The Springboks were really struggling to find any kind of pattern and a lot of what they were doing was very antiquated,' confirms Griffiths. Wider issues were also emerging. 'Drugs were in the game without a doubt. It was all slightly Wild West-ish.'

Griffiths, regardless, swapped journalism to become SARFU's chief executive. The World Cup was looming and the winds of change were blowing. The week before the tournament opened, however, the national team were booed at a warm-up game in Cape Town because they were perceived to be the Transvaal Boks, coached and led by Christie and Francois Pienaar respectively.

Any local confidence ahead of the opening match also seemed to be underestimating the defending champions, Australia. So when one of my old Reuters comrades, Anton Ferreira, wagered a bottle of wine on a South African victory, I duly backed the Wallabies. That week the Boks had seemed understandably wound up while the Wallabies appeared relaxed and confident. It was all an illusion. On a beautiful clear day, the purposeful hosts surged to an exciting 27–18 win. The next day even *The Sowetan*, a newspaper that began as part of the liberation struggle, led on the rugby, splashing 'Viva Amabokoboko!' across its front page. The Africanisation of the Springboks, or at least the blurring of old boundaries, was finally beginning.

This was precisely what Griffiths had hoped for. Earlier that week, outside the Woodstock Holiday Inn, he had asked for a sign to be erected displaying the squad's slogan for the tournament. It read: 'One Team, One Country' and, even at the time, it felt perfect. 'It was about harnessing the force which has always been there,' recalls Griffiths. 'To make it a direct goal. We're not three teams or 10 countries, we're one team, one country.' With the squad learning all the words to *Nkosi Sikelel' iAfrika*, Mandela popping into training, and confirmation that the national U23 side would in future have to contain a minimum number of Black players, crucial seeds of hope and reconciliation were being sown.

Even more dramatic was the pool game between South Africa and Canada in Port Elizabeth, watched by some of us on a massive screen at the Stellenbosch Wine Festival. (A decent bottle of wine cost nine rand, which then equated to about £1.50.) The punch-ups which saw three players sent off and floodlight failure delay the kick-off were striking, but Griffiths has another abiding memory. Right opposite the TV cameras, on the far side of the ground, stood a guy waving a big, old-school South Africa flag. In an effort to try and resolve the situation, Griffiths walked out of the main stand and around the ground to the open terrace to speak to the individual concerned.

'Please can you just put it down. The message you're sending is not the message I think you want to send.'

'Sorry, Mr Griffiths.'

The Canada game was significant in another respect. Chester Williams, the only black player in the Springbok squad, had been plastered across every billboard prior to the tournament – only for disaster to strike in the form of a hamstring strain. Now, with the winger Pieter Hendriks cited and banned for stoking the brawl against Canada, an opportunity had presented itself to restore Williams to the squad. 'I think he did have a sore hamstring, but the pressure of being the face of the tournament was also huge,' says Griffiths. 'Without Chester we were also an all-white team. And what does the poster boy go and do? He scores four tries against Samoa.'

Surreal is the best way to describe the rest. Rob Andrew's drop goal to help England beat Australia in the quarter-final was followed by that epic semi-final smashing of England by the All Blacks. In the other semi-final in Durban, a waterlogged pitch momentarily threatened to rain on South Africa's sporting parade. 'With 60,000 white men in the stadium I can remember very well six Black women being sent out to mop up the deluge,' confirms Griffiths. 'Marcel Martin, the president of the French Rugby Federation, and Louis Luyt were stomping around in the changing rooms, with us knowing that if the game was called off we'd be out because of the sending-off against Canada.'

Nine times out of ten Abdelatif Benazzi would also have been awarded a late try rather than having it disallowed by the Welsh referee, Derek Bevan. With no ability to refer the decision to a Television Match Official, however, the Springboks were saved. 'I can still remember sitting on the bench and thinking France had scored that last try,' admits Griffiths. 'I thought we were finished. The game was a crazy mess, but somehow we got through.'

By now the whole country was entranced. Little did anyone know an alleged poisoning plot would also enter the equation. Rumours about a mysterious waitress called Suzie deliberately poisoning the All Blacks on the eve of the game still circulate even now, but Griffiths remains adamant the source of the outbreak was far more mundane. 'My view on it would be they ate seafood in the week before a World Cup final, which was probably not the brightest thing to have done.'

Inside the South African team room on game day, either way, Griffiths was experiencing pressure of an unprecedented nature. 'I can remember very well sitting in the team room when I got a call asking for a jersey for President Mandela and organising for one of Francois' jerseys to go to him.' Before the president went outside, there was the equally unique sight of a 747 jumbo flying so low over Ellis Park it seemed about to clip the roof of the stand.

Even Griffiths in the tunnel was momentarily taken aback. 'You didn't know what it was, it just felt like thunder coming.' Then came an even more unforgettable moment when Mandela walked on to the field wearing the no. 6 jersey. The predominantly white audience in the stadium started to chant, 'Nelson, Nelson, Nelson'. It was same kind of force that lay behind the playing of *Die Stem* three years before – the same passion, the same energy – but now it was being channelled in a different way.

'Afterwards I remember saying, "Life is going to be an anti-climax after this."'

A tingle went down Griffiths' spine. 'I remember standing next to Mark Andrews in the tunnel after the president had come off and saying, "Whatever we do, this is just going to work out." Sure enough, Andrew Mehrtens missed his late drop-goal attempt and the game, tied at 9–9 after 80 minutes, went to extra time. Mehrtens and Joel Stransky swapped penalties to make it 12–12 before the moment of truth arrived two minutes into the second half of extra time. Direct from a scrum, Joost van der Westhuizen's pass found the lurking Stransky, who dropped the decisive goal to spark delirium.

Amid the celebrations, Griffiths and others instantly knew they would never again feel such a sense of pure elation. 'Afterwards I remember saying, "Life is going to be an anti-climax after this. We'll never have anything like this again, it's all downhill from here."' For many home supporters it felt almost otherworldly. 'In the stadium afterwards, it wasn't noisy. When the team walked around the field with the World Cup, it was almost like people were going, "I don't believe that." It was almost a serene atmosphere.'

Less mellow was the end-of-tournament function when Luyt ostentatiously presented referee Bevan – 'the most wonderful referee in the world' – with a gold watch. He then suggested that, had they been involved, South Africa would have prospered at the two previous World Cups as well. 'There were no true world champions in 1987 and 1991 because South Africa were not there,' Luyt informed the assembled dignitaries. A mass walkout involving several teams swiftly followed. 'It was a nightmare,' confirms Griffiths. 'I'd written him a speech, but he left it in his pocket.'

When the team and Griffiths returned to the Sandton Sun in the northern suburbs of Johannesburg, there was another twist. 'I had the World Cup in this silver box, went up to my room, opened the door and there were three people asleep in there. My luggage had already been moved out.' When I went back down to reception they said, 'Oh, we thought you'd left.' The three surprise guests were the children of team manager Morné du Plessis so, rather than disturbing them, Griffiths took the World Cup back to the bar, where Stransky joined him for another quiet couple of hours of warm, fuzzy reflection. Elsewhere in the country the celebrations were more raucous. Was this the dawn of a new age of enlightenment? As our little group marvelled at the genuine multi-racial joy outside the Radium Beerhall, that's how it felt.

* * * * *

One of South Africa's victorious squad members that day is less convinced. Brendan Venter was an injury-time replacement for James Small in the final, but ask him now what the outcome meant to people in his country and the phone threatens to melt. Venter is adamant that sporting outcomes alone do not, ultimately, shape lives. 'It was only an incredible time because of the result,' he insists. Is he absolutely sure? 'I don't think so, I know so. The one nice thing about the World Cup in 1995 is that everyone remembers where they were when it happened.'

There was also a lovely little cameo immediately after the final whistle when Venter saw a young kid holding the match ball and asked him if he could have it. There was some natural initial reluctance, until Venter offered his playing socks in exchange and the deal was done. The ball now resides at the StoneX Stadium in north London, part of the remarkable collection of sporting memorabilia built up over the years by Nigel Wray, the long-time Saracens benefactor.

The point Venter is keen to make, though, is a fundamental one. To him Stransky's drop goal and Mandela's no. 6 jersey and the post-match euphoria were not, ultimately, what really mattered. He even disputes that representing your country is, in itself, a crucial motivation, at least for players like him. 'For me – and it's a harsh thing to say – I didn't play for the spectators. When I win the spectators are happy, and when I lose they are sad. From very early on I understood I could not get my motivation from external people I don't know. Life is about real people with real relationships, emotions and feelings. South Africa as a country is a dead thing. It's not a live thing. But the people around you are real. You basically play for yourself, your teammates, your coaches and your family.'

In other words, sporting patriotism is an overblown concept. 'If you as a coach want to motivate people by saying, "You're doing it for your country", you will be 100 per cent disillusioned. Because when you lose you will be spat out. That same country will turn on you. There's a transactional relationship. When you're winning, it's: "I like you, I'll support you, you're a superstar." When you lose, it's: "I want nothing to do with you." It's very primitive. It's a case of: "You made me feel bad when we lose, you make me feel happy when we win."'

To back up his argument Venter points to a couple of subsequent World Cups when South Africa fared less well. 'How was the feeling in South Africa after the 2003 World Cup? Catastrophic. I played in the 1999 World Cup and got a red card against Uruguay. How was the feeling in South Africa after that tournament? Dreadful. Because it was seen as a failure. We lost in extra time to the first drop goal Stephen Larkham had ever kicked in his career. Unfortunately we want to link things to good outcomes. For me the challenge in life is when you don't get the outcome and you can still stay level-headed and keep your key relationships intact.'

Venter has carried that ethos with him through a notable coaching career, combining his life as a doctor with prominent rugby roles in both hemispheres. Ask him about the 2007 and 2019 tournaments, both won by the Springboks, and he insists they mostly prove the crucial part that fortune plays in sport. 'There were a lot of things that could have gone wrong and didn't. If you look at 2007, South Africa ended up playing Fiji in a quarter-final, Argentina in a semi-final and England – who they'd beaten 36–0 in their pool – in the final because other results went their way. In 2019 they lose to the All Blacks in the pool and end up playing Japan in a quarter-final, Wales in a semi and England in a final. You need a bit of luck. Maybe it was just meant to be. Sometimes we have less to do with it than we think.'

'I learned more from what coaches did wrong than what they did right.'

It is Venter's belief, furthermore, that deifying coaches who win World Cups or other major tournaments is a flawed concept for that precise reason. 'As a player at different times of my career I learned more from what coaches did wrong than what they did right. Sometimes coaches are too motivated by the own agendas and their own ambition. The moment it's all about your own ambition, you're doing it for the wrong reasons.

'What's your book about? *When we got the outcome, look at the change it made.* Sure, it did when the Allies won the war in 1945 and people were happy. But we tend to link all our memories to outcomes, good or bad. What if Benazzi had got over the line in that semi-final? In modern rugby the question would have been "Is there any reason not to award the try?" And they would have been awarded it. So that's why I'm so critical about outcomes.'

My mind spools back to another interview with Venter almost 20 years previously, in a stairwell at London Irish's old ground at Sunbury. That day the force of his personality seemed to rebound off the brick walls and time has not obviously diluted his conviction. 'When I look at people who link things to outcomes, I actually feel sorry for them. How many people do you know – actors, singers, sportspeople – who are really successful and still stay nice people? Are they happily married? Do they still have a relationship with their children? Do they meet up with their old friends? It's a minority. A lot of people seem to feel a certain outcome makes them superior.

'The older generation were, I feel, much better equipped because there was no social media. I've met a lot of former internationals. All of them impressed me because the highs and lows of rugby moulded them into wonderful people. That's the biggest reason I want my boy to play rugby. I'm saying to him, "This can mould you like nothing else in the world, if you know what to look for. If you experience the highs with humility and attack the lows with courage you become an amazing person."'

In other words, Venter believes those gauging their personal worth in shiny trophies need re-educating about the true benefits of sport. 'As a coach the impact my words, my actions and my deeds had on individuals whose faces and family I knew is, for me, rugby's value. It is not the trophies we won, it is the way we treated people and how we all remember our time together.

'If the relationships were dysfunctional and we got it wrong, we missed the point of rugby and sport. Because the joy is in relationships not outcomes. I'm not looking for happiness as an outcome. I'm looking for joy. You cannot control winning the World Cup. You can coach an U12 side and have an unbelievable effect on them for the rest of their lives by building them up and being positive. That is making an impact.'

Quite so. Greatness, as we have already seen, can be defined in different ways. The legacy of 1995 in South Africa was also not what it might have been. Griffiths, Pienaar, Christie and Du Plessis, for various reasons, were all gone from their respective roles within 14 months. No one has ever pretended it was a totally harmonious ship and Griffiths concedes as much. 'There were lots of rows, it wasn't all happiness. It's a big group of people with different views.' No one individual, he suggests, should take overall credit. 'Francois was an inspirational captain of the team, but would it have happened without him as skipper? Yes, it would. I'm not downplaying anyone. He found the right words at the right time and obviously developed a chemistry with Mandela. But success has a million fathers and failure is an orphan. It was bigger than just Francois. It was bigger than all of us.'

The intervening years have also encouraged a few fanciful myths, perpetuated by the makers of *Invictus* among others, that have failed to stand the test of time. Griffiths reckons a couple of misconceptions, in particular, need addressing. '*Invictus* needed to find a hero, so they had Mandela standing in front of a wall chart of the tournament. They made him look like the coach. It was absolute nonsense.

'The other reality was there were very few Black people in the stadium for the final in 1995. Mandela was everywhere, but that's the reality. Of the 65,000, I would say at least half – if not two-thirds – were the same people who had wanted to sing *Die Stem* three years earlier. It wasn't a revolution, it was the same people, just directed in another way.'

So was the legacy of the tournament maximised? 'Definitely not. There was a huge opportunity to really take the game forward into the Black community with coaching, equipment and facilities. There had been an election, the ANC had taken over and the country seemed to be going quite well. This benign grandfatherly president wasn't marching Afrikaners into the sea. There was a kind of reconciliation going on even before the tournament came along. But basically SA Rugby took fright. I'd allocated 40 per cent of World Cup profits to new facilities, but I was fired in February 1996 because the executive committee of SARFU saw it as me giving rugby to the Blacks.'

The fates have also been cruel to some of those who made it happen. Kitch Christie died of cancer aged 58 after a 19-year battle with the disease, while Van der Westhuizen, Small, Williams and the outstanding flanker Reuben Kruger all died between the ages of 39 and 50. Van der Westhuizen succumbed to motor neurone disease, Kruger died of brain cancer aged 39, and Small and Williams suffered heart attacks.

The great Lomu, the tournament's dominant figure, is not around either, having passed away aged 40 in 2015 of a heart attack linked to a long-standing kidney disorder. It would be a heartless sport, though, that diminishes the impact he and the others had on an event that set the bar for every subsequent global tournament. 'What happened in 1995 is still an important memory and a symbol,' insists Griffiths. 'No one can ever take that away. South Africans had a glimpse of themselves and what they could be as a country. It was like we were being propelled along a big river. We were all part of something special.'

11

2003 AND ALL THAT

You'd have gone to your grave regretting that
moment if we'd lost.

Two decades have passed since England became the first northern-hemisphere nation to lift the men's Rugby World Cup. It remains a *Where were you?* moment and, increasingly, a cautionary tale. Did English rugby properly maximise the legacy of Sir Clive Woodward, Jonny Wilkinson, Martin Johnson, Lawrence Dallaglio, Phil Vickery and all the other household names who delivered the fabled pot of gold? Or was it simply a high-class blip, the product of a remarkable bunch of players who would have stood out in any era?

At the time it felt slightly surreal. England arrived at that tournament as indisputably the best team in the world. It was, everyone agreed, their World Cup to lose. No one had ever said that about an English men's side before. Or since. And the real beauty of 2003 was the fact it took six years to complete the puzzle. Those of us trying to describe the journey were lucky to have been close-up witnesses to such a fascinating, multilayered mission.

Even now I find myself arriving good and early to meet Sir Clive just up from London's Embankment. This is the man who championed the idea of doing 100 things 1 per cent better – not least the importance of punctuality and, ideally, being 15 minutes early for meetings. The idea of Lombardi time – named after the gridiron coach, Vince Lombardi, who pioneered it – became addictive. Could excellence really start even before you entered the building to begin your day's work?

Woodward was never in any doubt. To slide in even a minute late was to waste your teammates' time and risk being seen as that most dreaded creature: an energy sapper. Even the doziest of hacks grew accustomed to turning up promptly, pencil sharpened and notebook fresh, for press briefings and team announcements. Woodward won't remember, but he once phoned me up at 6.45 a.m. to complain about a line in that day's paper. The fact he'd already read it before I'd opened the bedroom curtains was another valuable lesson learned.

Something else Clive used to stress also lingers. Unusually among England coaches he actively encouraged his players to engage with the media. It wasn't a chore to be endured, he insisted, but an opportunity. Not only would it raise individual profiles, it would help to place rugby at the forefront of more imaginations. More eyeballs, more column inches, more sponsorship, more public attention generally . . . everyone would be the winner. It contrasts sharply with the 'No comment, but don't quote me' mindset of some of rugby's supposed guardians these days.

Which is a roundabout way of saying England would not have won the 2003 World Cup without Woodward's involvement. That is not to suggest it was his triumph alone or that, conceivably, someone else couldn't have stitched together a successful side from the quality ingredients available. Clive, on occasions, had some terrible ideas; by the final stages of the 2003 tournament, some senior members of the team were hoping their head coach would keep any eleventh-hour brainwaves to himself.

But when it comes to identifying the catalysts behind England's rise, there is no question that, along with world-class players such as Wilkinson, Johnson, Dallaglio and Richard Hill, Woodward was a vital cog. If nothing else, he was determined to ensure everyone aimed that little bit higher. He didn't want players to do the bare minimum or just enough. He wanted them to be positively un-English and to reach for the stars. Nothing overly radical there, you might think, but more recent history says otherwise. Woodward has been as frustrated a subsequent onlooker as anyone. 'If we'd sat down in 2003 and you'd said to me, "England won't win another World Cup for 20 years", I'd have said, "You've got to be joking. That's ridiculous." There's a big part of me that really wants England to win the World Cup because it allows you to move on. While they keep stuffing it up – and they do keep stuffing it up – you look in the mirror and think, *I should still be there.*'

Which makes it well worth reinvestigating, two decades later, exactly what set Woodward and his players apart. The coach, lest anyone forgets, was well down the list of candidates prior to his appointment in 1997, having worked at Henley in the early 1990s before moving onwards to London Irish and Bath. 'I think they possibly spoke to Graham Henry and Ian McGeechan but, for some reason, neither of them was keen on doing it.

'Looking back, when I got the job, I don't think the RFU knew what they were taking on. Rugby was in a totally transitional stage. I was coaching the England U21 side as an amateur. My whole background was in business but, as well as having played for England and the Lions, I did four years at Loughborough University and qualified as a teacher. I never went into teaching because I didn't feel I could do that and play for England.'

Having taken a job with Xerox instead and gone on to set up his own successful leasing and finance company, however, he knew all about calculated risk. 'If you work for a big company you're protected. A lot of chief executives in rugby have never run their own business when you've got to put your house and all the rest of it on the line.' He remembers an official from the Rugby Football Union being taken aback when he visited him at home. 'Crikey, Clive, I didn't know you had such a lovely house. What do you do?'

The challenge was to apply his business brain to the flabby, underperforming world of English rugby in the early professional years. 'All my business background was saying, "Don't do it." It was effectively a new start-up business and you're the first in. I was the new kid on the block. They're the ones who make all the mistakes and get all the hassle. Then the next person comes in two or three years later and cleans up. I think the reason I was successful in the end was because I could apply all my small business knowledge to working at the RFU.'

Radical change was not going to happen overnight. 'When I walked in on day one, I had no office, no phone and no secretary. What really threw them was when I started looking at balance sheets and all the RFU's finances. They just thought I was some ex-rugby player.' But not only was Woodward critiquing the budgets, he was planning for the long term. 'I was just being totally logical about it. England had more talent than anybody else and, more importantly, more money than anybody else. Put those two things together and, to me, there was no reason why we couldn't be the best in the world. Then I started getting really excited.'

It helped that Woodward had played international rugby himself – 'I think that was important, it gives you kudos' – winning 21 caps for England and touring with the British & Irish Lions in 1980 and 1983. He also knew what he didn't want to do. 'Playing for England was a massive thing for me, but I look back at it with massive disappointment. Apart from the Grand Slam in 1980 and one fantastic game against Scotland, we hoofed the ball up the field the whole time because we had a monster forward pack. I think my frustrations as a player came across in my coaching. I wanted to get 85,000 people on their feet at Twickenham and going nuts because of the way we're playing. That was the vision. Now how are we going to do it?'

Exploring options that other people casually dismissed also came relatively naturally to him. During a spell working in Sydney late in his career, he even came close to representing Australia as well. 'When I was in Australia and playing for Manly, I got to know Alan Jones really well. He wanted me to play for the Wallabies and I went and trained with them. I'm sitting there with these Aussies and I can see them thinking, *What's he doing here?*

'I said to Alan, "I can't do this." He said, "Never say Can't. We're going to change the rules." I felt pretty uncomfortable about it but I think I would have got in the team. There was no doubt in my mind. I was captain of Manly and playing really well. Jones was adamant I was going to play for Australia.'

It didn't happen in the end, but Woodward's spell abroad was a formative period. 'I just came back from Australia thinking that, in rugby terms, we should be way ahead.' Early in his England tenure he also spent an instructive time in America. 'Nike got me into the University of Colorado in Boulder. I spent two weeks there and then had a few days with the Denver Broncos. That was just eye-opening. They were totally professional and way ahead. There were more coaches than players, it was just brilliant.' It persuaded him that specialist coaches were the way ahead. 'I remember ringing Fran Cotton and saying, "Fran, we need a specialist defence coach."'

'I needed every individual – whether they were a prop, a scrum half, or Jonny Wilkinson – to become the best player in the world.'

Woodward also wanted players who could solve problems for themselves. 'What the players weren't used to was me saying, "What do you think?" We really started to get this two-way programme going. The biggest skill of a leader is to listen. You've got your own ideas, but you have to listen to people. And we had a bright team.' To motivate them further, the management recruited some outside help. 'I got Steve Redgrave in early on. He just sat there in jeans and a T-shirt, with the players around him, and talked about what he did.

'It was a lightbulb moment for me. He was talking about his first gold medal in 1984 and telling us the amount of time the four of them were together in the boat was tiny. It's the same with a rugby team. So what he did outside of that to become the best athlete in the world was huge. I needed every individual – whether they were a prop, a scrum half, or Jonny Wilkinson – to become the best player in the world and, like Steve Redgrave, to have a gold medal around their necks for being the best in their position in the world. I do not think Eddie Jones ever understood this. Can you get gold medals around their necks?'

It was a while, even so, before England became consistent winners. For a time we spent our time chronicling their chastening defeats, notably to Wales at Wembley in 1999, Scotland at Murrayfield in 2000 and, subsequently, Ireland at Lansdowne Road in 2001. There was also the unsuccessful 1999 World Cup campaign, when England bowed out to a fusillade of Jannie de Beer drop goals in the quarter-finals, not to mention the 1998 Tour of Hell when a depleted England lost 76–0 to Australia. 'That first two or three years were really hard. Imagine sending any team on tour to play Australia, the Māori, two Tests against New Zealand and then flying to Cape Town to play South Africa. And I was there with my third team. And my dad died while I was away.' Stir in the toxic politics of the time – 'I reported in to the 57 old farts, Graeme Cattermole, Brian Baister, all those guys' – and it was not the smoothest of rides.

In some ways, though, it helped to forge the single-mindedness that Woodward's England ultimately needed. 'The lessons of the first World Cup were huge. Going to Paris, getting smashed by the Springboks, everyone's after your head. I had Francis Baron and Fran Cotton on the phone going, "Calm down, it will be fine." What they were worried about was that I was going to resign.'

As the criticism bubbled in the papers, it was his wife, Jayne, not for the first or last time, who proved a vital sounding board. 'Her big thing was always: "High ground, statesmanlike." She still says it now. And she was always right. If I'd been a journalist, would I have been writing that stuff? Probably even worse. These guys haven't got two heads. I can honestly say there's not a single journalist from that time I wouldn't meet for a coffee, a chat or a beer. We went through good times and bad together. And without the media you haven't got a job. The media are putting rugby in the newspaper or on TV . . . you have to take it seriously.'

What no one disputed was that England needed to find another level. For those of us following their every move, a fundamental turning point came on the tour to South Africa in 2000, when England beat the Springboks in the second Test in Bloemfontein with Wilkinson contributing all 27 of his side's points. It was only the third time England had ever won a Test in the thin air of the Highveld. Afterwards as we huddled around the still-callow fly half, sitting wearily on a concrete step beneath the stands, it was blatantly obvious England had an unusual talent at their disposal.

For Woodward, though, the key game had been four months earlier. 'The biggest one for me personally was just after the 1999 World Cup when everyone was after my head. We went to Paris and won. Do you doubt yourself? Of course. But once we won in France I felt I was good enough to do the job. I sold my business and said to Jayne I had to get rid of every distraction. You have to be totally and utterly focused.'

It is remarkable to think now that, post-Bloemfontein, England lost only three of their subsequent 40 Tests up to and including the 2003 final against Australia in Sydney. There was the delayed 'foot and mouth' game in Dublin when Ireland deprived their rusty visitors of a Grand Slam, plus two games in France, one of which was a World Cup warm-up with a below-strength side. By the time their depleted forward pack had triumphantly held out in a famous goal-line siege in Wellington before heading to Melbourne to beat Australia 25–14 less than four months before the tournament, they were unquestionably the team the rest had to beat.

That said, the tension was rising steadily as England approached the promised land. Wales gave them a scare in the quarter-finals and the throng of supporters in and around the team's Manly Pacific hotel was growing by the day. Woodward sensed it was time to refocus everyone's minds. 'I sat down with the team straight after we beat France in the semi-finals and said, "Right, this is what's going to happen. You're going to be inundated with friends, family, agents, sponsors, media, whatever. Just look me in the eye now and promise me you'll give me one more week. If we win the World Cup, do what the fuck you like but do not get distracted. And if you see any member of this team doing so, pin him to the wall and smack him one." We had this really heavy meeting. I told them we could win this thing but only if we didn't get distracted.'

I remember interviewing Phil Vickery in the middle of a massive scrum of people that week and, for the first time, wondering if the pressure might yet prove too weighty. In hindsight the squad had also probably peaked on that summer tour. It is all sepia-tinged legend now – Lote Tuqiri's early score, Robinson's 38th-minute try, the never-say-die resilience of Jones' Wallabies – but after 80 minutes it was still only 14–14. For Woodward and everyone else on England's bench, it was increasingly uncomfortable viewing. 'I've watched it a couple of times and we didn't play that well. The referee was a bit weird, it wasn't our best game by a mile. But in many ways, it was. The pressure to win that game was colossal. No one had ever done it before. You're playing away from home in Australia.'

As extra time wore on, though, it still required someone to pull the trigger. And when the ball finally came back to Wilkinson – courtesy of a spot-on pass from Matt Dawson – everything unfolded in slow motion. Was that really Jonny using his right foot rather than his famous left? From our vantage point in the press box, the ball almost seemed to hang in the air, with the faces around the stadium frozen as if captured by a modern-day H. M. Bateman. And then through the posts it floated, sparking delirium far beyond a rain-dampened Sydney. As Woodward says now, 'Everybody remembers that game, even if they don't follow rugby or sport. I've spoken to soldiers who were on the tops of mountains in conflict areas . . . so many people were watching. Time seemed to stop.'

'Everybody remembers that game, even if they don't follow rugby or sport.'

I certainly remember the morning after. In theory I was meant to be ghosting an England player's first-person column. In practice the individual concerned had been up all night and could barely speak. 'Ha-ha-ha-ha!' he giggled, as we stood outside the Manly Pacific. 'He-he-he-he!' Thank you, William Wordsworth. Tactical nuances or heartfelt recollections were clearly going to be a struggle. But, hey, what a snapshot in time it was. And every time you saw someone out kicking a rugby ball, hands clasped together à la Wilko, you were once again reminded of the promotional impact it had.

No wonder the all-English management – Woodward, Andy Robinson, Phil Larder, Dave Reddin, Dave Alred *et al.* – still meet for celebratory annual reunions even now. But how would they have felt had Wilkinson missed and England lost? Woodward believes it would have soured him for the rest of his days. 'I don't think I'd have turned out a very nice person. I really don't. I think there would have been a bitterness I would have massively struggled to get rid of. To have arrived at the World Cup as favourites, having not lost to a southern hemisphere team for a long time . . . I don't know what would have happened to me.'

It is an occupational hazard for all international coaches. 'We all love sport, but it can be horrible at times. I said to Eddie, "Do you ever think about that game?" He said, "Every day." I fully understand that. I don't think about winning the World Cup every day. You kind of move on. But in our house we have this great saying: "Well done, Jonny Wilkinson!" When we're in a lovely restaurant, having a lovely meal and a glass of champagne someone will say, "Well done, Jonny Wilkinson!" When we're skiing with the kids in Verbier, my daughter Jess will go, "Well done, Jonny Wilkinson!" If we'd not won the damn thing, it would have been almost impossible to get over. You'd have gone to your grave regretting that moment.'

Okay, but could they have won even with Mickey Mouse in charge? With Martin Johnson as the team's strong persuader and Richard Hill, Neil Back, Lawrence Dallaglio, Jason Leonard and Will Greenwood all offering wise, experienced counsel? Arguably, but Woodward's view is that the collective is always stronger than the individual. 'We had a great team. No doubt about it. But I remember Arsène Wenger being asked that question. I loved his answer. "What's more important, the team or the coach? You need both. I can be the best coach in the world but unless I've got a great team I'm not going to win. Equally they could be the best players in the world but without a great coach you're not going to win." I've never forgotten him saying that.'

If selection was often relatively straightforward – 'You haven't got to be a genius to pick Lawrence Dallaglio, Martin Johnson and Richard Hill . . . they're in the team' – there were also one or two key positions which needed filling. Woodward remains particularly thankful for the work done by coaches such as Simon Hardy and Phil Keith-Roach which helped to transform a player like Steve Thompson – 'In 2003 he would have got in to any team in the world' – into such a key asset. 'I kept looking at the hooker position. Richard Cockerill, Dorian West, Mark Regan . . . they were all good players, but I didn't see them getting into the South African or New Zealand team. It was the one position in the whole team where I felt we had a hole.'

Handling a workaholic talent like Wilkinson also required some care. 'You can't compare Martin Johnson with Jonny Wilkinson or Jason Leonard or Jason Robinson or Lawrence. You've got to treat them as individuals. My favourite moment? I learned that in American football they put their quarterback in a vest in training. No one can touch him. I thought that was pretty cool. You can have a great training session but, ultimately, you're judged on what happens at Twickenham at 3 p.m. My big thing was always getting my best team on the pitch. I didn't want Phil Larder battering them to death.

'But then somebody said, "Look at that." I turned round and Jonny had ripped his vest off, gone in and smacked somebody. I ran on to the pitch, got hold of him and said, "What the fuck are you doing? I'm in charge here. Put that vest back on. If you take it off again, you're out of here." All the players were laughing because it was the first time Jonny had ever been told off. But that's him. He's so single-minded. It's just the way he's wired. He'd have no qualms at all about keeping the coach waiting for an hour while he did his goal-kicking. We're all sitting on the bus and he won't give a monkey's. He's a very deep, intense person, but you love him to bits.'

* * * * *

Twenty years on from 2003 and the million dollar question hanging in the Twickenham air is an achingly familiar one. When will England next be in a position not just to win a men's World Cup but to lecture everyone afresh on the world-leading structure underpinning their success? Woodward, whose tenure ended less than a year after his team's finest hour, makes no attempt to massage the truth. 'I always felt we won the World Cup despite our system not because of it.'

Since leaving in 2004 he has been interviewed no fewer than three times to return to a high-powered role at Twickenham, none of which has eventuated for various reasons. The passing years have left him increasingly exasperated with the way the RFU operates and, in his view, have highlighted some crucial managerial shortcomings. 'I don't think English rugby is in a great position, I really don't. Participation numbers are going down, there's all the stuff around concussion, but you just don't feel there's a huge amount of leadership.'

To Woodward's mind there remain serious unanswered questions, in particular about the way England approached the 2019 World Cup final.

'I was in Tokyo for the last week of the 2019 World Cup. I saw quite a bit of Lawrence Dallaglio and said to him, 'They're going to lose this. They think they've already won it.' Jones was organising book launches and inviting his mates in from Australia to watch training. He just got totally distracted. And he knows I think this. They left a game early.

'Why? It's never come out because no one who really knows what went on was allowed to go in and question Jones and Bill Sweeney about what really happened in that week. You had people put on a committee to say all the right things. That's why rugby doesn't deserve, at times, to be successful.' What would he say to the current England team? 'It's not your shirt, you're just the custodians of it. Make the most of it and don't get distracted. Those guys who lost in Yokohama, unless they win the next one, will always have that in the back of their minds.'

Woodward, though, was already clutching his head and rolling his eyes long before Jones walked through Twickenham's front door. England's failure to make it out of their pool at the 2015 Rugby World Cup on their own turf was another massive own goal and Woodward still feels that trying to shoehorn the rugby league signing Sam Burgess into the Red Rose midfield was a major miscalculation. 'In 2015 they just got Burgess totally wrong. He wasn't an England centre, he wasn't good enough. I think they fudged it and it cost Stuart Lancaster everything. You need guys who are really quick and Burgess wasn't quick. You can't play in the centre unless you've got real pace about you. Especially if you're coming to a game you've not played all your life.'

In his own case, it was a row over how best to kick on from the 2003 triumph that precipitated his abrupt departure from office. 'It was a power thing in the end. I wanted to be in control of the players because they were playing too many games and getting bashed up. Jonny had been beasted, no one had thought about his health. I said, "I want to be able to have an adult conversation with the clubs. If I say he's not playing on Saturday he's not playing on Saturday." I think it would have worked, but the RFU said they wouldn't pay more money to the clubs. Now they've almost moved to that model. England players hardly play for their clubs during the Six Nations.

'I just felt people were folding their arms. Someone said to me – and I believe it was minuted – that senior people were saying, "It's okay, it's all bluff, he won't leave, he loves the job too much." I'd been a big fan of Francis Baron, but he definitely changed after the World Cup. I think a lot of jealousy – not from Baron, I must stress – came through. I've subsequently been told there was massive resentment around me getting a knighthood. It was huge. You don't apply to get a knighthood, it just arrives through the post. But that did me no good at all. They were clearly saying, "If you thought he was tough before, he's going to be out of control now."'

'I've subsequently been told there was massive resentment around me getting a knighthood.'

Then there was the time when, with Nick Mallett being tipped to take the England head coaching job that eventually went to Stuart Lancaster, Woodward decided to throw his hat into the ring. 'The reason I wanted to do it is that I didn't want Nick Mallett to get the job. I didn't want a South African to be coaching England. I didn't think they'd even think about Stuart Lancaster because he hadn't coached anybody of note. Then I got a call from Nick Mallett. He said, "You know it's a total stitch-up. You and I are being used as stalking horses." I just laughed.'

He also came close to returning as the RFU's director of rugby before backroom political manoeuvres saw Rob Andrew appointed ahead of him. It was a position for which Woodward felt he would have been ideally suited. 'I didn't want to coach England, I wanted to be the director of rugby and to support the coach, which I think I'd have been good at doing. Not doing a Rassie Erasmus but sitting in a suit and tie in the committee box and making sure the head coach has everything he wanted.'

It is a recurring English oversight, he believes, whether it be in football, rugby or cricket. Selecting coaches is a particular skill. 'We pick people to be chief executives, their feathers all plump up and it's absolutely ridiculous.' Woodward argues that Jones' sacking as head coach in December 2022 was an accident waiting to happen. 'I blame Bill Sweeney and Ian Ritchie. I'd say to them, "Why did you not appoint someone below you to make that appointment and report to you with their recommendations?" They'll say, "We spoke to loads of people and all the players." That's ridiculous because they don't know either. Just because you've played the game doesn't mean you're qualified to pick a coach or to understand what the job is really is.

'The real problem is that the person making the decision has not got the skill set to appoint that coach. The whole appointment system is totally flawed. It's still an old boys' club.' If asked, would he still be interested in a role now? 'If someone came to me, I'd look at it like anyone else. I'd never say never to anything. But I think that boat has well and truly sailed.'

Similarly dated structures, he argues, are also holding back the global game. 'Europe should be way ahead of where it is at the moment. To me the Six Nations are culpable for not inviting other people to the table and having promotion and relegation. We're not trying to ditch Italy. It's the complete opposite. We're trying to say if there's a side from Georgia or Romania or Spain that is good enough, they should be given the opportunity. That's when you get more money coming into the game. Why is rugby not played at a high level in, say, Germany? Because there's no incentive to get to the top table. If rugby wanted to make a change, they'd have put Gus Pichot in charge when he ran for the chairmanship of World Rugby. Instead the old school just backed each other. The game is retreating at the moment, it really is, with the exception of France. It's so sad.'

Which is why he believes France are the side to watch, both in the short term and for the foreseeable future. 'The scary team is France. They're like England in 2003. Since 2019 they've moved well ahead of England.' And having a Frenchman in charge, argues Woodward, makes them even more formidable. 'No national head coach has ever won a World Cup when not in charge of their own country. Fabien Galthié is a clever guy with a business background. It was an inspired decision.'

It is another good reason, in his view, to fancy Les Bleus in the 2023 World Cup. 'To be at home is a huge, huge advantage. If 2003 had been at home, I think we'd have won by 30–40 points. We'd have been unbeatable. Playing away from home levels things out a little bit, especially with the match officials.'

Before he heads off there is one last Woody-ism. Even now, after everything he has done, he could never be accused of a lack of enthusiasm. 'If I was in Galthié's shoes, I'd be getting seriously excited. He's got a real chance of doing something people will never, ever forget.' Make the most of this priceless opportunity, in other words. Because, as every English supporter will testify, it might be another 20 years before it happens again.

12

THE BRAVE AND THE FAITHFUL

People liked the fact that, if we went down,
we went down swinging.

High up on the list of the greatest brainwaves of rugby's professional era was the Heineken Cup. The original idea was simplicity itself: to pit Europe's leading sides together in a competition that would take the club and provincial game to places that amateurism could not reach. The first edition, in 1995–96, involved just 12 teams from Wales, Ireland, France, Italy and Romania. Toulouse eventually beat Cardiff 21–18 after extra time in the final at Cardiff Arms Park, with 21,800 curious spectators.

Over the next couple of seasons, the concept slowly gathered momentum. Brive smashed Leicester in the 1997 final, again in Cardiff, and Bath became the first English winners the following year. Until the 1998–99 season, when the English clubs boycotted the tournament, there had been no Irish representation in the knockout stages. This prompted euphoric scenes when Ulster defeated Colomiers in the 1999 final at Lansdowne Road.

In the early years, even so, the whole adventure still had a relatively homespun feel. The average quarter-final attendance in 1999 was a little over 8,500. There were few obvious signs as to how big the tournament would become, let alone the side who would elevate the tournament to another stratosphere of popularity. Without Munster the trajectory of European club rugby would have been much gentler.

Even those clad in the red jersey did not initially see it coming. Working in a garage in Tipperary town, for example, a young Alan Quinlan knew of Munster's illustrious past and their famous wins over

145

New Zealand and Australia, but his initial affiliations were with his local side Clanwilliam and, subsequently, Shannon RFC. When he played his first game for his province in 1996, it felt 'special', but professionalism was still such a novelty no one really knew what the future held. 'When I started in the garage there was no such thing as professional rugby. Some days you had to pinch yourself. *I'm not going to work in the overalls, I'm putting on a tracksuit, I have a nice sponsored car and we're getting paid to do something we could have been doing anyway.*'

Gradually, though, Quinlan and his mates looked around the dressing room and realised they had the makings of a decent side. Mick Galwey, Keith Wood and Anthony Foley were all influential leaders. At half back were two likely lads, Ronan O'Gara and Peter Stringer, with a bit about them. Stringer was just 1.52 metres (5 feet) in tall, but his top-of-the-range passing ability neatly complemented O'Gara's tactical savvy and kicking skills. Knitting everything together was Declan Kidney, who had first coached Stringer in the U13s at Presentation Brothers College in Cork. Kidney spoke quietly but he was canny and hated losing. In that autumn of 1999, Munster strung a few wins together before heading over to play Saracens in the pool stages of the Heineken Cup. Having trailed 21–9 at half time, the visitors snatched a thrilling 35–34 victory via a last-gasp try from Jeremy Staunton and conversion by O'Gara.

There were only 40-odd Munster fans present, but a seed had been sown. The following January, Saracens were narrowly beaten again, this time 31–30 courtesy of another late O'Gara conversion that bounced in off an upright. Having finished top of their pool, Munster saw off Stade Français 27–10 in the quarter-final and headed to Bordeaux to face Toulouse in the semi-final with excitement soaring almost as high as the pitchside temperature at Stade Lescure. Even those of us sitting in the press box were feeling the heat, and Toulouse were similarly red-hot favourites.

It was to prove a truly remarkable occasion. With Toulouse leading 18–17, their Kiwi centre Lee Stensness knocked on with a four-on-two overlap available. Instead it was Munster who seized the moment, a slick 80-metre attack ending with O'Gara scoring at the other end. The final score was 31–25 and the post-match scenes were epic. Galwey even took a long-distance mobile call from the actor Richard Harris, away filming in Mexico but desperate to share in the joyous moment.

Irish rugby's finest hour in France was meant to have been the previous March when the national team achieved their first success in Paris for 28 years. This, though, was a vintage result in anyone's language. 'The performance that day was phenomenal,' confirms Quinlan. 'It was the start of the whole fairytale of Europe: what it meant to us as players, the way we embraced it. It was an incredible high – followed by an incredible low in the final against Northampton. But suddenly we were more than just competitors. It wasn't just about taking part. We started to believe we could have a crack at winning it.'

'It was the start of the whole fairytale of Europe: what it meant to us as players, the way we embraced it.'

For a while, though, it seemed destined not to be. O'Gara missed four place kicks in the final at Twickenham as Northampton won 9–8. Two years later, Munster were beaten finalists again, this time by Leicester in Cardiff after Neil Back's sly hand had dislodged the ball from Stringer's grasp at a crucial juncture. The bitter disappointment simply made Munster's players hungrier. They were not about to shrug their shoulders and slink away.

The ultimate proof was forthcoming in January 2003. Not even Munster's most faithful fans foresaw them beating their fancied opponents Gloucester by four clear tries and 27 points, the implausible margin required to reach the knock-out stages. Somehow they nailed it, with O'Gara crucially converting John Kelly's 80th-minute try to complete a 33–5 win. Munster didn't do cool and trendy; I remember '(Do) the Hucklebuck' booming out of the public address system before the game. But Thomond Park possessed a rugby soul like nowhere else. Of all the club days I have attended live in Britain and Ireland, the so-called Miracle Match still ranks as the most remarkable.

What made it even more striking was the sense of a shared passion linking the players and supporters, mixed in with old-fashioned ambition. 'We had a lot of high achievers and guys who had real motivation and desire to be successful with Munster, to play for Ireland and to get the best out of themselves,' confirms Quinlan now.

'We weren't really sure what we had because we didn't know what everyone else had. But what we tried to create was a real hard edge and an honesty. We had great fun, we were great friends and we pushed each other together. I looked forward to going into training and meeting those guys every day. It was a collective effort of drive and desire from individuals who didn't even play for Ireland. If you turned up, and worked hard, you were respected. That was the minimum requirement.'

The unflashy, hard-nosed Quinlan was a prime example. The great Paul O'Connell wrote in his autobiography that his teammate 'epitomised everything I thought was great about Munster. He was a savage trainer, a fantastic footballer, incredibly committed and unbelievable craic.' Quinlan himself also believes star players were not, ultimately, Munster's trump card. 'Paul would be the first to admit some of the most inspiring people in our group were guys who didn't have glitz or glamour. Someone like John Hayes didn't want to talk to the media. He'd just want to jump in his car, leave the University of Limerick and get home in the evening. He epitomised the environment of accountability and sacrifice. Figuring out how you can get as fit as you can and how you look after your body. Not going out drinking, not eating shit food.

'We had great fun, but the most enjoyable part was trying to understand and embrace professionalism. Understanding that we needed to be fitter, that we needed to train harder and act and behave better off the field.' Old pros like John Langford and Keith Wood helped set the tone, showing the rest what 'maxing out' in training looked like. 'We had incredible days and nights out, but as we got older and grew as a team those nights out weren't the same. We were starting to embrace and understand what was really required. The sacrifices you have to make, as a player and as a team. It went from people going back and having a few pints wherever they wanted on a Saturday or Sunday, or during the week, to picking your nights out and saying, "Maybe we'll have a few pints at the end of the month."'

The beauty of Munster, though, was that characters were not merely tolerated but celebrated. The craggy old prop Peter Clohessy, for example. 'Claw did what he wanted, when he wanted,' recalls Quinlan. 'He trained when he wanted as well. Claw never killed himself with the fitness thing because he was coming towards the end of his career. But he was an incredible player for us. He and Mick Galwey were around for a number of years before a lot of us . . . they were mentors and guys who reminded us what it meant to pull on the jersey. It was like they were handing over the baton to the new generation; Mick Galwey kind of handed it over to Donncha O'Callaghan, Claw passed it over to Marcus Horan. We had a team that if you didn't train hard or look after yourself you'd feel guilty because you were letting everybody down.'

There was also Kidney's softly spoken influence. Rugby teams, to him, are like a chair with four essential legs. Without skill, fitness, mental strength and a life outside rugby, there can be no proper balance. Being local, he also knew exactly how people were feeling; from day one he also encouraged them to aim high. 'He would convince us that some day we'd win Europe,' recalls Quinlan. 'We thought he was crazy. But there was a massive mindset shift over the years and he would have been integral to that. He was very clever. He tried to get to know the individuals. At the start we didn't click, but we became great pals and had great respect for each other. No coach will ever please everyone, but he was a phenomenal part of our success.'

Munster were lucky to hire another shrewd guru when Kidney spent three years elsewhere between 2002 and 2005. Alan Gaffney had spent years coaching at Randwick and was smart enough to realise there was no need to reinvent the Munster wheel. The arrival of another Australian, Jim Williams, added a further layer of steel in 2001, even if Quinlan was slightly taken aback when his signing was announced. 'Lots of us would put pressure on to see if we could sign more players to improve the squad. I was probably one of those who was always trying to do that. We knew that at times we'd be coming up against teams who had bigger stars and bigger budgets than us. And then they went and signed Jim Williams right in my position. I remember thinking, *I should have kept my mouth shut.*' Luckily Williams fitted in seamlessly. 'He bought into the ingredients that we demanded out of people. A hard edge and a toughness. And the sense that if you wanted to beat Munster back then, you were going to have to earn it.'

Making the mix even more potent was the fact that Foley, O'Connell, Hayes, Quinlan, David Wallace, Jerry Flannery and others were all Munster born and bred. Some of their bristling intent was modelled on Leicester – 'We would have mirrored ourselves on them: the tradition, the packed stadium. It was a similar scenario to Thomond Park' – but much of it was home-produced. Playing for Shannon, whose clubhouse was at Thomond Park, Quinlan grew up knowing precisely who he was representing. 'Something I was always really proud of was the picture of me being put on that wall as a club international. I used to look up at the pictures of Mick Galwey, Gerry McLoughlin and Brian O'Brien . . . suddenly, from my group, between seven and 10 of us got capped.'

And when the going got tough, or whenever 'The Fields of Athenry' was being belted out, Munster responded like men possessed. 'Axel [Foley] would always say, "You've just got to turn up, play and remember you're wearing the Munster jersey." People often ask me what I miss the most about playing and the thing that comes to mind the most is being able to look around the dressing room and see the bond that had been created. We had less expectation, less social media and fewer internet chat rooms. By and large we had less pressure. There's so much scrutiny nowadays. But nothing has changed for me when you put on that jersey. I felt special every time. That's what always stands out for me. I was wearing something that was historic and we were always mindful of the previous people who had done so. Declan Kidney was really good at getting that message across and so was Jerry Holland, our manager.'

Add in the devotion of their fans in following their heroes to all parts, and it became a shared crusade that transcended mere sport. Quinlan calls it 'a unique journey' and he is right. 'One of the biggest drivers was having good coaches and good people around us. But, ultimately, it was having incredible characters and players who have gone on proving themselves. We were lucky as well. The mentality of modern sports people is that they want to play in the Champions League in soccer and challenge for trophies. We didn't really have people saying, "I want to go to Leinster or Toulouse or Bath". From 2000 we were already knocking on the door in Europe.

We never had a situation where people were wanting to go somewhere else to win trophies; we were in there rolling the dice. That's a brilliant environment to be in.'

* * * * *

Munster's quest to secure a European title, though, remained an itch everyone desperately wanted to scratch. Toulouse had beaten them in the semi-finals in 2003 and Wasps had done likewise in 2004. While the latter game ranked among the all-time great Heineken Cup contests, that was scant consolation. In 2005 they were beaten in the quarter-finals in San Sebastian by Biarritz. On New Year's Eve that year, a 35–23 away loss to Leinster in the Celtic League prompted a furious Roy Keane-style post-match tirade from Ronan O'Gara in the dressing room. The gist was that Munster needed to aim higher and make scoring tries more of a priority in big games, rather than relying on penalty goals in ferociously tight contests.

Occasionally O'Gara's teammates would call him Victor Meldrew because of his constant refusal to settle for mediocrity. He was usually right and a few ruffled feathers were worthwhile if collective improvement resulted. At home on the Île de Ré, having just returned from a game of padel tennis, O'Gara chuckles afresh at the old nickname and says little has changed. 'After almost 25 years it's just become the norm. You probably don't understand how demanding you are. But I don't think you want to change that. It's the same with people like Owen Farrell. That's what makes them tick. It's what makes me tick. When you play 10, you need everybody humming to bring out the best in you. Particularly if you're not a physical freak of an athlete, which I wasn't.'

Reminiscing with O'Gara about Munster is even more fascinating since he has become a trophy-winning coach elsewhere. When his Stade Rochelais side won the Heineken Champions Cup in 2022, it was hard not to draw parallels with the Munster sides in which he played: a team from outside the big-city elite with a fanatical following, seeking to break new ground with a heady blend of mental resilience, character and ambition. Had La Rochelle worn red instead of yellow and black, the comparisons might have been spooky.

O'Gara will also tell you he has learned much from his time coaching at the Crusaders, particularly about not putting high-profile sides like New Zealand on too high a rugby pedestal. 'That was just the way we were coached and brought up. With hindsight, it was very frustrating for me. If I'd known that as a player, I'd have had a very different mindset going into games.'

'Sport rarely happens like that . . . where all the pieces of the jigsaw come together on the biggest day in your calendar.'

His outlook, though, remains fundamentally shaped by the Munster ethos in which he was reared. As a Cork man himself, O'Gara always knew where his side's super strength lay. 'It was based on local players, albeit with some quality input, and I can't emphasise that enough. I think the only way a team succeeds is if you have a lot of young local boys who come through the academy. Without that core I don't think you have any heartbeat. For me that's crucial in trying to plan for success.' La Rochelle's European final success over Leinster in Marseille also had echoes of Munster's glory days. 'At 18–10 down and with a yellow card against a super team, it would have been easy to fold. That's hopefully the Munster spirit that has been ingrained into La Rochelle. That's why it was incredibly special. But I'm smart enough to realise that only happens occasionally in your career. Sport rarely happens like that . . . where all the pieces of the jigsaw come together on the biggest day in your calendar'

At La Rochelle, though, they believe O'Gara has also imported something else: a winner's mentality. As his former captain, the ex-All Black Victor Vito, once told me, 'Ever since Ronan got here, he's asked the same question: "Why not us?" He's just an ultimate competitor. I'm sure he was like that when he played, but he just wants to win so bad.' The cultural change at 'La Rog-chelle', whose Stade Marcel-Deflandre ground is named after the former club president executed by the Nazis as a Resistance leader in 1944, has been striking. 'When I got here, guys were smoking round the corner of the changing room,' laughed Vito. 'Now at least they drive somewhere else to do it.'

That steely edge was very much Munster's trademark, without a great deal of sophistication involved at the outset. Even the master motivator Kidney, reckons O'Gara, was feeling his way at times. 'You've got to remember he was my schoolteacher. I'd had him since fourth year and he was very much learning on the job. It just doesn't happen like that in sport anymore . . . the system doesn't leave holes for people like that to coach. That's not having a go. He did a lot of good things for me. We were brilliant for caring for each other but we probably needed a little bit more of a technical aspect. To win European championships you needed an all-round game and that's where we got to in the end.'

What Munster did possess was a fortress which made even the best visitors quake. Limerick is not a cosy kind of town, and the old Thomond Park had a no-frills concrete hardness to it even before you factored in their fanatical fans. 'Thomond Park was an incredibly daunting venue to play in,' recalls O'Gara fondly. 'The absolute respect for the opposition goalkickers also made them shit the bed. They just couldn't handle it. Looking back at the old footage, the tone set by the supporters is barely believable. Those occasions were something else.' The victorious pool games that stick out for him, against Sale in 2006 and Wasps in 2008, were perfect examples.

It also helped that, in common with many of the sides featured in this book, they had the right individuals in the dressing room. 'Strong characters, yeah, but good people who really had their teammates' backs,' confirms O'Gara. 'A lot of us were Munster stalwarts for 10 to 15 years: we were essentially a real family. That's gone out of the team in Munster nowadays, but there was an incredible connection between the supporters and the team. There were plenty of times we got beaten, but it was very rare for it to be down to a dishonest performance. That became our DNA: people liked that these boys in red would show up. I played 10 European Cup semi-finals. Maybe we lacked a little bit of quality, but I think people liked the fact that, if we went down, we went down swinging.'

At long last it all bore fruit when Munster beat Biarritz 23–19 in Cardiff in 2006. There must have been 55,000 Munster fans in the stadium with another 20,000 ticket-less supporters outside and thousands more looking on from Limerick's O'Connell Street. For many, the cheeky try scored down the blindside by Stringer was the keynote image, but O'Gara's abiding memory occured before a ball was even kicked. 'One of my clearest memories, and a lot of it is lost, would be walking on to the pitch at the Millennium Stadium. It's a nice entrance into a gladiatorial ring. I just remember Paul O'Connell saying, "We've got to play, boys. We've got to play." In the previous two finals we were playing not to get beaten. Against Biarritz we expressed ourselves better.'

The fact the Holy Grail had taken since 2000 to materialise also heightened the sensation. 'Six years in sport is an eternity. The initial reaction was enormous relief as opposed to complete and utter joy. It was a team with a lot of talent and guts; there were nine of us from the one club initially picked to go on the 2009 Lions tour to South Africa. There were a lot of special players, but standards weren't necessarily pre-established. It was very much a case of learning on the job to be the best you could be. Sports psychology was in its infancy. We understood it was important but it's way more advanced today. That's probably why it was so special. You felt like you were winning Europe with the most basic of ingredients.'

The comic-book narrative was further enriched by some entertaining old yarns. Like the time Donncha O'Callaghan, with the aid of two packets of cornflakes, smuggled several ducks into Munster's team room just prior to a meeting. Those, however, who assumed Munster were primarily a bunch of messers were missing the other half of the equation. 'Everyone thought it was pints all weekend, but we were bloody serious,' stresses O'Gara. 'We sacrificed a lot. It was a serious set-up, very competitive and ruthless, as it always has to be to get the best players on the pitch. But you have to have fun. If it's not fun, it drags. And the minute you find the day dragging, you may as well pass it to someone else. You haven't created the right environment.'

By the time 2008 came around, with Kidney poised to take over as Ireland coach, everyone knew what was required. The squad even had some extra southern-hemisphere backline class in the shape of Doug Howlett, Rua Tipoki and Lifeimi Mafi. 'We started becoming an attractive proposition,' recalls Quinlan. 'People wanted to come and play for

Munster. There was maybe an intrigue about us. I still meet French players who tell me how much they would have loved to have played for Munster. You might be picking the French sides ahead of us as regards quality, but our work ethic and desire made a difference. There was never a point where we reached the end of a season and said, "Well, that's great, we've got to another semi-final."

'Nothing was completely perfect, we had our limitations. We didn't have the same purse strings as some of the French clubs. But we made the most of what we had. Certain characters like Ronan O'Gara and Paul O'Connell were obviously rare leaders who would leave no stone unturned in terms of how they and the group could get better. You could have regrets and say, "We won two, we could possibly have won four." That's not being unrealistic or cocky. We could have done. We were in the mix. That was really special.'

Either way, the nerves prior to the 2008 final were still savage. For some it was the conclusion of a wild ride and Quinlan, for one, will forever savour the 16–13 final victory over Toulouse. 'That team in 2008 was probably one of the best Munster teams I ever played with. Even as we got older, we were getting fitter. I won a Heineken Cup aged 34 and probably played some of my best rugby because of the likes of Paul, "Rog" and John Hayes. A lot of the time we were training behind the scenes. Most of the forwards were in Limerick, but Donncha and Frankie Sheahan would even come up from Cork for extra sessions on weekends when we didn't have matches. A lot of that stuff went on. If we heard the Cork lads were doing extra training, we'd feel guilty in Limerick.'

All of it paid off in the end. Munster may have subsequently endured a few lean years, but European rugby still owes them a sizeable debt. Their legacy also reflects the ferocious competitive desire of players like O'Gara, still far and away the tournament's highest points-scorer. 'If he has his mind set on something, then he will achieve it,' said Donnacha Ryan, his assistant coach, following last year's European finale. 'He has been a success as a coach at Racing, Crusaders and now La Rochelle. It is not an accident that has happened.' The same applies to Munster's golden era, still as vividly clear in the mind's eye as it ever was.

13

DISTANT HORIZONS

We'd be running in with knees, there'd be head butts,
there'd be fighting.

As every journalist knows, the easiest way to grasp a complicated subject is to go and ask someone smarter than yourself. That explains my presence on the outskirts of Abingdon, plodding through the February drizzle to meet the author of one of the most perceptive and enjoyable books ever written about rugby. At this point, clearly, I must prostrate myself at the feet of Stephen Jones, Donald McRae, Stuart Barnes and every other oval-ball Hemingway out there. Forgive me, fellas. You're all still up there on Mount Olympus. It's just that Richard Beard's *Muddied Oafs* nailed rugby's sense of brotherhood so perfectly it should be a set text for anyone interested in this imperfect sport.

The following quotation from page one should be stuck on every clubhouse wall from Wiveliscombe to Wanganui:

My cheek and eye are crushed into grass and mud, several half-naked strangers are piled at angles beside and on top of me and softly, from the sea-grey sky, it starts to rain. Which is when I think, I seriously think: *God I love this game.*

Brilliantly evocative, no? Two decades on from the publication of his seminal work, Beard has agreed to have lunch and to revisit some of the life lessons learned during his various amateur club stints in England, Scotland, France, Switzerland and Japan. All I have to do is listen to his literary brain humming. And nod sagely, as if it were an everyday occurrence to hear some of my own half-baked theories being so smoothly articulated.

Because the crux of *Muddied Oafs* is what makes rugby special: that wherever the game is being played around the world, the participants share a universal *esprit de corps*. 'Everywhere you go, every rugby club will give a different version of a sense of belonging,' confirms Beard. 'That'll be very different in an agricultural community in Scotland to the sense of belonging in Paris. Each club has its own identity.'

Very often, he reckons, these identities will involve playing up to certain stereotypes. 'When I was playing on the west coast of Scotland and we went down to Glasgow, we'd be the sheep shaggers. And everyone in the group played up to that. In Paris you are the intellectuals: you're effete and dilettantes. You're expected to wear a bow tie, you're expected to buy into it. There's a conformist aspect at any club – but at the core of it is the utmost respect and admiration for the courage of everyone else on the team. Even the ones who aren't the best players – you can't help but admire the fact they turn up. Someone's got to be the least skilful player in the team.'

And pretty much everywhere Beard went he discovered something else. 'I found what rugby had always claimed: that it would welcome you and give you a sense of belonging. To find that actually happening felt like a miracle. It turned out that all these places, whether it was in Geneva or Japan, were much more similar than they were different. It allowed me to stay quite grounded in the communities where I was. And to meet a huge number of very interesting people, which I'm not sure I would have done in any other way.'

Beard also still found playing the game strangely therapeutic until well into his mid-30s, a release from the cares of novel-writing and almost everything else. 'It's like a switch. When you're playing rugby, you cannot think about anything else. You've got 16-stone guys trying to run you over. You're not going to think about anything else. You're genuinely getting a Saturday off. You're not going for a walk and thinking about your book the whole time. It's like a washing-machine cycle for your brain. It just completely cleans you out and then you can start again. I think that's the joy of it. And staying around for a few beers afterwards is part of it. We've all been 'cleaned', we've all been through this cycle and wasn't it amazing?'

Fair enough, but what about those people who don't instinctively get that buzz from the faint waft of Deep Heat or the clatter of metal studs in a dressing room corridor? Or those with a low pain threshold? I wonder how Beard would sell the essence of the game to non-converts. He rises to the challenge like a literary salmon. 'Imagine having a line of large people in front of you, all of whom want to knock you to the floor.

'It's a moment of utter transcendence and joy I've never found in another sport.'

Then, somehow, you find a way through without anyone laying a hand on you and space miraculously opens up. It's a moment of utter transcendence and joy I've never found in another sport. It's also terrifying because everyone is now trying to catch you up. But that moment, when the whole field opens up, is just fantastic.'

If asked – and possibly even if not – he will also happily talk you through the finest moment of his own playing career, which occurred at Gordano RFC when he was 35 years old. 'Everyone knows Gordano. It's on the left as you go down the M5. It was just a stonking try . . . I took a great line, stood up the last defender and went outside him. I remember just thinking, *This is what it's all about and it'll soon be gone.*'

Okay, okay. But we still haven't discussed that hoariest of rugby clichés. There is an argument that the classic put-down – 'Rugby's a middle-class sport' – does more to hold back the English game, in particular, than almost anything else. Beard, conveniently, is also an expert on this subject having written a searing book, *Sad Little Men*, about the psychological after-effects of a public school education. He cites the example of a certain former British prime minister, educated at Eton. 'Remember the famous Darius Guppy tapes? He's asking Boris Johnson to give him the address of a journalist so he can beat him up. There'll be a few rib injuries but "nothing you haven't suffered in rugby". It's clearly part of his mental landscape, as it is a lot of public schoolboys' mental landscapes.'

Perceptions, in other words, can be hard to shift. Beard recounts another telling story about a phone call he received after the publication of *Muddied Oafs* in 2003. Someone at the *Guardian* – bless 'em – wanted him to investigate whether rugby was actually more of a people's game than was popularly assumed. 'They said, "Shall we do a piece about the reach of rugby?" I said, "Great, come to Bristol. There are 32 rugby clubs there, a huge mix of people, all walks of life." And they said, "Oh. We were thinking of going to Henley."'

It is another good example of how rugby and those who play it are often viewed. There are millions of people who assume rugby players only drink beer through their underpants and exchange endless fart jokes. This, as everyone knows, is rarely true: the underpants were probably lobbed through the skylight of the team bus several hours earlier. Beard, though, does not accept such caricatures. 'There is this assumption that rugby players don't read, that it's not a literate community. But at the same time people want to say it's a middle-class game. You can't really have it both ways. Regionally the story is not the classic one of public schoolboys and old men in blazers, insisting on their right to be first to the bar. There's a limited imagination about it sometimes.'

Lunch is almost over, but before Beard jumps on his bike we briefly skim through some of rugby's most famous chroniclers who, at various times, have helped to elevate the game to a different level. Arthur Conan Doyle and P.G. Wodehouse definitely make the match day squad, along with James Joyce who, as reflected in *A Portrait of the Artist as a Young Man*, was a slightly nervous schoolboy rugby player in Co Kildare. 'He kept on the fringe . . . out of the reach of the rude feet, feigning to run now and then.' A little youthful apprehension on a rugby field, reckons Beard, did Joyce's writing no harm at all. 'Maybe it's the way to make an artist: to introduce them to rugby as a young person. Give them a hard time of it, but later on they'll write *Ulysses*.' Something to cling to there for quivering fifth-team wingers praying for their waking nightmares to end.

* * * * *

But what about keen wannabe players who grow up in parts of the world where rugby is either a minority sport or the national side is a pimple on the hairy backside of the established order? We once asked the German-born Phil Christophers, who made his debut for England in 2002, whether it had been a childhood ambition to wear the Red Rose. He smiled politely at us. 'Ambition? It's more like a dream,' he replied. 'If you grow up in Germany, it's difficult to think *I'm going to move over to England and play for my country*. You've got to think realistically.'

In his case, the combination of a rugby-mad father, a few imported videos featuring David Duckham and a decent work ethic helped him make the leap from Heidelberg, his home until the age of 16, to the hallowed turf of Twickenham. His father Gerald met his Berlin-raised mother Katrin when he was working as an international salesman in the chemical industry, and he took his son along to their local club at the age of four. 'In Germany there are two towns which are particularly interested in rugby, if you wanted it,' Christophers told us. 'I was fortunate enough to grow up in one of them.'

It was only in his teens, when he was sent away to Royal Grammar School, Lancaster and went on to represent England at U16 and U18 level, that bigger rugby doors started to open. A gap year in France after attending Loughborough University saw him end up in Brive's first team, and signing for Bristol helped propel him into the England team at the age of 22. He scored a lovely try against Argentina in Buenos Aires on his debut, jinking past the full back Ignacio Corleto, but won just two further caps through a mixture of injuries, family issues and relocating back to France.

There are many others who, simply by dint of geography, have to jump through hoops that players from bigger nations simply cannot conceive. I particularly remember being approached by a Latvian contact who told me I should write a piece about the unshakeable pillar of his country's rugby team, Uldis Saulite. There are only five clubs and 500 active players, women and children included, in Latvia and most of their citizens follow ice hockey and basketball, viewing rugby as a minority pastime for 'crazy people'.

In his native city of Jelgava, the young Uldis did not play the game until he was 16. Naturally big and strong – 1.98 m and 127 kg (6ft 6in and 20 stone) – he caught the eye of two former Latvian internationals, one of whom gave him the money to pay for the late bus home from training he could not otherwise have afforded. He grew steadily fitter and sought to combine rugby with his day job as an apprentice carpenter.

Shortly after he had turned 21, a Latvian referee based in Russia advised him that Enisei-STM, a club side in Siberia, were trialling new players. Enisei are based in Krasnoyarsk, where winter temperatures routinely dip to -40°C (-40°F). Even so, Uldis fancied trying his luck 5,000 km (3,100 miles) east on the banks of the frozen Yenisei river. Early in 2001, in the depths of a harsh Siberian winter, he arrived in Russia to pursue his dream.

The early days were predictably tough. The club's forwards coach ran a hotel and allowed him to stay rent-free in exchange for basic chores, but Uldis's rudimentary skills were not deemed good enough to earn an immediate contract. In just his second practice session he accidentally broke a first-team lock's collarbone, which endeared him even less to his new teammates. He stayed put only because 'I didn't want to return to Latvia as a loser.' In order to discover the true depth of his resolve, the club's captain subsequently challenged the Latvian incomer to a fight. The latter's blunt refusal to back down convinced the squad it might be wiser to keep their big new recruit onside.

It still took six months before he received his first wage packet, which was seven times smaller than his carpenter salary in Latvia. 'I wanted to play professional rugby so badly that it didn't bother me at all.' He also put his body on the line internationally for Latvia, once turning up to represent his national team despite recently broken ribs. Refusing to let his country down, Uldis strapped himself up with a chunk of old bed mattress, had a pain-killing jab and played on. Back in his native Latvia they nicknamed their hero the Siberian Bear and took immense pride in his exploits.

Finally, in 2010, the big man's break materialised. Never having had an agent, he had struggled to attract interest from overseas clubs, but the

French club Bordeaux Bègles urgently needed someone as injury cover. Finally he had the chance to swap the Siberian gloom for the vineyards of south-western France – until disaster struck. Major surgery was deemed necessary to correct a long-standing back problem. Now the wrong side of 30, he had no choice but to remain in Krasnoyarsk, where he had also married the club president's daughter. One day, with the temperature at -44°C, he recalls his shoes almost cracking in the extreme cold. Still he soldiered on in the second row deep into his late 30s. 'The hope dies last,' he told our mutual friend. Good luck telling the Bear – or, for that matter, Chile's long-serving Pablo Lemoine or the flinty Georgian legend Mamuka Gorgodze – that rugby is a game whose beating heart is primarily to be found on the playing fields of English public schools.

* * * * *

On the edge of the Kalahari desert in Namibia, Jacques Burger is another warrior with an extraordinary tale to tell. These days the former Saracens flanker is a sheep farmer on a 5,666-hectare (14,000-acre) property near Stampriet, some 300 km (185 miles) and a three-hour drive south of the national capital Windhoek. The first couple of years of this new life coincided with one of the worst droughts in Namibia's history. Not for nothing does the Kalahari take its name from the Tswana word *Kgala,* which translates as 'the great thirst'. Then came COVID. 'It was a very tough time,' admits Burger. Coming from one of the toughest men ever to play rugby union, that feels like an understatement.

He is living proof, too, that overcoming vast odds is often a matter of belief. In his early years representing Namibia, he played in African Cup fixtures which would have traumatised most people. 'I played games in Tunisia, Zambia and Ivory Coast where anything went. Back then the refereeing was terrible. There were punch-ups every time, eye gouging, kicking. In World Cup qualifying games in Morocco and Tunisia I've been shot at by supporters using slingshots to hit players on the pitch. They'd be waking us up in our hotels as well. It was crazy.'

To survive as a young player there was just one option: front up or be taken apart. 'Anything went. We'd be running in with knees, there'd be head butts, there'd be fighting. You had to take it and, unfortunately, dish it out as well. Especially as a back rower, I needed to get stuck in. They were tough times, but they definitely grow character. We went to Uganda once and in the morning at breakfast there was just bread. We asked if there was anything else and the guy from the hotel said, "Listen, this is not England."'

'Back in the day it was war. You'd go out and smash each other and then you'd run to your bus and get out of there.'

So much, too, for the romantic guff about rugby values and gentlemanly conduct. 'A lot of countries haven't got that rugby culture of respect for each other. I think a lot of African countries still have to learn what that means. There wasn't a lot of love . . . everybody just wanted to go to the World Cup. Back in the day it was war. You'd go out and smash each other and then you'd run to your bus and get out of there. That's the way it was. It sounds like 100 years ago, but the game has changed so much in a short period of time.'

Even making it out of his Namibian homeland and into the foothills of the professional game required a state of mind that went way beyond youthful enthusiasm. It soon transpired that the crooked-nosed, shaggy-haired Burger had a remarkable blend of inexhaustible desire, focused aggression and almost suicidal bravery. 'The mentality of throwing that first punch, so to speak, has always been in me. I grew up living with my grandmother and never really had a great relationship with my parents, until now. When I was younger, I always felt like I had to battle things on my own. I got into a lot of trouble with a lot of confrontational things and when you're a kid you don't always do it the right way.

'It was similar in my rugby career. Every time I stepped on the pitch, for me, it was a battle: it's me or you. I wanted to make that first impact, I wanted to be that spark in a team that sets everybody at ease. I just tried to get involved as soon as possible. The game is about skill, physique, power and pace, but it is a mental game as much as it is a physical one. If you impose yourself and get stuck in, there are a lot of guys who are not going to enjoy that part of the game. I wanted to unsettle people, get in their faces and plant that seed of doubt in the other team's head.'

His fondness for the game was also fostered by hanging around the dressing rooms at the Wanderers club in Windhoek where his father was the manager. 'He did everything: he put out the shirts, did the strapping, gave painkilling injections, the lot. That's how I fell in love with it. We didn't get a lot of the UK leagues on TV, so I used to set my alarm at 2 a.m. and watch Super 10 games.'

In some Namibian clubs they have been known to present a stuffed warthog's head as a post-match trophy, and the bone-hard pitches also breed a certain resilience. Burger's ethos, though, was simple. 'A lot of youngsters ask me to find them a club because there are no opportunities here. It is a lot easier to be seen in countries with professional set-ups . . . we haven't really got a proper structure to grow the game in Namibia, which is a bit worrying because we are a country which really loves our rugby. But what I believe is that if you play well enough and work hard enough it doesn't matter if there are only 10 or 20 people watching. Someone is going to see you and take note that this kid really wants it.'

In Burger's case it was a tour to the UK with the African Leopards, coached by a certain Brendan Venter, that eventually led to a contract offer at Saracens. 'We beat the British Army and I remember having a big gash in my chin from some Fijian's boot. Brendan had to restitch my stitches afterwards.' If Venter was an all-action player, Burger was even more energised. 'At that time, I was really hungry. That was the main thing that drove me: to use my opportunity and to play rugby. Being on the pitch is an amazing feeling. There's nowhere to hide.'

Also encouraged by Namibia's wheelchair-bound coach Danie Vermeulen, he was no. 8 in the Namibian squad for the 2007 Rugby World Cup. He and his teammates lost their warm-up game against South Africa 105–13. Less than four weeks later they restricted Ireland to a 32–15 victory in Bordeaux, a triumph of mind over matter if ever there was one. 'Every time I played for Namibia and put that shirt on, you think of where you started and the limited opportunities you get in a country like ours.'

The 2011 World Cup, though, was the one where Burger truly forged his indestructible reputation. Namibia, shamefully, were forced to play Fiji, Samoa, South Africa and Wales in the space of 16 days and Burger played every minute, even after suffering a fractured cheekbone against the Springboks. In total he made 64 tackles in four games, much of it on one leg. 'I had so much fluid on my knee that after every match I had to get it drained and couldn't train. I just kept going and going. Every time you play in a World Cup it is special, but looking back at it now I was tired. But I was still a youngster and the body could take it back then.'

After the tournament he was named among the top five most impressive players in the tournament on World Rugby's website, as recognition for the supreme effort he made. As captain it also fell to him to try and instil belief in the battered part-timers alongside him. 'We only trained together for about a month before the World Cup and most of the guys are amateur players. You want 22 or 23 guys willing to do exactly what you want to do. But then you look around and you see a plumber or a dentist. A lot of guys are numb in a strange kind of way. They know the experience is going to be so big, it's exciting for them just to be involved. To get belief into guys is the toughest thing of all. But you have to put that frustration to bed when you start playing for Namibia.'

Then, in 2012, he suffered a knee injury so bad it kept him out for two years. Subsequently he took to carrying the metal plates and screws in his kit bag to remind him of what he had overcome. 'Until the age of 28 I was never on the physio bed. I thought I would play the game for ever. Then I got my first knee injury and then my shoulders went. The last three years of my career were agony. I don't think there were a lot of guys at Saracens who thought I'd start playing again.

'On match days I'd walk down the stairs and not be able to put any pressure or weight on my knee. *Jeez, how am I going to play a match today if I can't walk down the stairs?* Then you'd play anyway. It's amazing what you can put your body through. I was always in pain, but I think it's something you get used to.'

One Saracens game underlined it better than most. They played a supposedly hard-edged Clermont Auvergne at Twickenham in the

European semi-finals and won by the staggering margin of 46–6. Burger put in 28 tackles in 70 minutes, none of them remotely half-hearted. As he joked afterwards, 'Luckily I've got a face that hides pain well.'

A second Premiership title with Saracens followed in 2015, but by the time he retired at the end of the 2015–16 season his body was in pieces. 'I went to discuss a shoulder surgery before I came back to Namibia and the specialist said to me, "Listen, it's like rearranging the deckchairs on the *Titanic*. It's not really going to change anything. You need it to be replaced."'

These days the challenge is a slightly different one. Adjusting to life after rugby – 'It takes a while to accept that it's over, that you've done your bit on a rugby pitch' – is tough for everyone but all the more so for people who have donated as much of themselves to the cause as Burger. In tandem with the farming – 'We've had some good rains in the last two years, things are looking up' – he is keen to put something back. 'I've got a massive passion for it and I think it would be selfish not to do anything. We've got so much talent here, so many kids who grow up in a rugby culture. If we can get things in place and play in more competitive tournaments, we'll be a force and you'll see special things coming from Namibian rugby.'

For that to happen, though, the financial ship will need steadying. 'There are so many stories of money being invested into Namibia and just disappearing. We need selfless people who really want to grow the game rather than going on a free trip to a World Cup for the perks. We are getting better but there's so much more that can be done. If the money goes to the right places in all the developing countries . . . look at what Georgia are doing. You need the right people at the top and there are a lot of people willing to get involved. I'd like to be involved because I think we can do some special things over here.' If anyone can make it happen, it is Africa's most uncompromising rugby export.

14

FIRST AMONG EQUALS

You've just got to get the ball to this young kid.

You know it when you see it. It might only be a half break or a deft little pass in a humdrum club game, but sometimes it is enough. You can just tell. Not, necessarily, that a newcomer will go on to win 100 Test caps but definitely that their ability will set them apart. And you never forget those moments of sweet revelation. For me, in a half century of watching rugby union, it has probably happened 'live' on five occasions.

A couple of the quintet are still soldiering on. France's Gaël Fickou has taken a while to be properly appreciated but finally he is fulfilling the precocious promise he displayed as an 18-year-old on his Heineken Cup debut for Stade Toulousain against Leicester in 2012. With Toulouse down to 14 men shortly before the interval on a damp afternoon at Stade Ernest-Wallon, a greasy ball fell to the ground just inside the home side's half. In a flash, Fickou had transformed the entire picture, chipping in behind the cover and coolly burning off every chasing Tiger. Look up some of his other early tries on YouTube, and his soft-shuffling footwork is as deliciously deadly as you could wish to see.

Then there was Danny Cipriani, who before the fracture/dislocation of his ankle and leg in May 2008 was threatening to emerge as the kind of once-in-a-generation player even England could not ruin. As Ireland had found at Twickenham a couple of months earlier, there was almost nothing he could not do. What a sensational talent he was before the real world tapped him on the shoulder.

The third was a slightly unlikely looking golden boy from Dublin called Brian O'Driscoll, to whom we will return shortly. The fourth was another centre, a 19-year-old Jeremy Guscott, carving London Irish apart at Sunbury in the mid-1980s. People overuse the phrase poetry in motion, but in Guscott's case it was entirely accurate. The coltish pretender did not so much run as glide, with an occasional sway of the hips, leaving defenders confounded. He also knew he was good, which gave him an extra edge.

And the most striking of them all? The greatest? In June 1983, as my working holiday in Australia drew to a close, I made the pilgrimage to the Sydney Cricket Ground to worship at the shrine of Mark Ella and co. The Wallabies were 'only' playing the United States, but I was also curious to see if the 20-year-old playing on their wing was as good as people were saying. It was David Campese's fourth Test, but inexperience was clearly not an issue. There were nil traces of self-doubt as he contributed four tries to equal Greg Cornelsen's individual Test record for Australia.

Admittedly the opposition was modest and the back field wide open, but it was akin to watching a cheetah outpacing a herd of wildebeest. Even Ella was pinching himself. 'Campo was like a fourth Ella to a certain extent,' says his old teammate, face brightening at the memory. 'I remember we went on tour to France in 1982 when I was Wallaby captain. After one match I said to everybody, "I don't care who you are and I don't care how. You've just got to get the ball to this young kid." Then we just supported him. He was a freak.'

The young kid from Queanbeyan had it all: pace, attitude, showmanship and a sense of mischief all rolled into one. It would have been a dereliction of duty not to try talking to him for this book, so I sent a nice, polite message into the ether. Nothing happened for months. And then, out of the blue, one hot August Sunday lunchtime, an email pings in from the Gold Coast. 'Mate, call me.' 'Ripper!' as we say in southern England.

Sure enough, Campo is on the line the very next morning. He is more than happy to talk and has much to get off his chest. 'My wife Lara's from Zimbabwe and she cannot believe the amount of crap I cop. When we lived in South Africa, everyone knew who I was. It's the same elsewhere around the world. In Australia, they don't give a fuck because I'm outspoken and I get in trouble for saying this and that. It's very sad because I just love rugby.'

It is a real shame. You tell him every rugby fan of a certain age in the UK still reckons he walks on water. The tone softens momentarily – but he is off again soon enough. 'In Australian rugby, for some reason, they're intimidated by us [former players] because we're not going to agree with them. Especially me. You ask me a question and I'll give you an answer. That's the way I've always been. That's not always politically correct but it's what we did in our day. I didn't go to a private school, my father's Italian and as far as some people are concerned I'm a wog. I come from a government school background and I didn't finish school. My education has been rugby and the world.'

And what a rip-roaring adventure it has been. That 1984 Grand Slam, the 1991 Rugby World Cup triumph, some of the greatest tries ever scored. Until Bryan Habana nudged past him a few years ago – the flying Springbok registered 67 tries in 124 internationals – Campese stood supreme as the leading try-scorer among the top-ranking rugby nations. Sixty-four tries in 101 Tests, in addition to all the others he scored for Randwick, his state team, and for Padova and Milan during his Italian sojourns. Not bad for someone who started out weighing just 79 kilos and went from fourth-grade rugby with the Queanbeyan Whites to his Wallaby debut within three years.

Not everyone, though, relished his occasionally sharp-tongued manner. He used to particularly relish the Anglo-Australian rivalry, having spent much of his childhood glued to the Ashes. 'We were brought up on Lillee and Thomson and not liking the Poms. I don't disrespect them, it's just the rivalry you had. To me that's always been good.' His teammates grew accustomed to taking the rough with the smooth. 'As a teammate on the field you always loved him,' recalls another ex-Wallaby World Cup winner, Phil Kearns. 'The holy trinity back then was Farr-Jones, Lynagh and Campese. The relationship those three had on the field was quite special. Off the field? Look, if all your friends were perfect, you'd have no friends. Campo is a difficult personality, but that's part of him.'

The public, on the other hand, loved Campese because he was never remotely dull or predictable. It is a lesson he believes a few of modern rugby's finest should heed. 'They're in big trouble, even in New Zealand now, because rugby league is dominating. People want to be entertained. They don't want to watch rugby because the game is so stop-start. It's not entertaining. We played because we loved it. The game used to be about enjoyment. For the players these days it's a job. Who's happy now? The guys walk around town looking sour. The game has changed, I understand that. But I think the values of the game have changed as well. It's all about me, me, me. We've diluted rugby by professionalism. The game now is about defence. It's not about attack.'

'**We've diluted rugby by professionalism. The game now is about defence. It's not about attack.'**

Nicely warmed up now, he is also dismissive of coaches who try to dictate every move their players make. 'We used to get together three days before a Test match. Now they've got six weeks and there are still guys running on to talk to them after three minutes. Really? They're highly paid athletes and you've got people running on telling them how to play the game?' He reckons the 1984 Wallaby team, transported by the Tardis through the years to play an in-house game this weekend, would wipe the floor with their modern, gym-raised, structure-obsessed successors. 'We would flog the current team because of our angles of running and our knowledge the game. Half these players have no idea what their role is.

'Take someone like Marika Koroibete, who I think is a bloody good player. I sometimes wonder if he has ever been taught how to play rugby properly. I'm old school, but my knowledge isn't. I would love to teach these guys how to understand their roles and what they should be doing. I love coaching. I go out every day and coach kids. I coach six-year-olds to first-graders because I think I've got a lot of knowledge to pass on. But in Australia they won't let me get involved. How about getting in people who have won things? You name it, I've been there. But it means jack shit. When I was involved with Rugby Australia, half the people there didn't know who I was.'

Bitter ex-player or ahead-of-his-time visionary? When Campese wrote his autobiography *On A Wing and a Prayer*, he suggested in the final chapter that rugby was a dying sport in Australia. The intervening period, until the award of the staging rights to the 2027 Rugby World Cup, has frequently threatened to prove him right. 'Around the 1991 World Cup things were fantastic. We were on terrestrial television and doing adverts and all that. Now in 2022 there's no free-to-air coverage and we struggle. It's very frustrating.'

And while some used to compare him to Sir Don Bradman on the basis of his prodigious scoring feats, the sportsman to whom he bears a much closer resemblance is probably the late Shane Warne. Campese worked harder than people realised – 'I was a professional well before professionalism: I wanted to be the best' – but he liked to out-think opponents, too. In Italy he played at fly half, which further helped him to learn how to manipulate defences. 'As a finisher I was a creator. When I went and played Test rugby, it was so easy to understand what was happening. It wasn't difficult, it was about reading the game. When I marked Rory Underwood, I knew he was an in-and-out, in-and-out kind of player. But I could sidestep, I could swerve, I could do the goose-step, I could catch and pass and kick. The poor guy opposite was thinking, *What's this guy doing?* The whole idea of sport is trying to have something over the opposition.'

The ultimate example, perhaps, was that famous assist against New Zealand in the 1991 World Cup semi-final in Dublin. Looking back now at the nonchalance with which he gathered Michael Lynagh's chip, jinked right and left and then threw a reverse over-the-shoulder pass to Tim Horan is to see a gifted player creating his own time and space. 'Firstly I was going to kick the ball but it bounced up to me. I had John Timu in front of me, so I stepped one way and then stepped the other. As I stepped off my right foot, I saw Timmy Horan coming. He was a great communicator and I just passed it to him. You don't practise those things, they just happen. But that's what happens when you have instincts. We were very fortunate. Bob Dwyer, Alan Jones and the other coaches I played under allowed me to experiment. Sometimes it worked, sometimes it didn't. But if you don't try, you'll never know.'

There it is: the genius of Campese in one pithy sentence. And if he could share one other motivational secret with the world, it would be the critical importance of doing the basics well. 'Why are Lionel Messi and Ronaldo the best football players in the world? Week in, week out they

173

perform. You know why? Because they do the basics correctly all the time. You cannot do the hard things if you cannot do the easy things. My life was about doing the simple things – and then you experiment. Simple.' There has only ever been one Campo and he remains as singular as ever.

* * * * *

There is only one Brian O'Driscoll, too. The great Irishman is a different type of character from Campo – more self-aware, less provocative – but they share two important traits. The first was the uncanny ability to bend rugby matches to their own bidding. The second? For better or worse, both have experienced the white heat of intense public scrutiny that can sear the naive or the unwary. Any search for greatness still leads directly to their front doors.

In O'Driscoll's case his entire career was floodlit by the unforgiving glare of professionalism. For a while he was the biggest fish in Ireland's sporting pond and generating attention in places where rugby players had previously not registered. 'I didn't help myself on that front,' he concedes now, looking faintly rueful. 'When you've got long blond hair and you're dating certain people, you're going to bring that scrutiny. It was just immaturity and not knowing how to navigate a simpler path for yourself. But I wouldn't change anything because that ends up shaping you into the person you subsequently become.'

O'Driscoll, along with his contemporary Jonny Wilkinson, duly became a poster boy for the shiny 'new' sport of rugby union emerging from the quaint old amateur era. Finally the players were being properly paid and, as part of the deal, were becoming public property in ways only a legendary Welsh fly half could recognise. Financially it certainly helped. O'Driscoll used to joke with Ronan O'Gara that without rugby he would have been eating cheese sandwiches on the bus en route to a dull office or bank job somewhere. Instead he found himself at the epicentre of a whole new and rapidly expanding ball game.

Fame, as with Campese, arrived young. Previously he had little inkling that it might be heading down the tracks towards him. 'I came out of school in 1997. The game had just gone professional, but we weren't thinking like that. In truth I fell into it. We were winging it and totally oblivious to what the expectations were. The current crop come out of school and have this plan to be professional rugby players. There was none of that with us. There was no vision.'

Nor was everyone loudly hailing the one-time scrum half from Blackrock College as the next big thing. 'There was nothing at a schoolboy level that was particularly headline material. I was just one of the crew.' The Leinster environment he entered was not exactly the smooth-running machine of today, either. 'You have to understand the players had been playing as amateurs and were suddenly professional. The reality was we couldn't move on to the next iteration of professional rugby until all those guys had retired. That's through no fault of theirs. It's just that when you've experienced one thing it takes a lot to change. It took lots of good nights [for us] to get our act together.'

Some 141 international caps and 47 Test tries later, the long-time Ireland captain has travelled a long way from his Clontarf and Blackrock College roots. As the former Leinster coach Michael Cheika once said, 'Whether it's the southern or northern hemisphere, Mars, Jupiter or Venus, he's recognised as one of the greatest players in history.' The son of two doctors – his father Frank played twice for Ireland against Argentina in 1970 – he was not obviously massive or power-laden and had below-average eyesight. With and without the ball, though, he was an unstintingly competitive menace. You could say he was a jack of all trades and master of all of them, good enough to win his first cap in Australia at the age of 20. Getting picked opposite one of his boyhood heroes, Tim Horan, was one of the catalyst moments of his career. 'Once or twice he made me look pretty average, but for the most part I survived it.'

The second big moment came in 2000, when he scored a hat-trick of tries against France as Ireland famously recorded their first win in Paris since 1972. He was instantly propelled into the big time, a far cry from the previous weekend which he had spent out on the town in Dublin, drinking cheap white wine in Buck Whaley's in Leeson Street with, among others, a guy called Oran, a friend of his sister, Jules.

'When you next score for Ireland, I want you to give me the big O.'

'Yeah, sure, right.'

A week later, having just touched down his first try in Paris, that conversation came back to him. He duly made a celebratory 'O' sign with his fingers. Same again when he scored his second. At which point even he began to realise it might be time to rein things in a touch. 'By the time I'd scored the third I was thinking, *Oh, my God, this is getting serious. I can't be taking the piss any more.*'

There was no shortage of other green giants that day, not least his centre partner Rob Henderson and fly half David Humphreys who slotted the winning penalty goal, but it was O'Driscoll's display which caught the public imagination. 'The three tries aside, it was one of my better all-round performances, on both sides of the ball. The first two were almost put on a plate for me, but I had to do a bit of work for the third. I was on the blindside of the ruck and not anticipating the ball coming out. Then Peter Stringer gets hit, the ball gets knocked out of his hands and it lands at my feet. It was a good pickup and all of a sudden you're accelerating into space. *Jesus, this could be on here.* Then you look up ahead. *Ntamack's at full back, this is going to take some work.* But I arced on the outside and he doesn't even attempt to get me. Then you're just thinking about getting it under the sticks as close as possible.'

In hindsight certain other things now strike him. 'There was so much heads-up rugby back then. Look at that game and it's so disorganised, there's so little shape. Guys were doing their own stuff, ad-libbing to what lines people were running. I was also probably ignorant of the fact we hadn't won in Paris for 28 years. I certainly didn't feel that baggage. It was my first outing there, it was a fast track. You're playing scared because it's France and they've been heroes of yours. But you just stay in the hunt because there are no other experiences for you to lean on when things went badly.'

Amid the subsequent post-match frenzy, even he began to understand that a switch had been flicked in the Irish psyche. 'It was the reaction of others that made you realise it really was a big deal. At schoolboy and U20 level we'd been accustomed to beating England and France and Wales. Granted we lost to Jonny Wilkinson's England Schools side, but we didn't feel we were significantly inferior. Now, suddenly, there was mad stuff going on. After the France game one of the sponsors put up one million euros for anyone who scored four tries in the next match against Wales. We were talking as a team about whether we'd have to share it or not. *Gosh, maybe this is a new era.* There was reason to be hopeful.'

Another magical moment duly followed on the 2001 British & Irish Lions tour to Australia. In the wake of O'Driscoll's spectacular solo try in the first Test in Brisbane, his parents were on a bus heading back to their hotel when everyone around them suddenly started singing their new favourite song, to the tune of 'Waltzing Matilda'. 'Waltzing O'Driscoll, Waltzing O'Driscoll!' His parents could barely believe what they were hearing. Only now does their son freely acknowledge what the rest of us were saying and writing at the time. 'It was a cracking try. You can score those tries in club matches and occasionally in Tests. But to be able to do it against a world-class, World Cup-winning defence is what really landed with me after a few years. People still talk to me about it now.'

As, inevitably, they still do about the first Test of the 2005 Lions tour to New Zealand. Maybe the touring side would have struggled to win the series in any event, but pretty much the entire trip was a disaster. The morning in Christchurch had dawned deceptively clear and calm, but by nightfall an icy storm had swept into town. Barely had the game kicked off than O'Driscoll was being gang-tackled and speared into the ground by Tana Umaga and Kevin Mealamu, his tour over with a shoulder dislocation. At the time he was understandably upset – 'I describe it as deliberate foul play, dangerous, a cheap shot' – but nowadays he is more philosophical. 'I genuinely don't believe I was specifically targeted as in *Let's try and take him out.* It's a hard physical game and I think what happened is that two guys didn't realise where they were.'

O'Driscoll also now wishes he had not stuck around as the inevitable media typhoon intensified over his tour-ending injury. 'I should have been gone the next day. I didn't want to be seen as jumping ship, but there's no place for an injured player, captain or otherwise, on any tour.' Nor does he look back at his relationship with the media with total satisfaction. 'I wish I'd been advised a bit more. I was on the very guarded, wary side of it . . . they were a little bit the enemy rather than your friends.

But that was a result of the environment I'd come into and what I'd inherited from those who'd been in it before. It takes someone very strong-willed to break from the mould.

'Maybe I should have come in with a better energy, but I was so nervous around what I was going to say and what negative consequences it might have that it felt draining rather than something I should have enjoyed. I work in the media now and talking about these things is fun. It could have been fun back then. I just didn't know that was the attitude I should have been going in with.'

'I didn't want to be seen as jumping ship, but there's no place for an injured player, captain or otherwise, on any tour.'

As an example he cites an incident on the 2001 Lions tour. 'Naively I alienated one of the Sunday journalists because he had written a couple of unfavourable articles about a couple of my pals, one of whom had to retire. I remember thinking, *He's the enemy*. Talk about shooting yourself in the foot. My career lasted for another 14 years after that. He had to go back to his editor and say he couldn't get an interview with the guy who was just breaking through. It was a bit of stubbornness and maybe a misplaced loyalty to others around me. I could probably have handled the criticism myself, but I felt protective of others and dug my heels in. I wish there had been someone who had helped me to navigate that a little better.'

In the main, though, his rugby did most of the talking for him, both with Ireland and Leinster. 'The Six Nations Grand Slam in 2009 was huge because we hadn't won one for 60 years, but winning European Cups with my home team was really important. They're your really close pals, they're the ones you soldier with every day and still bump into most often. They're the ones you're still on WhatsApp groups with and the stick is still flying.

'I still look back with huge fondness. If we hadn't won those Heineken Cups, would we have that bond? Absolutely not. But we won three in four years. I almost went to play in France, but I'm so relieved I won it with my home team and that we started something great. It's very close to being as important provincially as it is internationally. You live in each other's pockets and do everything together.'

Interestingly, though, the teammate he nominates as perhaps the best of them all is an Englishman. O'Driscoll only lined up alongside the World Cup-winning flanker Richard Hill in a Lions jersey, but it was enough. 'Having played with him he was just a phenomenal player. One hundred per cent commitment, low error count, huge commitment and confrontational.' Then there was Wilkinson. 'Talk about someone getting professionalism from minute one. It was almost as if he was ahead of his time. He had the ability to understand at a very young age the need to get the very most out of his ability. Maybe he didn't achieve everything his talents deserved because of the injuries he had to deal with, but he was a trendsetter of the best kind.'

And maybe O'Driscoll's own most striking achievement was the way he reinvented himself once his body started to dictate terms ever more loudly. 'From 2009 through to 2011, I had a really bad shoulder and ended up having a neck fusion as a result of it. In that 2009 Heineken Cup final, I literally couldn't pass the ball more than two yards. People will say, "Nothing changed there", but from right to left I had absolutely no power in my right arm. You're kind of hiding these things and missing opportunities as a result.

'I would say I was still at my peak in 2009, but then slowly started falling off a cliff after that. I had to try and modify my game, but it wasn't how I wanted it to be or how I remembered it earlier in my career. By the end of the 2011 World Cup, I wasn't enjoying it. I was having to manage my way through games and it wasn't a true reflection of who I was as a player any more. It's a significantly inferior version of who you want to be. I thought, *I can't do this any more. Maybe that's it.*'

All credit, then, to the sheer willpower that got him back and on to one final Lions tour to Australia in 2013. Only to receive a significant public kick in the nether regions, courtesy of Warren Gatland's decision to omit him from the winner-takes-all final Test in Sydney in favour of Wales' Jonathan Davies. 'It felt very, very bitter at the time. Missing out and not feeling part of it. But I'm able to look back at it differently now. It's far more important that we won a series and I didn't play than vice versa. It isn't about one person.'

And Gatland's hunch ultimately paid off. 'As much as the outpouring from Ireland was lovely, there was very little of that from Wales. The game is about winning series and getting the job done by whatever means. As I discovered, there's very little sentiment in the game. Whether you feel hard done by or not is irrelevant. Even teammates like Sexto . . . I'm sure they felt sorry for me, but they felt bloody happy for themselves that they had a chance to play in a series decider.'

Which is why, a decade on, he harbours no resentment towards the man who dropped the guillotine. 'Gats was never afraid of the tough call. Giving me my first cap as a 20-year-old, from something he'd seen at a training session, was ballsy. Bringing in five uncapped players after we got ripped apart by England in 2000 was a brave call. In 2009 he knew there would be a storm of abuse from certain elements of the supporter base, but he was doing what he thought was best for the team. All you can do is make a decision in the moment. Sometimes you don't know if they're right or wrong. You're almost in a haze. But that was one which, in hindsight, you can't help but think he was justified.'

But what about the future of the game more generally? As with Campese – and also echoing Duckham, Ella, Davies, Fitzpatrick and others – Drico has his concerns. 'I hope we're not closed-minded. I hope the power players have an open enough mindset to growing the game and are not just trying to line their own pockets. It's a great game but we've only had four winners of the World Cup. We need to broaden our horizons, not just in sevens but 15s. The only way that happens is by letting people in a bit more, even if sometimes that hurts you slightly in the pocket.'

And his advice for the next Irish wunderkind, with the team's 2023 Grand Slam having further heightened their collective profile? To seize each and every day. 'I don't think I ever took any matches for granted, but they're magical times. Pitting yourself against the best players in the world in the biggest games. The margins between the very best and everyone else have squeezed significantly since I started in 1999. I'd encourage everyone to take it all in and not to let it pass you by. Because you don't know when your last one is coming. It might not be your call, it might be someone else's. You have to lap it all up.' In BOD we all still trust. Amen.

15

POSTCARDS FROM THE EDGE

In our era a concussion was a bit of a badge of honour.

Journalists are meant to be relentlessly thick-skinned. The story is the story; never mind the emotional debris strewn across the page. And then you pick up the phone and dial a number in New Plymouth. To listen to Carl Hayman, one of the most indomitable All Blacks of his generation, discussing the constant headaches, changing moods, corrosive anxiety and forgetfulness from which he is suffering in his early 40s is to be sharply reminded that everyday life is precious and never remotely to be taken for granted.

The situation is a desperately sad one. Hayman is among the growing band of former players to have been diagnosed with early-onset dementia and probable chronic traumatic encephalopathy (CTE), with World Rugby and several individual unions now facing legal action on behalf of hundreds of professional and semi-professional ex-players with irreversible neurological impairments.

On the Wednesday lunchtime when we speak, though, Hayman sounds relatively upbeat. In a few days' time, he is due to travel to Mexico to take part in a groundbreaking medical trial which he also hopes will shine a light for others like him. If there is the remotest chance of a cure, he and his family are naturally keen to try and seize it.

The reality of his situation, though, is laid bare from the moment Hayman begins to speak. A tale of matter-of-fact horror and everyday pain spills out, starting with the day in July 2021 when he was diagnosed at the age of 41. As his partner Kiko Matthews subsequently told my *Guardian* colleague Michael Aylwin, he has considered ending it all. 'Carl has joked about going out to sea on his boat. Put in so much fuel

181

and just go in one direction. And, you know, the fuel's going to run out eventually . . .'

You do your best to reassure Carl that, collectively, he and Kiko are inspiring millions of others with their honesty. The unvarnished truth, even so, is horrible. 'I'm often anxious and I get headaches pretty much continuously. The anxiety can fluctuate depending on a number of things: what's going on around me, for example, or if I am sleeping well. I have sleep issues – if you're not getting good sleep, then sometimes your symptoms the next day are worse.

'I definitely felt invincible. That's how you had to look at it.'

'The bit of the brain that is affected is essentially the nerve centre to your whole body. Forgetfulness is quite a big thing, so I try and have a place in my house for everything. If you can't find things in 10–15 seconds, you start to turn into the Incredible Hulk. I'm trying to put those little things in place to make life easier. When you can understand, you can plan and do a lot of good things to improve life and how you function. When you don't, it's a pretty scary place, that's for sure.'

For those who did not see Hayman play, or know him only by reputation, it is important to stress that, for a lengthy period, he was renowned as the best tighthead prop in the world. He played 45 Tests for the All Blacks between 2001 and 2007 before becoming one of the game's highest-paid players. During his time in Europe he played for Newcastle and Toulon, with whom he enjoyed three European title-winning campaigns prior to his playing retirement in 2015, and was later employed by Pau as a forwards coach.

Which is why Hayman is such a powerful witness now. International rugby is famously tough, but he, and everyone else, thought he could take it. Only now, looking back, does he wonder if the combination of his own durability and the savage toll of his chosen trade might have been an accident waiting to happen. 'I definitely felt invincible. That's how you had to look at it. Your body is an amazing thing and it does get accustomed to those impacts over a period of years, certainly from a scrummaging point of view.

'It takes years of training to build up that strength and resilience. That was certainly my mindset – once you moved past the fact that medical people compare those collisions to a small car crash. To perform at the elite level, you had to go through that. If you didn't, you wouldn't have much of a career as a professional player. The front row is not everyone's cup of tea, and to play in that position well you need to be a bit of a hard arse or to have something about you. At the time I thought I was pretty robust, which I still believe I am to some extent. But I had no idea that what I was doing was going to have some pretty serious repercussions further down the track."

At one point, as his symptoms worsened and his moods fluctuated, he thought he was going crazy. Those big-money contracts are at least now helping to fund his treatment, but at what cost to his health? 'I probably played over 150 games in five years in France. I was averaging 30-plus games a season, on top of a 10-year career in New Zealand where, in those days, there was only one substitute prop. There were probably less than half a dozen games when I didn't play 80 minutes. On top of training. And in those days the Bs would play the As at Tuesday training. Whoever survived got to play on Saturday. It wasn't quite that extreme, but there was a lot of contact training. Which has ultimately led to the position where rugby is at now.'

He cannot prove it definitively but, in his personal experience, the way the game was played in Europe might well have been another factor. 'The rugby from a forwards point of view was physical. In New Zealand it was faster and the skill level of the forwards at that time was higher. Among our generation a real strength of New Zealand forwards was that most of us could catch and pass. At that time in France and England if you wanted to walk round the field and scrum you could do that.' There was also less emphasis on rugby as an evasion sport. 'Instead of having people who were going to stop you, you had people who wanted to run over the top of you and dominate you physically. The whole European game was based around strong forward play and intimidation. You just had to look through the England team of those days. That was their mindset at that time.'

After initial misgivings – 'It sounds arrogant to say it was difficult to get my head around, but I was so used to doing things in a certain way' – he grew to enjoy it. 'I started to appreciate European forward play and the importance of mauling and scrummaging. I realised you don't have to run the length of the field all the time and make amazing offloads and passes to beat teams. It sort of helped my rugby intelligence, to understand there are different ways to succeed.'

Worryingly, though, Hayman was already experiencing random flashbacks during games which, for the life of him, he could not explain. 'I had quite a lot of experiences like that, especially at Toulon. I'd be running to a point in play and just having a real sense of déjà vu. It was a really odd feeling.' It did not stop him, though, from reporting for duty every week. 'I was one of those guys who wanted to be on the field the whole time. A week off seemed a bit odd.

'I might have had a different view on things if I'd known a bit more, but wanting to be on the field was probably part of the reason I was the player I was. I was competitive and motivated. I accepted that we were *tranches* [slices of meat], as the French say. Once we finished there was always going to be someone else to take your place. The ship would keep sailing, so to speak, and no one is bigger than the game. I always understood that.'

Along with every top-level rugby player, he also knew there was a longer-term pact to be made with his battered body. 'I understood that if I had a sore knee or a sore back in later years, I wouldn't mind that. There are guys I played with who can't go for a walk up a hill because they've got no cartilage. You sort of expect that stuff . . . a bit of a grizzly ankle, a bit of arthritis in your hands. But there was never a conversation around your head.'

Which is exactly what Steve Thompson, Ryan Jones, Alix Popham and so many other players of a similar vintage have also been stressing. Yes, they knew rugby could be a dangerous sport. But, no, it was never fully explained what damage it could do to their brains. 'In our era a concussion was a bit of a badge of honour,' confirms Hayman. 'You got knocked out and you could go back on the field. If you were aware of the long-term damage you could potentially do, either from one of those or the repetitive hits over a long career . . .'

Now they all know better. 'The research is out there in other sports, I believe, saying there are real problems coming for some of these guys just in terms of the repetition of what they're doing. What I was told was that after seven years of a rugby career you can be put into a high-risk category. Even when I was playing at NZ age-group level, they were pretty tough games of rugby. I'm sure it all has an impact. And back then we were all playing cricket in the summer and rugby in the winter. There was a decent-sized off season.

'Looking back on it now, it would be nice if there was more education around it. I've heard talk of player passports in NFL, monitoring collisions and being given a certain amount per year. I think stuff like that can only be good for the safety of players and the overall health of the game. At the end of the day rugby players are not going to care for their bodies when they're playing on a Saturday. It's about education and putting the right things in place, and working out what is an acceptable level of games to be playing. Once you have that in place, people can be responsible for their own decisions.'

But as Hayman also points out, growing problems exist well below the professional strata. 'Even at a pro level, it's difficult as to who takes responsibility for the HIA [Head Injury Assessment]. The other day I saw a comment from a referee who said, "I'm not a doctor, it's not my job to tell them to go off." When you get to club level, those sorts of problems double.' Which leaves rugby with no alternative but to take even greater care of all its participants. Hayman pauses again, when asked if he would personally propose anything specific. 'I think a universal protocol for rugby would be great. So that they can understand the risks and are educated on what potentially could happen to them over a period of years.

'Then it's about putting support in place for people who do struggle for various reasons, whether it's a one-off concussion or, as in my case, a hard paper round for a number of years. It would be great to see the game of rugby move on. And for everyone to sort out what that looks like and how we shape that for players moving forward. There are so many good things about the game of rugby that we love.'

It is heart-wrenching, nevertheless, that one of the sport's finest cannot bring himself to watch the sport a great deal these days. 'Sadly, I don't really. I watched the French Top 14 final last year because I knew a number of people involved, but other than that I have had very little to do with rugby since I left Pau. I've sadly lost my love for it. It was a great part of my life which I really enjoyed, but it's nice to go and do other things. One day, hopefully, that will return and I might get involved with the game again. But at this point I'm just enjoying what I'm doing, I guess.'

His phone also continues to ping with messages from old teammates and friends, some of them increasingly concerned about their own future health. 'I've been contacted by a number of guys, some of whom are having issues themselves. There are a lot from my generation – the first senior players of that professional generation now getting towards their 50s – who are worried.

'I think there are a lot of people who are concerned about their health and may already be experiencing symptoms of some kind of brain injury. Moving forward, it would be great to have some support in place for these guys because people who don't have family or clinical support don't do too well.'

Depressingly, a little while after we speak, there is another development. Hayman was pulled over by police in Opunake, some 70 km (45 miles) down the coast from New Plymouth, and breathalysed. The 42-year-old was found to be four times over the legal driving limit. In court he pleaded guilty, adding that 'he wasn't in a good place' due to a combination of depression, his early onset dementia and the recent death of his mother. Was rugby primarily to blame? It is impossible not to offer up a silent prayer for big Carl and all those trapped in similar nightmares.

* * * * *

Nearly 20,000 km (12,000 miles) away in Northampton, Bill Ribbans knows precisely how people like Hayman are feeling. As an orthopaedic surgeon with over 40 years of medical experience, he is among the world's leading authorities on sporting injuries. Walk into his clinic on Billing Road, and you instantly feel in the reassuring presence of an insightful expert who cares deeply, both about the game and the thousands of patients he has encountered over the years.

In his time he has treated athletes ranging from Greg Rutherford, Paula Radcliffe and Jessica Ennis-Hill to Michael Schumacher, as well as working for the British Boxing Board of Control, Northamptonshire CCC, Northampton Saints and the England rugby union team. In rugby he has helped nudge the Saints to Premiership and Heineken Cup titles and worked alongside the likes of Ian McGeechan, Wayne Smith and Clive Woodward. Which is why it resonates so strongly when he says rugby has a problem it urgently needs to address. As he wrote in his thought-provoking book *Knife in the Fast Lane*, 'It could be argued that the game turning professional was the worst thing that could have happened in terms of player welfare.'

'It could be argued that the game turning professional was the worst thing that could have happened in terms of player welfare.'

This is not some distant clinician talking. Ribbans played rugby at a junior level until the age of 43 and knows what a compelling fascination it can exert. 'I always felt rugby was a dangerous game, but it was kept in check, up to 1995–96, by the fact we all had to go to work on a Monday. The moment the game went professional and you allowed the guys to be in the gym and training full-time, we saw the change in the size of them.

'I've never actually admitted this to anyone before, but I did fall slightly out of love with the game: the way the ball is always taken into contact, the constant recycling. I always have to rein myself in from saying it was better back in the day. But if you went into contact 30 years ago, you'd failed to some degree. The idea was to avoid contact. The problem is that in rugby now there's no longer a place on the pitch for you regardless of your size.'

In his book Ribbans also quoted Dr James Robson, the British & Irish Lions doctor, after the massively intense second Test against South Africa in 2009. It was among the most compelling games of Test rugby ever played, but no fewer than five Lions players required hospital treatment afterwards. Robson was clear in his own mind that something had to change. 'The balance is wrong between power and skill,' he wrote. 'We are reaching a level where the players have got too big for their skill levels.'

In making that statement, Robson was simply echoing what he had been saying for years. Years earlier – the final week of the 2001 Lions tour to Australia in Sydney, in fact – he was sitting in front of the press corps and telling us that players needed better care. 'Something has to be done about the season . . . at present it's like someone punching holes in you.' He warned that the game had become '40 per cent more physically demanding' since the Lions toured New Zealand in 1993 and revealed there had been only one day on the entire five-week tour to that point when he had not had to deal with a new injury. He told us he had been required to rise from his bed on 22 of the first 29 nights in response to requests from players or management for medical assistance. 'Everyone needs adequate rest, otherwise we're just going to have lots of young rugby players. Players are setting themselves up for a lot of problems in the future.'

How prophetic those words seem now. Another backstage veteran of four Lions tours is Phil Pask, among English rugby's most unselfish, loyal servants. Ask anyone who has ever dealt with him, and they will confirm 'Pasky' is a 24-carat legend. Generations of Northampton players do not know how fortunate they have been to have had easy access to the talents of both the former Saints flanker, who has also worked at six World Cups, and the dextrous Ribbans. Injured players of all ages could not ask for a better duo than the Batman and Robin of sports rehabilitation.

Fighting the good fight, though, can be draining. And just occasionally both men wonder if their expertise might be putting their patients at even greater risk. 'Are Phil and I part of the problem?' asks Ribbans softly, glancing across to his right at the seated Pask. 'We're putting them back together again. People have become very specialised in terms of surgical expertise and we're able to get these players back.'

In other words, all that medical excellence, multiplied by the relentless pressure to be on parade felt by every professional sportsperson, risks players returning to the fray prematurely. And for years few people have been interested in applying the handbrake. 'It's not only the pressure from the player, it's the coaches, the agents, everybody,' continues Ribbans.

'Phil has to see it all the time. It's that balancing act: getting them back too early and risking re-injury or getting them back too late and risking the wrath of the coaching staff.'

It is not a subject often aired in public, but there is increasing research suggesting a rapid return is not always good news. 'The evidence now is that for every month over 10 months you can prolong their rehab it reduces their injuries by 25 per cent,' says Pask. He and his colleague Barney Kenny once helped the outstanding England flanker Richard Hill return from a serious ACL injury in six months, with the help of the renowned US-based surgeon Bill Knowles. They now believe a more gradual return to play would have been preferable. They also recall the case of South Africa's Joost van der Westhuizen, who required major knee surgery three times in four years and, by his own admission, played in the latter stages of the 1999 Rugby World Cup on one good leg. Van der Westhuizen was subsequently diagnosed with motor neurone disease and died, aged 45, in 2017.

Pask, still involved with Northampton Saints, has been at the sharp end of this vexed debate for decades. Take the 1997 Lions tour, generally regarded as one of the all-time great tours. The lesser-known side of the story is that numerous players needed patching up even before they arrived in South Africa. 'Matt Dawson had a knee injury and we didn't think he was going to go,' recalls Pask. 'Paul Grayson wasn't fit and Gregor Townsend couldn't tackle with his left arm for the first half of the tour because he'd injured it playing against France. They were going on tour with injuries then.'

Yet whenever Pask suggested certain players needed more time to recover, he found the responses tended to be unsympathetic. 'I got fed up with coaches saying, "You're always keeping the players back." In the end – and I did this with England as well – I'd get a copy of the team sheet and write down the injuries that people were carrying. We were probably fielding about 10 out of 15 starters who had something we could probably have pulled them out with. The coaches got fed up with me doing that after about a year.'

It is a staggering detail. Two-thirds of an English match day squad kicking off a game in significant pain? It is also a stat to make anyone – players, fans, administrators – wince. These days there is greater awareness surrounding play welfare, but the game itself grows ever more brutal. 'Twenty-five per cent of our playing squad are injured at any one time, according to our latest audit,' reveals Pask. 'We've got 21-year-olds who have had four operations already. The game's not soft. I once got told off for comparing it to being in a 24 mph car crash twice a week. These days it's more like 50 mph. People like big hits . . . but it comes at a cost.'

Some collisions remain etched on his memory even now, not least one involving Jonny Wilkinson down the blindside in a physical game against France. 'Jonny steps into the tackle and Barney Kenny and me are looking at each other thinking, *Oh no*. He hit the French guy flat out, the ball seemed to shoot about 20 foot in the air and both of them were left on the deck. By the time we got to Jonny he was awake, but by today's standards he should have been off. In those days he did all the tests we had and he played on.'

So what next? Ask Ribbans how he perceives the medium-term future and the answer is not encouraging. 'Am I sanguine about the next five years? I don't think so. I don't think we've topped out yet.' Nor is it as simple as suddenly lowering the tackle height to waist level and below, particularly in the elite game. 'With the skill the modern professional players have got, they'd score every time they got the ball,' says Pask. 'They're so good at passing out of contact anyway.'

Both Pask and Ribbans believe, though, that a change to the regulations surrounding replacements would be beneficial. 'I'm a big fan of not having replacements,' says Pask. 'Tiredness makes cowards out of people. Spaces open up, mistakes get made and suddenly the game takes on a different character.' Ribbans also believes the injury data supports a rethink. 'When you look at injuries in the last 20 minutes of games, they're far more likely to happen to people who've been there for the full game. You could say it's because they're tired, but maybe it's because they're being hit by fresh players. But it's a proposal the players will always be against. At the top level it means losing caps and wages.'

Accidents can clearly occur in any walk of life. Pask cites the example of the childhood day when he ran smack into a lamppost and knocked himself out, long before he had encountered a rugby ball. He remains keenly aware, though, of the risks that exist beneath the professional game at youth and junior club level. 'Sometimes I look at it in fear. The medical staff won't pick everything up, they haven't got video replays. I think it's actually more dangerous to play at that level than it is for Saints versus Bath.'

Not so long ago he happened to be watching down at his local club, Olney, when a player suffered a fracture/dislocation of his ankle. 'When I got to him, he had no pulse. I got his mate to hold his hand and then had to reduce his ankle without any pain relief. It took nearly an hour for the ambulance to get there and another 20 or 30 minutes to get him to hospital.

'If we're going to protect our internationals and Premiership players from concussions and head injuries, we've got to stop them having them in the first place.'

Afterwards it makes you think: *Had I not been there, he might have lost his limb.* At that level, though, there is no spare cash for extra medical help. They say, "We've got physios, but we can't afford to pay them and we can't afford paramedics." For me that's where the RFU should be looking to put finance into. At Saints you can't move for medics, but at other clubs you feel vulnerable. I felt vulnerable and I was only watching it. I also saw a number of head knocks. If that was Saints v Bath we'd have four or five Head Injury Assessments because we're trained to look for them. It's kind of scary. Are we looking at the right end of the game?'

Ribbans, along with the Progressive Rugby lobby group, also has concerns around the women's game, with the death of Scotland international Siobhan Cattigan in November 2021 among the more sobering case studies. 'I feel very strongly about women's rugby. I feel we've got to make the changes at schools and community level. The evidence for me is pretty clear.' Youthful brains and heavy collisions are an extremely worrying mix. 'If we're going to protect our internationals and Premiership players from concussions and head injuries, we've got to stop them having them in the first place. We'll never know if, in the cases of players like Steve Thompson and Alix Popham, it started when they were teenagers. I suspect it did.'

Calls for 'brain passports' and more criteria-driven rehab, rather than simplistic catch-all timelines, might help. There is also the flip side, as perfectly articulated by Pask, that rugby can be a character-building force for good. 'People who play the game have got something about them. They wouldn't play it otherwise. You're that type of person . . . you want to challenge yourself.'

Maybe, too, science, will become more sophisticated and steer the game away from the abyss. 'Whichever coach works out how the game is going to be played in five years' time is going to be a successful coach,' says Pask. 'Because then people will be thinking differently. What are the physiological demands? Do we need big, heavy forwards or the more athletic type? Or the French model when they're big and skilful? That will filter down to the strength and conditioning guys and then to us.'

But how many Haymans, Thompsons and Joneses do there have to be before attitudes change radically? Ribbans is as passionate a rugby fan as any but, with lawsuits against World Rugby and individual unions having now been launched in the United Kingdom, Ireland and France, his closing diagnosis is stark. 'The thing that is potentially going to make rugby authorities change is the legal case. And if schools and parents start stopping their kids playing. That'll make them change.' Rugby's existential threat is real enough, and those who deny it are either closing their eyes or sticking their fingers in their ears.

16

FIGHTING THE GOOD FIGHT

The biggest hurdle for me was being a woman.

To be in Eden Park on 12 November, 2022 was to witness something as uplifting as it was beautiful. The bold, ambitious rugby with which the Black Ferns secured the World Cup title at England's expense made for sensational viewing, but even better was the sparkly-eyed congregation watching it unfold. Beneath clear blue skies more than 42,000 people had come out to worship at the altar of women's rugby inside the All Blacks' traditional sporting cathedral. It was a historic moment, regardless of your nationality.

Until a few weeks earlier, no one had ever been able to flog a ticket to a game of women's rugby in New Zealand. Now there were a further 1.3 million Kiwis glued to their screens, as keen to see what Ruby Tui, Portia Woodman, Ruahei Demant and Stacey Fluhler (née Waaka) could do with the ball as they would have been had their male counterparts been involved.

Up in the stands it was no wonder Farah Palmer could feel tears welling up. A former Black Ferns captain and a three-time World Cup winner (1998, 2002 and 2006), she played in an era when crowds for women's games could be measured in the dozens. She rose from a rural Māori background to become the first woman to sit on the board of New Zealand Rugby, so the sight of an entire nation rising as one to salute players of Māori heritage like Woodman, Demant and the ever-smiling Fluhler was understandably emotional.

Tui's family history was slightly different – Scottish and Irish ancestry on her mother's side and Samoan on her father's – but it all added to the joyous sense of diversity, celebration and acceptance that elevated the women's World Cup to new heights. Palmer, whose husband Wesley Clarke was part of the Black Ferns coaching team, felt intensely grateful to have played a part in paving the way. 'I was just crying, jumping up and down and crying some more for them. Everyone was going, "Well done, well done." But for me it isn't any one person, it's a whole lot of people who have helped it to get to this moment. And I'm just so proud and feeling very fortunate I've been a part of that journey.'

There is a strong argument, though, that none of it would have been possible had Palmer and others not fought the good fight for years. Off the field, the 49-year-old has become a noted academic and figurehead for Māori women and in 2023 was made Dame Farah in the New Year Honours list. During her playing days the Black Ferns lost only once under her captaincy and she did not miss a single Test through injury between 1996 and 2005. Not for nothing has the provincial women's tournament in New Zealand been named the Farah Palmer Cup in her honour, even if her children initially found it hard to grasp. 'When it first came out the kids were saying, "Why do they keep mentioning your name, Mum?"'

The story of Palmer's early years is an inspiration in itself, particularly for those who wonder if their origins might be an insurmountable hurdle. Growing up in the small settlement of Piopio – 'It's the sound the birds used to make' – some 37 km (23 miles) south-west of Te Kuiti on New Zealand's North Island, Palmer did not have an easy start. Her father refused to acknowledge he had a daughter and played no part in her early upbringing. For the first seven years of her life, she was brought up by her Māori mother and Māori grandparents, before her Pākehā father, Bruce Palmer, whose family hailed from Cornwall, belatedly entered her life and the reconnected family moved to a nearby farm. Moving from a small village 'with a very Māori sense of everything' to even more isolated surroundings was another major test of her resilience.

Only when she won a scholarship, partly funded by the Māori Women's Welfare League, to study as a physical education teacher at Otago University in distant Dunedin did another kind of life beckon. 'I was completely out of my comfort zone and freaking out. I'd never been to the

South Island. It was such a culture shock. *Holy moly, there are hardly any brown faces down here.'*

In her desire to fit in with her fellow students, she resolved to join the university netball club. Wandering past the table advertising the university rugby club, she noticed they had a female recruiting officer as well as a male one. She hesitated momentarily.

'Would you like to play rugby?

'Yeah, I wouldn't mind but I'm not sure.'

'Well, just come along.'

It proved an instant revelation. Palmer loved the way she could run with the ball, having barely experienced the game before. 'They used to have a married v singles men's game in our village and thought it would be a laugh to get a bunch of women to play in the curtain-raiser. So I'd had no coaching at all . . .' Then, one day, someone showed her a King Country programme from 1972, the year she was born. 'My dad's name was in there. He was a back row forward who played over 50 games for King Country during the latter years of Colin Meads' career.

'In some ways it all made total sense to me. My dad must have thought he was on the trajectory to becoming a great rugby player and didn't want to be tied down with this child. I'm not saying what he did was okay, but I kind of got where his head might have been. He realised he was going to be a dad and he wasn't ready. It's been quite interesting, my whole relationship with my dad . . .'

Whatever was driving Palmer, it was a potent force. Playing at hooker, she weighed, at most, 70 kg, but her opponents rarely had any respite. 'I wasn't very big but I had a high pain threshold. I didn't really feel anything. I also had pretty strong legs and I could scrummage all day. That was fun. So was going into rucks and mauls.' Her mother was considerably more nervous. 'My mum doesn't like risk. She'd always be, "Are you sure?"'

In her first match as captain of the national side, New Zealand beat England 67–0. The game, tellingly, was played at an army base just south of Christchurch, and a recently arrived England had no answer to their formidable hosts. By 1998, when the World Cup was played in the

Netherlands, the sense of collective purpose in New Zealand's dressing room was even stronger. 'All we wanted to do was to put New Zealand women's rugby on the map because we'd missed out on the 1994 World Cup.

'We also wanted to prove to people back in New Zealand that we deserved to get just as much recognition and attention as the All Blacks. We had amazing athletes – Vanessa Cootes, Annaleah Rush and Louisa Wall – and it was just a really great team. If we took that team and had the same kind of resources they have now, I think we would be quite competitive.'

'The papers had started calling us the Lady Blacks and the Gal Blacks. So we had a team meeting. *Ugh, no way are we being called that.*'

After they had beaten United States in the final, though, one crucial thing still needed resolving. As Palmer recalls, 'The papers had started calling us the Lady Blacks and the Gal Blacks. So we had a team meeting. *Ugh, no way are we being called that.* I don't think we even had a team room in those days, so everyone just squished into one of our bedrooms. We said, "What is it that we represent?" The Black was something we wanted to keep and the fern is something often associated with female sports teams in New Zealand. *Why don't we just call ourselves the Black Ferns?*

Soon enough the idea went public. 'We went on the *Holmes* show, which was what everyone in New Zealand used to watch at six o'clock at night. Paul Holmes interviewed a group of us and said, "Everyone's calling you the Gal Blacks." And we said, "Actually we've got another name we'd like to be called." So I announced on television that we'd like to be called the Black Ferns. By then we'd found out that, in Māori, the black *mamaku* tree fern was the matriarch of the fern family in the forest. But we still had to wait another six months until the NZ Rugby marketing team had done their research and said, "Yes, that's fine."'

By the time Palmer played the last of her 35 Tests, steering New Zealand to a 25–17 win over England in the 2006 World Cup final, everyone knew the Black Ferns by name and reputation. 'I feel like we did kind of make some inroads in terms of getting attention. It helped that the All Blacks weren't doing so well at that time.' What was still lacking, though, was the investment to match from the New Zealand Rugby

Union. There seemed to be a sense it was not overly urgent, given the Black Ferns were winning everything anyway.

Which was among the motivations behind Palmer becoming the first woman to join the NZ Rugby board in 2016. Given the union was founded in 1892, it is hardly surprising Palmer can remember her first board meeting. 'I wasn't sure what I should wear, so I just put on a white shirt and some black pants. I'm also a bit deaf in my left ear, so I wanted to sit on the right-hand side, close to the chair, so I could hear.'

As she went to sit down, however, two shadows appeared over her shoulder. It was the president and the vice-president, both former lock forwards. Apparently it was where they normally sat. 'It wasn't a case of me not feeling welcome, but it made me laugh that there were these traditions and things that happened around the boardroom table that, in my opinion, needed a little tweaking and challenging. After that it was "Can we sit anywhere we like?"'

It also swiftly became apparent that the 'male, pale and stale' brigade might need gently educating in other areas. 'At that very first meeting we had an independent diversity report tabled. The very first recommendation was there should be one female representative on the board. Because I was there, they were saying, "Well, we don't need that any more". That was a bit of an eye-opener for me.'

As well as serving as the chair of the NZ Māori Rugby Board and a board member for Sport New Zealand, Palmer has since become the vice-chair of NZ Rugby. "Initially you feel like a possum in the headlights . . . it's hard to hit the ground and start challenging things when you're not sure what's gone on previously. But there are times when I've felt my voice has been effective, either in raising things no one has considered or in questioning things from a different perspective. Challenging assumptions, making people aware of certain biases . . . often it is just a series of conversations. Very often it's not a one-off statement that makes a huge impact and leads to change.' Together with Dame Patsy Reddy, the former governor-general of New Zealand who was elected as NZ Rugby chair in December 2022, she has smashed the toughest of glass ceilings.

No one, certainly, is better placed to judge how New Zealand Rugby should best build on the legacy of their triumphant World Cup. 'After that big high it's about looking and planning at what we need to do at the next World Cup. And how we continue to prove women's rugby is something people want to watch and invest in. We've got to be careful we don't focus too much at the top level. There are going to be huge numbers of girls and boys who now want to play rugby. If we don't have our systems ready to take in that influx, we're going to miss that opportunity. We might even convince a few athletes in other sports to jump on over as well.'

Whatever happens, the images of that Eden Park finale will remain firmly etched in her mind. '*I don't just want to record this on my phone, I want to be in the moment.* It just felt so heart-warming that everyone else was feeling what we'd always felt. We always felt proud of representing New Zealand and playing rugby, because it was our national sport. Our families and close friends felt that. But to see 42,000 people – and to know everyone else was watching it at home – was mind-blowing. It's been the perfect storm in terms of taking women's rugby to the next level.'

* * * * *

When Maggie Alphonsi was growing up on a north London council estate, rugby might as well have not existed. She was born with a club foot and her only sporting role models were the ones she could see on television: Denise Lewis winning a gold medal at the Sydney Olympics, Venus and Serena Williams playing tennis in some faraway galaxy. 'They looked like me and were from similar backgrounds. I knew rugby, but it wasn't a sport for me, especially as a person of colour and coming from a low socio-economic background. Growing up in north London – it was very much not a rugby environment. You basically did football or athletics, whether you were a girl or a boy.'

Her Nigerian-born mother, Rebecca, also had her own ideas about where her sporty child should focus her efforts. 'She said to me, "If you're going to get into sport, get into tennis." She saw that as a sport where it looked fair, where it didn't matter who you were. You could still make it to the top. Twenty-odd years ago lots of sports had their stereotypes. I guess the perception was that someone like me would fit athletics or tennis better.'

Throwing the discus was her real forte – 'I used to watch the Olympics and wonder what could have happened' – but luckily for rugby Alphonsi was diverted down the road less travelled. To see her now, fronting assorted campaigns or working as a television pundit, is to wonder how many other young Black girls and boys might grow to love their rugby if they had the early encouragement. In Alphonsi's case a couple of enthusiastic teachers, including Liza Burgess, ended up steering her towards Saracens where her eyes were instantly opened. 'I don't like using the word *luck*, but I was so lucky I had a combination of things that fell into place at the right time. I had a few teachers who just loved rugby and saw the fact I was a good athlete rather than my bad behaviour at school. All the stars aligned.'

At first it felt like she had stumbled into some kind of secret society. '*Wow, there are so many people here.* You had to be fully involved in it to realise that people played it. It just wasn't visible.' When she looked around her U16s huddle, though, she swiftly felt part of the gang. 'I wasn't the only person of colour in that team. It wasn't super-diverse, but we had a mixture of different types of people.'

And as soon as those first crucial seeds were sown, the teenage Alphonsi sensed she might have found herself a passport out of Edmonton. 'I was always driven by wanting to progress, to move out of the flat and the estate. My childhood wasn't bad, but I was very determined this wasn't going to be my life. My dream was to live in a house and have a garden and a car. All the things I didn't have growing up with my mum in a single-parent family. That always drove me on. Then, as you get older, you start to be more focused. *I want to play for England, I want to win a World Cup.* The goals changed, but the aspiration was still there. I wanted to find a way out and that was it.'

It makes her among the best people, male or female, with whom to discuss the barriers of racism, class and sexism in rugby. The sport likes to cite its open-door policy but, in Alphonsi's experience, it is not quite that simple. 'Racism wasn't a big thing for me because I didn't experience it. But it doesn't mean it wasn't there. I just wasn't acknowledging it. The biggest hurdle for me was being a woman. We didn't really have changing rooms, we'd have to get changed in our cars. We'd be playing on the back pitch at Bramley Road which might have dog poo on it. The reality was, not many girls played. It always felt like we were the leftovers. Thankfully, times have changed and Saracens, in particular, is a very strong, supportive club for women and girls. But it took time and it was quite frustrating.'

'**The reality was, not many girls played. It always felt like we were the leftovers.**'

It is a measure of Alphonsi's inner drive that by 19, she was playing for England, initially as a centre. Injury then intervened, but soon enough she was her country's first-choice openside flanker, spurred on by a coach urging her to become not just the best in England but in the world. Maggie the Machine, as they nicknamed her, duly went on to win 74 caps and score 28 tries for England, her tackling so forceful she once put Owen Farrell on his backside at training. Along the way she helped to deliver a record-breaking seven consecutive Six Nations titles and, finally, a World Cup title for England at Canada's expense in 2014 after two previous final near misses. 'It was weird, I just didn't think we could lose it. Maybe in 2006 and 2010 there was an element of doubt, but in 2014 there was this relentless belief nothing was going to get in our way. I think the best teams, the ones who experience epic wins, have also had epic failures along the way. They know what the pain of defeat feels like.'

Having fought her way back from a bad knee injury to be involved in the tournament, Alphonsi was also very aware it would be her final fling. 'I knew 2014 was my last season in rugby. I was very fearful of going downhill and still keeping playing.' Following her retirement, though, she moved swiftly into another career, becoming the first former female player to commentate on men's international rugby when she was employed by ITV for the 2015 Rugby World Cup.

Several years previously the Rugby Union Writers' Club also awarded her their top annual prize, the Pat Marshall Memorial Award, when she pipped New Zealand captain Richie McCaw to become the first female winner since its inception way back in 1976. Such well-deserved accolades, sadly, failed to impress some of the internet's smaller-minded inhabitants. The worst racism Alphonsi has experienced has stemmed from her television punditry and made her more cynical about social media. 'I genuinely don't care what people say any more. Unfortunately, at some point you develop a thick skin. *Why am I listening to people I don't even know or value?*

'Some of the best male pundits out there, who have achieved a lot, get loads of adverse comments as well. If I spent my whole time trying to please people, I don't think I'd progress far. I just try to be authentic, I try to be myself. People are going to like you, people are going to hate you. If you work in the media and you're visible, you're always going to get negativity. But as long as I try hard to be the best I can be, that's all that matters. My career in punditry won't last forever, but my priority is to enjoy what I do.'

Her desire to accelerate change, though, was among her reasons for accepting the invitation to join the Rugby Football Union council in 2016. 'When I came on to the council in 2016, I was the first person of colour, the third woman and the youngest one in the room. Richard Hill and I were virtually the only people under 60. It highlighted that, as a council, we weren't necessarily reflecting all those who are part of the sport. I would say we're starting to evolve and are becoming more diverse. Off the top of my head I think there are now eight women on the council. In terms of other governing bodies we're trying to lead the way.'

You can only admire her continuing desire to smash down barriers in much the same uncompromising way she once did her opponents. What she cannot do is wave a magic wand and solve all the world's problems overnight. 'People say to me, "Will we ever eradicate racism?" And I say, "No, I don't think we ever will." I don't think things will ever get better.

'Some people might use the term *microaggression*. It's subtle.' Luther Burrell's stark testimony in the summer of 2022 that racism was 'rife' in the sport, prompting the RFU to issue the former international centre with an apology for the discrimination he encountered, underlined those fears. 'It saddens me and I admire Luther for being very open about that,' stresses Alphonsi. 'Shining that spotlight has allowed other people to come out and speak about stuff. But it also highlights the fact it's still out there. To what degree? Luther's experience is not the same as maybe my experience. But, either way, it's important people are talking about it. And it's important how we manage it and value people's experiences.'

The good news is that women's rugby continues to make huge strides in popularity. Alphonsi has always had a parallel passion for music – she used to play the acoustic and electric guitar and her wife has a degree in classical music – but she remains an equally firm believer in the power of rugby from the perspective of social and mental well-being. 'If it wasn't for rugby, I don't think I'd have done well in my GCSEs, or in terms of university. It was a really big driver for me to keep my discipline, to have a goal, to keep moving forward. When you play sport, rugby in particular, people are always pushing you. If you're having a low day, someone will be trying to pick you up.'

And, as she continues to prove on a daily basis, there is a place in rugby for anyone regardless of where you come from. 'My big thing is to push everyone into sport and then find the one that suits them. I don't want everyone to go to football. The best thing about rugby is that there are different sizes and shapes. I think that's why rugby works for most people.'

17

PACIFIC WARRIORS

The first through the glass is the one that takes the bullet.

Late in November 2005 I found myself in the clubhouse of Newbury RFC in Berkshire, not really knowing what to expect. The idea was to gather some material for a *Guardian* feature about bright young English rugby coaches who might one day thrive at a higher level. Someone had suggested popping down to Newbury, going well in National 1 at the time, to talk to their 34-year-old director of rugby whose methods were impressing even seen-it-all old stagers. 'Our players are saying, "This guy makes sense",' confided the club's president, David Smith. It was worth a punt, if nothing else.

Which is how I first met Ben Ryan, now widely known as the smart, empathetic coach behind Fiji's gold-medal winning Olympic sevens team in Rio de Janeiro in 2016. I knew he was refreshingly different when he told me his favourite relaxation on his days off was to visit the Tate Modern and gaze at the colourful abstracts of Wassily Kandinsky. 'I don't want to be arrogant but I don't think there's anyone else thinking as freely as I am,' he told me, breaking off from manoeuvring coffee cups around to demonstrate ingenious new ways of creating midfield space.

I liked him immediately and enjoyed writing up the thoughts of a man refusing to be shackled by convention or, worse, fear. 'I want to change the way people think about rugby in England,' he told me at one point. 'I don't think enough coaches appreciate there's more than one way to skin a cat.' He was also impatient for a Premiership job that, since he was not a big name, was proving elusive. 'People running clubs have tended to look for a well-known figurehead who will impress their friends in the bar. I think a glass ceiling does exist.'

It turned out fate had other plans in store for him, far beyond club rugby. He went on to coach England's sevens side but departed Twickenham in 2013 following a difference of opinion with Rob Andrew, the RFU's elite rugby director at the time. Little did he know it would offer him a springboard to a radically different life in perhaps the most rugby-mad nation on earth. Serendipity indeed.

Even now, sitting in a café back in Richmond, Ryan's eyes light up at some of his Fijian memories. Everything is still vivid, from the phone call to offer him the Fiji sevens job in 2013 – he was given 20 minutes to accept or decline – to the early days staying in Pacific Harbour, 40 minutes west of the capital Suva. 'We've got a place near the River Thames now and sometimes you get a smell that's reminiscent of the seaside, whelks and all. Whenever I get a whiff of it, it reminds me of walking out by the reef in Fiji.'

From the imposing sand dunes of Sigatoka, where the players honed their fitness, to the breathtaking Olympic final against Great Britain in Rio, the red-haired Ryan was at the heart of one of sport's most glorious stories. Fiji had never previously won an Olympic gold medal but, above and beyond that, this was a tale of remarkable people. Among them were their inspirational skipper Osea Kolinisau and the diminutive Jerry Tuwai who defied his impoverished background to become one of the world's best players. Tuwai learned to play rugby on a roundabout, barefooted with a plastic bottle for a ball. At one stage, Ryan revealed, his parents did not eat for a week to save up the money to buy their son's first pair of boots. After that Tuwai wrote the word *knife* on his left boot and *fork* on his right to remind himself of the sacrifices his family had made for him.

Little wonder a feature film, directed by the Oscar-winning director Orlando von Einsiedel and produced by the Los Angles-based company behind *The Lego Movie*, is in the works. The human interest stories are compelling enough even before the camera pans out to show the scenic backdrop. And if the soundtrack needs bolstering, there is even a Bob Marley-inspired remix – 'Because he's Iron, Like a Lion, Ben Ryan' – out there somewhere.

How, though, can you possibly recreate the almost poetic genius of the real thing? In their unforgettable final against an outclassed Great Britain, the Fijians came as close to perfection as any rugby team I've ever seen live. Fit, fast, adventurous, relaxed and confident, they were runaway 43–6 winners. Kolinisau set the early tone and by half time it was already 29–0. There were seven tries in total, followed by an equally unforgettable post-match ceremony at which all the Fijian players knelt humbly in front of Princess Anne to receive their medals.

Looking back now, Ryan has two other abiding memories. The first was on the morning of the final day in the Olympic village, where Fiji were sharing an apartment block with Australia. When the Aussies came down for breakfast, they saw the Fijian players laughing and joking in the pool, not remotely looking like athletes who had an Olympic semi-final and, potentially, a final to play that day.

And the second? 'It was in the changing room before the final. The players had total alignment and autonomy. I had a speech ready, but it would have been for me, not for them. If you'd looked at our warm-up in isolation you'd have said, "They're not taking this seriously." But when you've prepared for an exam perfectly, you don't want a teacher at the door saying, "Do you want to revise this?" You just want to relax them. When you've got a group of players like that, you just know there's going to be no problem.'

In short, it was coaching nirvana. That moment when a coach becomes, in the nicest possible way, superfluous. 'There was nothing I had to do apart from get them on the bus on time. They could probably have had a terrible breakfast and it wouldn't have made any difference. We were the only team not to have a performance analyst. Psychologists call it the zone of optimal function. It's when you're totally aligned and they make every decision correctly. Even if a pass is the wrong pass, it doesn't matter because they'll correct it immediately. I didn't need to be there.'

As a reward for the team's Olympic triumph, Ryan's face adorns Fiji's commemorative $7 banknote and its 50 cent coins. The heat, the darkness, the wide smiles . . . all of it has stuck with him even now he is the director of elite performance at Brentford FC, in English football's Premier League. 'In my head I occasionally disappear off around Fiji and it starts to feel like it wasn't very long ago. But then I'll be on a bus heading to Southampton and it's different.'

Few are better qualified, though, to articulate exactly what it is that sets Fijian rugby apart. Often this can get lumped together under the catch-all heading of 'natural talent', but Ryan's detailed insight is fascinating. 'If you were in a gym in Twickenham with a Fijian guy and an English guy, the English guy will generally be lifting or squatting heavier traditional weights.

'The Fijian players' functional strength is off the scale. It's like farmer strength – it's hard to measure.'

But the Fijian players' functional strength is off the scale. It's like farmer strength – it's hard to measure. That ability to use their strength and power for what is actually required – stepping off one foot, a fend, reading everything – takes them to another level.'

Ryan's experience with Fiji also taught him a few other things. 'They are very, very resilient and robust. Yes, there's an element of genetics. And upbringing. And coming from a developing country where they grow used to having less.' Equally crucial, though, is the way Fijians learn the game. From an early age, playing on crowded fields, they grow to understand the importance of offloading and communication. 'In the villages very little will have changed. It will still be a makeshift ball, a mismatch of people and on an uneven piece of land, after school or after work. Because it's so chaotic you've got to have good spatial awareness and your communication has got to be good.'

There are rather different cultural obstacles at play in, say, England. 'What every coach would say about young English players is that they need to talk more because they're used to being on their phones too much.' With Fijians the bigger issue is supporting players who, sometimes, are not appreciated at home as much as they are abroad. Even their all-time superstars like Rupeni Caucaunibuca and Waisale Serevi did not always enjoy universal love. 'You don't want anybody to get too big,' explains Ryan. 'Fijians can sometimes be quite happy to knock you down. With Waisale and Rupeni they always had detractors, rather than people always lifting them up. Their talent was undeniable, but the support wasn't around them.'

Look up the videos of the incomparable Caucau in full flight, not least in the 2007 World Cup in France, and it seems impossible that anyone would not appreciate perhaps the most naturally gifted force of nature there has ever been. Ultimately, though, he only played seven Tests for Fiji and Serevi, the sevens maestro, is probably the bigger name worldwide. 'Sevens was everything to him,' confirms Ryan. 'He was a pioneer in terms of the way the game is played. He took the fitness element seriously and his running and diet was probably ahead of everyone else, even the New Zealanders. That's why he carried on playing until he was 42.'

The next big question is whether Fiji can kick on in 15s under their new head coach Simon Raiwalui and build on the slowly improving facilities in the islands, which now include an artificial pitch and a gym that Ryan and others helped to crowd-fund. Women's rugby is also on the up, with Fijiana making encouraging strides. 'We set up their programme and put them at the same training base as the men. The value of women in society has gone up as a result of that. You look at those sort of spin-offs and think, "That's our legacy."'

The former Harlequins chief executive Mark Evans has now taken a guiding role with the Fiji Drua in Super Rugby, but Ryan believes it won't be too long before the world-beating men's sevens team is also being overseen by a Fijian with the requisite *mana* – a mix of aura, respect and presence – rather than another foreign hire. 'There's an argument that they need to go back to Fijians. Look at someone like Osea Kolinisau, who is now Chinese Women's head coach. He'd be better than me: he's not only got the playing pedigree, he's got that cultural *mana*.' The hardest part of the job, believes Ryan, is convincing Fijians they could be as good as anyone else out there. 'They just don't rate themselves. When a Fijian gets picked for New Zealand, they see them as a better player than the guys playing for Fiji. It's the same with coaches as well.'

A little piece of Ryan's heart, either way, will forever be in the Pacific. And, as he gazes out over the Thames, he wonders if the ultimate Fijian miracle might one day materialise. 'Leaving any sort of legacy on the Pacific Islands is difficult because, politically, things can be built on sand there. What we did do is change the mindset: there is no glass ceiling, Fijian teams can be on the top stage. We've now got consistent World Cup-class sevens teams, the Fijian national 15s team have bought into that and improved, and we've got the Drua in Super Rugby. The next step for them would be to win a World Cup.' Really? Could that actually happen? 'Yeah, I do think that's possible. In the USA in 2031? I wouldn't put it past them.' What a film sequel that would make.

* * * * *

I was similarly keen to hear from someone else with specialist knowledge of the huge logistical barriers every Pacific Island rugby team has to overcome. Hence the reason I am sitting in the Regatta – a handsome old pub known to locals of a certain age as the Regret-er – in the Brisbane suburb of Toowong. The venue, it turns out, is appropriately chosen. In 1965 the Regatta was where Merle Thornton and her friend Rosalie Bognor chained themselves to the public bar in protest at the law prohibiting women from drinking there. This is a place where people have historically been prepared to stand up for their beliefs.

Dan Leo, founder of Pacific Rugby Players' Welfare (PRPW), certainly fits that description. In his case the battle ground has been the unequal playing field upon which Pacific Island teams have long since had to operate. If you haven't seen his documentary *Oceans Apart: Greed, Betrayal and Pacific Island Rugby*, which focuses on the iniquities and challenges facing many Pacific Islands players, seek it out. 'The reason there will be no change is because the people who stand to lose from change have all the power,' says Leo solemnly at one stage. 'This sums up the game of rugby to me.'

Leo has been bravely championing the cause for years now, having grown up in a family where preaching the gospel to the unconverted was a daily ritual. His mother Vicky, a Kiwi from Christchurch, and his father Alesio, from Samoa, used to train missionaries of Pacific Island descent in South Auckland. It instilled in their son a similar desire to stand up for those who, for whatever reason, need a helping hand. 'I've always been that way. I think Pacific Islanders are often too concerned with hierarchy and not challenging authority. Even when it needs a bit of revisiting.'

As a player the tall, rangy Leo was a bit of a novelty: born in New Zealand, he moved to Brisbane at 18 and ended up representing his father's homeland. 'I was one of the first Australian-based players to come through to the Samoan team. People were saying, "Who is this guy?" I didn't really have much of a reputation because I'd never played any Age Grade stuff in NZ. No one really knew me.' One day in 2005, though, Samoa were about to play Australia in Sydney and needed some injury cover, prompting the former All Black legend Michael Jones to ring Leo out of the blue.

He was instantly propelled into a very different rugby culture. 'I flew into Sydney and the boys were in training. The team manager gave me the key to my room but didn't say much more than that. I went up to drop my bag off, opened the door and saw there was a double bed and a single bed. The single bed had a couple of suitcases on it. I looked at the name tags and it said, "Brian Lima". I was thinking, *This guy is a legend*. I'd grown up watching him and was totally in awe of him. And he'd taken the single bed. Then I began to wonder: *Is this some kind of trick?* So I put my stuff in the corner.' It proved to be a shrewd move. 'It was the right thing to do because it totally was a test. If I'd taken the double bed, I don't think I'd have lasted 3–4 days.'

Messing with The Chiropractor – Lima's nickname because of all the opposition bones he rearranged – was not an option. Leo also swiftly discovered there was a strong back-of-the-bus culture. 'It was pretty scary because there were a lot of protocols. You didn't get told anything, you just learned from your mistakes. I remember one of the newer boys pulling out his Sony Discman to listen to some music. He got blasted. I remember Brian Lima saying, "That's a sign of disrespect. Do you not want to get to know us? That's what it says to me if you sit there and listen to your own music."'

The new caps also learned it was their role to do the laundry for the squad. 'We didn't have a budget for washing, so myself and five other new caps were put on it. First we had to scan the whole field and changing rooms for any rubbish and make sure that was tidied up. Then, at the end of the day, we had to pick up all the laundry from everybody's rooms and take it to the laundromat because we didn't have a budget to use the hotel service. So we'd go down to the laundromat, sit there and get it washed. They'd send you with a bag of 50 two-dollar coins and you'd be sitting there slotting them in for two hours. It was a great time . . . you got to know people really well. We also learned pretty quickly that you don't then just chuck all the washing in the team room. You had to fold it all up and deliver it, particularly to senior players. I remember having to fold our captain Semi Sititi's clothes. And drop them off to his room. You didn't get to sleep until 2 a.m. by the time you'd done that.'

Leo, not wanting to risk the consequences, did what he was told. When his debut game against Australia came around, the Samoans lost 74–7, but complaining was not remotely an option. 'You learned pretty quickly. It was pretty old school . . . you might get a slap around the ears if you didn't pull your weight. Or get your head taken off by Brian Lima. Given the choice, you'd opt for a slap around the ear every time. There were no financial fines because no one had any money. For some of the boys coming from the islands, $10 was their daily salary. They had to find other ways.'

The lack of funds to buy even the most basic of performance-enhancing essentials was also an eye-opener. 'I remember playing in the Pacific Nations Cup. It was my second or third tour and it was to be my first away series in Samoa, Tonga and Fiji. The email we received said, "Bring your own strapping tape. When you're at your clubs, just grab a couple of rolls." I remember thinking it was a joke, but it wasn't. I discovered later that what Wasps spent on strapping tape alone was more than what Samoa spent on physios, doctors, strapping and rehabilitation.'

Signing for Wasps in 2005 – opting for Samoa meant he was no longer eligible to play for an Australian Super Rugby franchise – gave him a glimpse of a parallel universe. He did not play as much as he would have liked, but vying for back-row selection with Lawrence Dallaglio, Tom Rees, James Haskell and Joe Worsley was never going to be easy. Prior to the 2007 Rugby World Cup he also found himself summoned back to Samoa to compete for a place in their tournament squad. It proved to be another eye-opening experience. 'In one of our pre-World

Cup camps, they dropped us off on a deserted island. The idea was to make it a back-to-your-roots experience. If you were New Zealand-born, you got partnered up with one of the local players so that, basically, you didn't die.

'With some of the guys there was a bit of friction. They didn't really want to help the New Zealand guys out too much. Luckily the guy I was partnered up with was from my dad's village, which was helpful.' Leo soon realised he would require all the help he could find. 'They released a whole truckload of pigs into the bush and said, "Right, you know they're out there. That's your food for the week. Go out and survive." It was crazy. We had Eliota Fuimaono-Sapolu with us. He's an activist now but back then he was all about animal rights. He didn't want to kill a pig and was saying, "Nah, I'll be vegetarian for the week." After four days he was eating pork because there was nothing else.'

By the time Leo became a senior player, though, the off-field issues facing the squad were once more becoming even harder to stomach. In 2011 the Samoan captain Mahonri Schwalger was dropped after heavily criticising the conduct of the team's management during the World Cup in New Zealand. He alleged that officials treated the event like a holiday, disappeared for days and drank heavily at the team hotel. Then, in November 2014, the squad threatened to go on strike before their international against England at Twickenham over poor pay and conditions. Samoa's prime minister compared the players to 'foolish children' and Leo, one of nine players who wrote a letter to the *Samoa Observer* backing Schwalger after the 2011 World Cup, decided enough was enough.

Having discovered that team staff had been giving away the players' match kit to supporters in return for small favours while simultaneously asking the players to reuse their jerseys, he told the squad it was time to stand up. 'I told them that we couldn't go through what we went through in 2011, with money going missing and all sorts of other stuff. I said to everyone that if we wanted to have a good World Cup in 2015 we needed to address things now. I had a whole lot of grievances, but the final straw was them just giving away all our uniforms.'

Leo knew that, by speaking out, he would be ending his own international career. And possibly making life very awkward for those closest to him. His parents were living in Samoa at the time and their missionary organisation was based on government land. 'They said to me, "You know you're going up against some of the top people here and that could make our lives very difficult. If we're associated with you, everything's at risk."'

'You're not just representing yourself, you're representing your village, your church, everyone.'

It was, accordingly, a massive decision for him. 'In the islands we are seen as a reflection of our parents. If your children behave well or not so well, that's what regulates us. You're not just representing yourself, you're representing your village, your church, everyone.' Ultimately, though, Leo decided the wider cause was too important, as he explained to his teammates in no uncertain terms. 'The first through the glass is the one that takes the bullet,' he told his teammates. 'I'll front it as long as you guys sit there and nod your heads.'

He also stressed the importance of improving the situation for generations to come. 'I said to them, "We're not doing this to rock the boat unnecessarily." But most of us, particularly those who have come through the system, realised something needed to give. The only way that was going to happen was if we stood up. I'm not saying we need to go back to 1970s trade unions, but unless players are willing to make a stand nothing changes. Pay had effectively not changed for years. Up until 2014–15 we were getting paid around £500 a week to play. The PRPW movement needed to happen.'

Sure enough, his World Cup dream evaporated on the spot. 'I knew that because I'd asked questions and embarrassed them a little bit this was probably the last time I'd be sitting in the room. I decided to release everything because it didn't matter anymore. It must have gone on for half an hour. Officially it was announced that I'd retired but they said to me, "We're going to give you an opportunity to go out with a bit of grace." I retired knowing they were showing me the door. By that stage I was holding on as a player, so it was probably easier for them, for the sake of what I was bringing on the field. The coaches did give me a call, to be fair. The head coach phoned me personally and said he totally agreed with the things I'd been bringing up but that he'd had a directive from the Prime Minister not to select me. I'd been pretty outspoken on a couple of tours before then.'

There is unselfish and then there is Leo's absolute determination to help future generations and push for change, no matter what. The basic rights for which the PRPW have lobbied seem pretty obvious now. Revamped eligibility regulations, which allow Pacific Islanders discarded by major unions like New Zealand to represent Tonga, Samoa or Fiji after a three-year stand-down period, suitability tests for administrators, World Rugby voting equality and increased match fees, etc. Leo still sees no reason why Samoa should play in front of 82,000 spectators at Twickenham and receive only a pittance. 'The away team gets nothing . . . hopefully the house of cards is ready to fall.' His time spent on the barricades has, if anything, left him even less tolerant of the self-interest that exists in certain quarters. 'It's the big unions who are controlling things. They're constantly just gaslighting us. That's one of the biggest realisations to me.'

The release of *Oceans Apart* has certainly concentrated a few minds. It only told a part of the story – 'We could only touch on a few things in the documentary . . . we were trying to cram so much into one hour' – but it successfully highlighted the debt rugby owes to the Pacific Islands, not least in exporting talent to almost every professional team in the world. 'At the moment we're reliant on handouts,' stresses Leo. 'But to me we've got a strong enough commodity and reputation worldwide to be more proactive. Fiji are a good example. Hopefully soon Fiji can say, "We don't have to play anyone for free anymore."' Getting rid of the glass ceiling that has previously existed, however, would not suit every so-called tier one union. 'It's a tier two or three thing, not just the Islands. I'm all for a global season but it's got to be equal opportunity. That's what's been lacking in the past.'

The clock is also ticking. For young Samoans, rugby league is increasingly attractive, with an NRL development officer now based on the islands. As Leo warns, 'Unless you have a heavier front-row profile or you're not any good, you're going to get snapped up by rugby league in

Australia. The sharks are circling, so we can't rest on our laurels in union.' At least the inclusion of the Fiji Drua and Moana Pasifika in Super Rugby is a step in the right direction, not least in terms of giving Pacific Island forwards greater exposure to some of the game's more technical requirements. 'The difficulty we've always had is around the set pieces,' confirms Leo. 'Hopefully now with the introduction of these Super Rugby sides it's going to lift the calibre of our set piece dramatically.'

Which brings us to Leo's ultimate dream. That, with the help of others, the Island nations cease to be simply a conveyor belt delivering talent to others and finally become competitive equals operating on a more level playing field. Whether or not it happens on his watch, his determination to stand up for the downtrodden deserves due recognition. 'World Rugby's like a big steam liner . . . it changes direction very slowly. But I believe God has given me the right people around me and the tools and influence to make some change. Whether I'll be the one who carries this torch forever, I don't know. But I'll be here for as long and hard as I can.'

On the following Saturday night, as Australia host England in front of a packed house at Suncorp Stadium, I find Leo's words still echoing in my head. The Wallaby side is full of players with Pacific Island heritage, not least Taniela Tupou – the 'Tongan Thor' – and the Fijian-born Marika Koroibete. England's no. 8 is Billy Vunipola, whose father captained Tonga. The evidence is right there in front of our eyes: the exodus of muscle to Europe, Australia and New Zealand, the exploitation of cheap labour and the loading of the dice in favour of the richest. Leo, and others, deserve all our thanks. Sometimes rugby greatness is as much about what you say and do off the field as what occurs on it.

18

RIDING THE BULLET TRAIN

Look, mate, we've got nothing to lose. If you think
we should have a go, have a go.

It is New Year's Eve in Tokyo and Eddie Jones is reflecting on the soaring peaks and painful troughs of international coaching. 'They never end as you like them to do,' he murmurs. 'That's the reality of it.' Less than a month previously he was England's head coach and looking forward to taking his squad to the Rugby World Cup in France. Now here he is waiting to find out what 2023 holds in store after his abrupt exit from Twickenham. It will be another couple of weeks before he signs on the dotted line and commits to a five-year deal to coach his native Australia for a second time.

He will be doing well if he rocks the world with the Wallabies in the same way he once did with Japan. Has there ever been a globally significant result to compare with the national team's RWC pool victory over South Africa in 2015? *The Brighton Miracle*, as they called the subsequent film, was more than a stunning rugby occasion on a beautiful seaside afternoon. It was a day to confound those who assumed rugby's so-called elite nations would forever hold sway over the tier two minnows – and to glimpse a future beyond the traditional boundaries of the sport. Heading home on the Sunday morning, I even saw people crossing the street near Brighton station simply to shake hands with random Japanese tourists.

Nor was it remotely a fluke. The Springboks were outplayed in almost every facet of the game by opponents ranked 13th in the world and boasting just one previous World Cup pool win in 24 attempts. The full back Ayumu Goromaru supplied 24 points, but it was the ability of Japan's key decision makers to keep their heads amid the craziness that ultimately counted most. The best example came in the final seconds when the hugely impressive Japan captain Michael Leitch twice rejected potential shots at goal which could have delivered a draw, preferring to chase glory instead. When the replacement wing Karne Hesketh rewarded that faith by diving beyond JP Pietersen into the left corner, the impossible fairytale was complete.

It was also a stunning triumph for Jones and his assistants, including Steve Borthwick, now England's latest head coach.

'With an Asian team beating a top tier country, that really makes it a global sport.'

'We talked about staying with them, putting pressure on them and what might happen if we were in touch after 60 minutes,' said Borthwick afterwards. 'That was exactly what happened.' At the post-match press conference, Jones compared it to Alfred Hitchcock's *Psycho* – 'It's like the horror story. If you go into the shower at midnight, you know what's going to happen next' – and admitted the 34–32 result had surpassed even his famously high expectations. 'I had to look at the score at the end to see if it was true or not. It's fantastic for the sport. With an Asian team beating a top tier country, that really makes it a global sport.'

It later emerged Jones had put his squad through as many as four training sessions a day, pushing them to breaking point with the aim of developing an absurdly fit squad, capable of playing a high-tempo game and keeping going no matter what. He had also picked the brains of Pep Guardiola, then at Bayern Munich, about training intensity and exploiting on-field space. Jones was wily, too: in a pre-tournament warm-up fixture, he put back-rower Hendrik Tui on the wing and started with nine forwards, specifically to throw South Africa off the scent. The man who battled his way back from a stroke in October 2013 had now cemented his reputation as one of rugby's most masterful World Cup tacticians.

Admittedly Japan's success was not wholly down to micro planning. Immediately prior to Hesketh's defining score in Brighton, Jones was yelling at his players to kick a score-levelling penalty instead. 'Just before the end I was screaming: "Take the three, take the three."' Then he recalled a conversation between himself and his captain earlier that day. 'I had coffee with Leitchy and said, "Look, mate, we've got nothing to lose. If you think we should have a go, have a go."' The rest is now rugby history.

Jones' relationship with the remarkable Leitch was a further compelling narrative strand. They first met when Jones coached his future captain at Tokai University, by which time Leitch was already familiar with commitment and sacrifice. 'You think about his story,' stressed Jones ahead of his side's 2022 Test against Japan at Twickenham. 'He is from a village in Canterbury, with a New Zealand father and a Fijian mother. At the age of 14 he gets offered a contract to play professional rugby in Japan, in Hokkaido. He didn't even know where Hokkaido is. He goes up to this high school where they train on a baseball field. Rolled clay, right? He is the only non-Japanese player there. Everyone else is speaking Japanese, he's from the backblocks of Christchurch. So you have got this tall, skinny, half-Fijian, half-New Zealander playing with these Japanese guys half his size.'

The story also goes that the locals started to refer to the steep hill overlooking Yamanote High School in Sapporo as Michael Leitch's playground. During Leitch's student days he used to run up it every day after training. It is supposed to take most kids around 30 minutes to climb. Leitch was doing it in 15 minutes by the time he left. To say Japan had – and still have – an indomitable captain is an understatement. The days of Japan losing 145–0 to New Zealand, as they did in 1995, are long gone as a direct consequence.

When Jones looks back, he does so with a mixture of emotions. Pride is definitely one of them. His deeds with Japan helped earn him his long-term England gig and the nation is close to his heart. As he wrote in his autobiography, 'The country flowed through my family like a river.' His wife Hiroko and mother Nellie are both Japanese and his working relationship with Suntory has now spanned a quarter of a century.

There is also a slight sense of wonder, even now. While he has never sat down and rewatched the South Africa game, certain images remain vivid. 'The memories are there, mate,' he murmurs. 'The big one for me was walking down from the grandstand at the end of the game and seeing Japanese supporters crying their eyes out in joy. That's the difference you make, and they're really good memories.'

Mostly, though, he cites the Brighton miracle as a perfect example of a fundamental human truth: that everyone is capable of more than they imagine. 'The thing that still sticks out the most is that you can't be limited by traditional thoughts. Your ability to look beyond what everyone thinks you're capable of doing is always there.' No one believed Japan could match the Boks, but that was before Jones' side redefined the nature of the challenge.

The other crucial aspect he still highlights is the impact of his erstwhile assistant Borthwick on the Japanese line-out. 'His role in that team was absolutely outstanding. He created a line-out that could compete at a world level even though the tallest guy we had was 6ft 3in tall.' The outcome, from a coaching perspective, was Jones' signature masterpiece. Such was the stratospheric interest in Japan that sumo wrestling and baseball were temporarily knocked off the back pages. It was also perfectly timed. Suddenly the 2019 tournament in Japan, the first in history to be staged in Asia, could not come quickly enough.

* * * * *

The decision to award Japan the 2019 event had been made 10 years earlier. The possible commercial benefits had outweighed significant concerns about logistics and the on-field competitiveness of the host nation. With 2015 having proved a runaway financial success, there was a collective view within World Rugby that the time had come to test out new ground.

There was just one snag: the dates of the tournament coincided with the annual typhoon season in Japan. When some of us sat down with Alan Gilpin, the tournament director, in a Richmond hotel in September 2018, we made a point of asking if the weather might pose problems given the biggest storm for 25 years had just struck the World Cup host cities of Kobe and Osaka. 'It's a real hot topic for us,' stressed Gilpin. The general view, nevertheless, was that it should be all right on the night.

We all reckoned without Hagibis. It was the strongest super typhoon to strike mainland Japan in decades and the deadliest since 1976. At its widest point it measured some 1,500 km (930 miles) in diameter. The organisers were braced for the worst by the time it made landfall in Japan on 12 October. Stuck in his 'war room' in his serviced apartment in central Tokyo, Gilpin had not slept for the three previous days, having been warned by his local meteorological advisor that there were three significant storms on the horizon. As Gilpin recalls, 'It started to become clear that we had a real problem. At least one of them was going to be enormous.'

Not everyone was quite so well briefed. 'It's pretty windy and wet when you play at Exeter . . . it can't be too different, right?' murmured England's Courtney Lawes as the weather warnings intensified. His wry gag felt less amusing as we sat on the 31st floor of a shaking hotel building in Tokyo, a 5.7 magnitude earthquake having simultaneously rocked the Japanese capital. By the time the mega storm had blasted through, it had caused billions of dollars of damage and over 100 people had lost their lives. The disrupted pool stages of a rugby tournament instantly became a relatively minor detail.

The tournament organisers will not forget that weekend in a hurry. 'We basically had a rule that if a pool match couldn't be completed on the scheduled day and hadn't been relocated in advance, it was cancelled,' explains Gilpin, taking a contemplative sip of coffee in a hotel in central Auckland. 'But it had never been tested in a World Cup, so everyone had kind of forgotten that. We were very bloody aware of it.'

Because of the tight turnaround times and the logistical difficulties of moving teams and, crucially, spectators around Japan, the options were limited. At one stage someone suggested relocating games to the covered stadium in Oita on the southerly island of Kyushu, only for the reality to dawn that the weather would severely impact fans travelling between cities. England's game against France, Italy's match against New Zealand and Canada's fixture with Namibia were all duly called off. It was the first time in history that World Cup games had had to be scrapped.

The biggest nightmare of the lot, though, was the scheduled game between Japan and Scotland in Yokohama. The only glimmer of hope for Gilpin and his team was that the weather might have eased sufficiently for the game to be played. A handful of members of the Japanese organising committee volunteered to hunker down in the stadium overnight so they could assess the on-site situation at first light. There was minor damage, but by 7 a.m. Gilpin had his answer. Japan and Scotland were advised that their game was definitely on.

Scotland were subsequently fined £70,000 following prematch remarks by their chief executive Mark Dodson that it might suit Japan if the game were to be called off and that the Scots should not be treated as 'collateral damage'. World Rugby strongly refuted any suggestion of favouritism – 'Nothing was further from the truth,' stresses Gilpin now – and the upshot was one of the games of the tournament. After a minute's silence for the victims of Hagibis, Japan tore into their opponents and scored four tries in 26 extraordinary minutes to win 28–21. 'This game was about more than just us,' stressed Leitch after his side had reached the World Cup quarter-finals for the very first time. 'A lot of people suffered in the typhoon for this game to happen.'

Gilpin, now chief executive of World Rugby, rates the atmosphere that Sunday as among the best he has ever experienced in sport. 'It was one of the most amazing experiences of my life. There were also 54 million people watching on television who probably wouldn't have been watching otherwise. That, for me, was the biggest moment of the tournament.'

The semi-final between England and New Zealand was arguably even bigger. It certainly produced the most dazzling performance by a team in white for years, setting up a re-run of the 2007 final between South Africa and England. Unfortunately for Jones' England, it was a foregone conclusion from an early point. If the outcome was disappointing for Red Rose supporters, the sight of Siya Kolisi hoisting the golden trophy into the clear Japanese night has become iconic. Just 24 years earlier, the world watched as Nelson Mandela congratulated Francois Pienaar in Johannesburg. Now here was a Black Springbok captain lifting the Webb Ellis Cup, having left the tough townships of Port Elizabeth to conquer the world. It ranked high among the greatest images in rugby history.

The tournament as a whole also felt as if it was ushering in a new dawn. From the hot springs of Beppu to the backstreets of Tokyo, Japan were wonderful hosts and some of the subsequently published statistics were jaw-dropping. The event was said to have added £2.3 billion to Japan's GDP, attracted 242,000 international fans from 178 nations and involved the selling of 1.83 million tickets.

At this point, however, opinions start to diverge. Was the legacy of the 2019 World Cup all it could have been? Robert Maes, a marketing executive with years of experience of promoting sport in Asia and elsewhere, told the *Guardian* in 2020 that he feared for the long-term future of the game in Japan. 'It all looked very nice to the outside world, but after 2019 there was nothing left. In Japan we're looking at the death of rugby. The future is very, very bleak. The clubs will still pay big salaries, but it's basically just a few rich companies pouring money in because they're old school and their executives played rugby. They talk about a World Cup legacy, but the sport is shrinking in Japan.'

'It all looked very nice to the outside world, but after 2019 there was nothing left. In Japan we're looking at the death of rugby.'

With another big World Cup approaching, it felt like an opportune time to reconnect with Maes and see if his view had altered. If anything he sounded even more pessimistic, citing the financial impact of the COVID pandemic. 'I like rugby. But if you ask me as a professional marketing expert I wouldn't touch it with rubber gloves in Japan because I can only lose money. Commercially it's dead. The number of registered players is going down and the talent base is getting smaller. Last year 609,000 more Japanese died than were born. Where are you going to get new fans from? The only thing keeping rugby alive is that it's pushed in universities. You're seen as a real man in Japan if you play it. And when they graduate, those same people continue to support it. It's always the same people who go to the rugby.'

Maes also points to the Tokyo-based Sunwolves dropping out of the Super Rugby competition, the recent decline of the Hong Kong Sevens, the political regime in China and a lack of 15-a-side tournaments to promote in the region. He also says floating fans are gravitating more towards baseball and soccer than the domestic Japan Rugby League One. 'Rugby will always have a place in Japan, but growing it? When I did some work for the Asian Rugby Federation I said to them, "What do you want me to sell because you don't have anything?" Everyone ignores reality. They're paying very high salaries to overseas players. The management of rugby has been crap and I think rugby is already over its ceiling. Rugby in China? Good luck. The only bright spot I see is the United States. If the American team starts doing well, the money will follow. In Asia it's only going to go down.'

Plenty there for expansionists everywhere to ponder. On the flip side, significant Japanese brands such as Taisho, Canon and Asahi are signed up as sponsors of the 2023 World Cup. A joint venture was also announced in December 2022 between the Japan Rugby Football Union (JRFU), Japan Rugby League One (JRLO) and the digital and entertainment giant Sony. A new company called Japan Rugby Marketing Inc. has been formed with the aim of increasing fan engagement and driving so-called 'audience development'. There has also been some recent on-field progress. The Brave Blossoms, driven on by the inspirational Leitch and a shrewd coaching team, lost only 38–31 to New Zealand in Tokyo's National Stadium in October 2022. There are growth possibilities around the women's game, too, particularly in sevens.

For all that, attracting the next generation is what ultimately matters and Japan's qualification for the latter stages of the 2022 football World Cup in Qatar further complicated that task. Gilpin, to his credit, openly accepts not all is totally Zen in the Japanese rugby garden. 'There are so many lessons from that World Cup. We'd only ever done World Cups in established rugby markets and we didn't plan hard enough for the legacy. We were so focused on delivering a great tournament, but I don't think we were partnered enough with Japan Rugby for what happened next. The combination of that and COVID has made it almost impossible to understand how you now drive that legacy.'

And while Gilpin still lives in hope – 'I do think they've done some really good things and the domestic league structure is better than they had before' – he does accept rugby in Japan still has a way to travel. 'For Japanese families, sport's not a priority. It's all about education. In the established rugby markets your parents will probably take you along to a club. In Asia the key to participation growth is through the schools and colleges.' There is also the small matter of regular terrestrial television coverage. 'Part of the challenge in Asia is getting cut-through on television. Maybe this is shifting, but it is very hard to build an audience if you're not on mainstream national TV.'

Hence Gilpin's renewed focus on making sure there are more longer-lasting benefits after the United States hosts the 2031 men's tournament and the women's equivalent in 2033. 'I look at it and say, "Can we take rugby's biggest moments to new markets and use that as a driver for growth?" Absolutely. "Are we confident we can put our major events on almost anywhere in the world, as long as the infrastructure exists?" Definitely.

'But that's not enough. Having a wonderful six weeks is fantastic. But you've got to build the audience and the legacy in advance. Then you have to be ready afterwards to do the rest of it. All the groundwork has to be done to be ready for that spike in interest.' While the 2019 Japanese experience was genuinely unforgettable, it also clearly taught World Rugby some salutary lessons.

From Jones' perspective, though, all is not yet lost. When he strolls around Tokyo these days, there may be less in the way of Eddie mania – 'It's dropped off a bit now' – but he has seen enough of it to be convinced the 2015 and 2019 successes have had a lasting impact on local perceptions. 'It built a new sporting Japan. COVID put a bit of a hold on it, but I remember going to a practice game after that 2019 World Cup and there were 7,000 people crammed into the training ground. To get out of there, I literally had to be rescued because of the fever for rugby.

'The Japanese are no different to many other nations. They like winners . . . if their national team is not winning, it's replaced by another team that is winning. At the moment the soccer team is the flavour of the month. But it wouldn't take much for Japan to get that back. Once you've done it and you believe you can do it again, you can resurrect that dream of a vibrant sport and encourage youngsters to play.'

As an example Jones cites a rugby school in Oita which he has visited twice, once before the World Cup and again more recently. 'Prior to the

World Cup they had eight players playing. Now they've got 30. While the numbers mightn't be what World Rugby want, there has been some incredible inspiration for young people to play rugby. You need young players to be able to dream they can make it at world level. That's the thing that makes the difference. There is NBA advertising all over Tokyo because a Japanese guy has made it in the NBA. Any time a player from your country makes it on the world scene, it creates a role model for young players.'

He also feels Japan's domestic season structure now gives the Brave Blossoms more quality time in which to prepare than almost any other squad. 'They've set up their whole domestic season to support the national team and they're going to have a four-to-five-months preparation for the 2023 World Cup. They had three months together before they played the All Blacks in November. They could have won that game. With that being a possibility again, we don't know what they can achieve.'

Beware, in short, underestimating Japan on the field. 'They've got high aspirations but they're going through a difficult little period because they've basically now lost all the really good players from 2015. They get older and the new group is still finding its feet. International rugby is difficult. But if they can get a couple of strong wins in the 2023 World Cup, the game will take off again. There's no doubt about that, mate.' As Jones' Japan proved in 2015, anything is possible if you really put your mind to it.

19

THE AMERICAS DREAM

Guys, we did something special. Never forget about this.

When Agustín Pichot was young, his parents took him travelling to Europe. Being a keen rugby family, they made a point of going to Twickenham and educating young Gus about 'the cathedral of English rugby'. Back home in Buenos Aires, that motivational spark never left him. One day, he promised himself, he would play rugby in the United Kingdom and beat the English at their spiritual home.

The gears of fate were duly engaged. In the early years of professionalism, Pichot signed for Richmond, and driving past Twickenham became a regular occurrence. Other than his passage into adulthood, nothing had really changed. 'When I passed the stadium I always had the same feeling. *One day I hope to beat England at Twickenham.*'

Which was why it was such a huge deal for Pichot, as captain of the Pumas, when the big day finally dawned in 2006. Often post-match functions can involve a litany of sleep-inducing speeches, but not this time. In the wake of their famous 25–18 victory, Pichot rose to his feet and told his players to shut up and listen. 'I just wanted to have that moment in time and say to the guys, "We made history today. For the first time Argentina has beaten England in the country where the game started." It was massive. I have so much love, respect and admiration for everything that England gave me and that was the moment to spell it out to those players who didn't have the same understanding of history. "Guys, we did something special. Never forget about this."'

In that moment he was also speaking, in some ways, for rugby 'outsiders' around the globe. All of them crave the same thing: recognition and respect from the establishment. After that the goal is simple enough.

To overturn traditional perceptions and shove yesterday's condescension and inferiority complexes where the 'elite' sun never shines.

It was this same driving force that powered the diminutive Pichot through and past bigger men and helped him burst out the other side as a can-do administrator looking to stand up for rugby underdogs everywhere.

'Rugby's a nightmare at the moment . . . it's not sustainable'

Without his crusading zeal, Argentina's addition to what used to be the Tri Nations might never have happened. There were few signs of it, though, in his early childhood.

As recounted in Rex Gowar's fascinating book *Pumas*, his parents were increasingly concerned when their five-month child grew pale and listless and would drink only soy milk. They were advised to consult a Brazilian witch doctor 40 km (25 miles) away, who ordered the child to be undressed, said a prayer, put a blue mark on his bottom and gave his mother a mallow plant. Pichot's parents were instructed to put mallow water in the baby's bottle and to bring him back to her every day for a week. By the end of the week the boy's health had been utterly transformed, and his surging energy and purpose has never left him.

Even on the end of a phone in Colorado, where he is conducting some business, Pichot exudes the same passion some of us witnessed in 2018, when he was inducted into the World Rugby Hall of Fame. Pichot was then World Rugby's vice-chairman, but there was no hiding his frustration that the game he loves was not modernising swiftly enough. 'If you ask me as a businessman, the business side of it is not working,' he said then. 'If you ask me about the playing side, it's not working. Is the international game under threat? I think it is. I'm not going to be an accomplice to rugby's ruin.'

What a line. And he absolutely meant it. Five years on and many of the same arguments about revenue, common purpose and the best ways to help smaller rugby nations endure. Pichot still has strong views on the subject – 'Rugby's a nightmare at the moment . . . it's not sustainable' – but he also wants to talk about Argentina's 2022 summer win over the All Blacks in New Zealand, another once-fanciful dream made flesh. Pichot was as impressed and quietly thrilled as anyone, but he cannot help but reflect on how much times have changed since the mid-noughties when he was still playing. 'The Pumas beating the All Blacks in New Zealand was an amazing achievement, but when you take into consideration the guys have been professional for a while it was a feasible possibility.

'With us back in the day it was more a case of *How can we make this happen?* We only had a few pro rugby players playing in the Premiership or France. How can they beat England in Twickenham? Or France in the opening game of the 2007 World Cup with the odds completely against them? It was because something special and extraordinary happened.'

Looking back now, Pichot calls it a 'beam of hope' that reached peak intensity in the opening game of that 2007 tournament against the hosts, France, in Paris. 'I've been to four World Cups, so I have experienced all the emotions, good and bad. But this one was special. I lived in Paris, five minutes away from the Parc des Princes and half an hour from the Stade. I used to have meals with my friends around the corner. It was like playing on my playground but, at the same time, playing against France.'

To be there in the stadium on that sultry opening night as a neutral observer was to be in a Gallic boulevard of broken dreams. Never had a World Cup opened with a visiting team showing a greater disregard for their supposed attendant role. By half time the Pumas had established a 17–9 lead thanks to a try from their long-striding full back Ignacio Corleto and the fury of their forwards. France tried hard to respond, but the calm goal-kicking of Felipe Contepomi had ensured a final 17–12 scoreline that shook the world. They subsequently delivered a stirring encore by hammering Les Bleus again in the third-place play-off, scoring five tries in a riotous 34–10 win. Pichot secured the man of the match award on his 72nd and final Test appearance.

At no stage in his career was he ever emotionally disengaged – he was an inexhaustible spirit, constantly urging on his forwards – but this outcome was extra special. 'How many times does the away team beat the host nation? If you count up the number of times it happens in life, it's almost impossible. It was epic. We lost to South Africa in the semi-final and no one could argue about the power of the Springboks or them winning the World Cup. They were a great team. Bryan Habana was a machine. But nobody will forget that France lost to Argentina. Or how quiet the Stade de France was in the 78th minute. I do remember that.'

It becomes even less of a surprise that the Pumas emerged triumphant that night when you discover what the skipper said to his teammates prior to kick-off. 'Sometimes I only needed to look at the players, sometimes I really pushed them hard. For that game I was very, very calm. I said to them, "We can do this. This is the start of a tournament we've all dreamed about. But never forget there are hundreds of thousands of Argentine kids who would like to be in your position right now. You have to play for them and all the others who aren't here."' In particular he implored them to win for the sake of Martín Gaitán, the Biarritz centre who had played the full 80 minutes against Wales at the Millennium Stadium just prior to the tournament but suffered a heart attack after the game. 'It was quite special. If you can't get pumped up thinking about all that, you're from another planet.'

It was also the launchpad, reckons Pichot, to everything that has followed. 'If it wasn't for 2007, we wouldn't have beaten the All Blacks in recent years or had a side in the final of Super Rugby or achieved a bronze medal in the 2021 Olympic Sevens in Tokyo. It showed that when you have a goal and you work with a lot of passion and intensity, then things can happen.'

Which brings us back to Pichot's stint in the corridors of power at World Rugby – and his abrupt departure in 2020 when he chose to stand against the incumbent Sir Bill Beaumont for the chairmanship. Ushering in a new era of change was never going to suit everyone and the vote duly ended up 28–23 in Beaumont's favour. Then, as now, Pichot was never going to compromise his beliefs. 'I loved it but I couldn't carry on unless there was going to be change. The way rugby works is very structured. Unless you can fulfil a lot of difficult conditions – economic, infrastructure – then you don't have a chance. And that's unfair.

'I didn't want to be the chairman of World Rugby just to sit in VIP seats. That's not me. I couldn't care less about that. I think Bill is a great guy but I thought we needed more teeth. Not a revolution – people were trying to paint me as a rebel or a cowboy. But those who know me know I'm a business guy. I have 600 employees in one company and nearly 400 in another. I'm not a cowboy. I love finance and I study it. My businesses are all based on cost-efficient models. It is very easy to understand. Unfortunately, the system is not sustainable. It's not rocket science. But I think World Rugby is doing the best it can. I've no hard feelings.'

Instead he has been trying to help build stronger foundations in the Americas, with the launch of the Superliga Americana de Rugby having already assisted both Chile and Uruguay to qualify alongside Argentina for the 2023 World Cup. 'We made a plan with Uruguay, Chile and Brazil and we're very happy with the health of the game in South America. I think we're in a very solid space. We are going to carry on fighting to get more games and to improve. We have 10 per cent more players in the clubs and financially the union is healthy despite the COVID pandemic cutting the budget by 30 per cent. We saw how Australia nearly went bankrupt. Then we saw how the European club owners were losing money. We were looking at how not to do it. We tried to look and learn, to be humble and to do things better.'

Some argue that, one day, a British & Irish Lions tour to South America might be another positive step in the right direction. Imagine a spectacular road trip through Chile, Brazil, Uruguay and some of Argentina's provincial strongholds such as Tucumán or Rosario, with three Tests against the fired-up Pumas and maybe a marquee fixture against a combined Americas XV as well? Pichot is less enthused, politely rejecting it as a catch-all catalyst for growing rugby on his continent. 'I'm not so sure the Lions are so relevant in world rugby today. I think they are a great brand and I love them, but it's not a sustainable ambition for many countries. It helps Australia, New Zealand and South Africa, but it doesn't help the rest of the world at all. The Lions do very little for the worth of Fiji or Samoa, say.

'The concept also doesn't inspire anyone in South America. What inspires kids there is watching Uruguay beating Fiji at a World Cup. Or watching Argentina. I wish the Lions would come to South America. But if they only come once every 8, 12 or 16 years what will that change? It's like the All Blacks playing in America. It doesn't change anything. One day you play in Soldier Field and you beat America by 70 points. What's the point? You just cannibalise the brands.' He pauses, as if belatedly remembering he is supposed to have turned his back on this stuff. 'I could carry on forever . . . '

It begs the question, though, as to whether he might be tempted to run again for high office at some stage? After all, rugby's answer to Che Guevara is still only in his late 40s. 'At the moment I'm happy where I am. Helping the Argentine union, helping South American rugby to carry on growing. I loved my time in World Rugby, but I've also loved my time out of it, looking back at it with a bit of perspective. One day you're an influential guy, but now I'm coaching young players at my club. I've made my dream come true. I've played for my country and now I'm teaching the U15s what rugby's about. I haven't had the space to think about World Rugby. I think it's healthy for the system that I've had three years out. Maybe one day, if people think things should be addressed, then we'll see . . . '

* * * * *

If World Rugby could have just one wish granted, it would be similar to the prayer offered up by every British pop act in history. *Guys, we're doing okay, but what if we can crack America?* All those contact-loving athletes, all those sponsors' dollars. And by inviting the United States to host both the 2031 men's Rugby World Cup and the 2033 women's tournament, rugby now has a ticking clock officially up and running.

So no pressure as rugby union seeks its own eureka moment in North America in 2031. Initially the Americans wanted to host it in 2027 but were prevailed upon to hold off and give their national team more time to become properly competitive. A shrewd move, as it turned out, after the US Eagles failed to qualify for the 2023 event in France. Once more there is a virtually blank sheet of paper where rows of lucrative dollar signs are supposed to be.

This is a good time, then, to talk to Dan the Man. Dan Lyle was the first American rugby import to make it big in England and is fondly remembered by all those who saw him play for Bath and the US Eagles. Occasionally, because he could, he would throw torpedo passes across three-quarters of the pitch at the Rec to remind everyone where he hailed from. The son of a two-star army general, he also captained the Eagles and has forgotten more about the battle to popularise rugby in the States than most of us will ever know.

It helped that he spent some of his childhood growing up on army bases in Germany. He also played soccer and basketball and was good enough at American football to be asked to train with the Minnesota Vikings before, belatedly, giving rugby a try. When he pitched up at Bath in 1996 – 'I took my pound of flesh, being called a Septic [tank = Yank] and all that stuff' – his ability to read a playbook and outdo people fitness-wise soon endeared 'Captain America' to all. 'I was a better athlete than just about everybody, but they were superior in a rugby context. Luckily soccer and basketball are not dissimilar to rugby. It's also about putting people into gaps, playing team defence, seeing the game. I was able to see the field and pick lines.'

The personable Lyle loved the whole experience and shared in Bath's European Cup triumph in 1998. He also played 45 times for his country between 1994 and 2003, enjoying some good days along the way. 'We beat Fiji, we beat Japan by 70 points, we beat Tonga. We gave South Africa a good game in Houston 2001 . . . we lucked into some players and some decent coaching at times. Right people, right time. But that's not a system, right?'

Lyle's view is that the likes of himself, Tom Billups, Luke Gross and Dave Hodges, all of whom played professionally in Europe, were the last of a certain old-school breed of American player. 'Rugby has always been a sport on the fringe in America, but there was a counterculture renaissance in the 1950s and 1960s. A lot of footballers and basketballers could also play rugby and found the camaraderie a release. My era was the last of the real crossovers. There's barely a crossover dialogue in America still. Some clubs in America have tried to get it going . . . the only flaw is that if you have 50 people who don't know how to play rugby, who leads it on the field?'

Lyle remains convinced, even so, that the potential is still there – assuming the game in America ever gets its administrative act together off the field. Financial issues continue to affect the domestic Major League Rugby competition and the national union has been in and out of insolvency. As a director for AEG Rugby and an analyst for NBC, Lyle is fully aware a successful rocket cannot be fired from a wobbly canoe. 'I'm probably more frustrated with our own rugby union than anything else. We've got a good product but we don't have a Steve Jobs. We're still a start-up company, we're still in a garage.

'We've got a good product but we don't have a Steve Jobs. We're still a start-up company, we're still in a garage.'

'We have never, ever written a plan. I quizzed a guy at World Rugby once. He was a little bit perturbed I knew as much as I did. But our dialogue turned into a conversation. I said to him, "You want to come to America and play games on your terms. But you don't want to come and create a system. You're giving $2 million a year to the USA in performance grants and grassroots grants. But have you ever seen a business plan out of the United States? And, by the way, have you guys ever written a strategic plan for the United States?" And of course the answer was "No". How do we continue operating in that way?'

Clearly patience is going to be required. It will be a while before rugby is on every billboard in, say, Los Angeles. But how would Lyle himself unlock the American dream? A wry chuckle rumbles down the Zoom link from Colorado. 'Some of the things I put down on paper in my early administrative career were laughed out of the room by people who said you had to have played rugby since you were five. But how does that work in New Zealand or England, let alone America? We're still clinging to our insular structure, but it's about being entrepreneurial. I work for the largest sports entertainment company on the planet, which has chosen to sniff around the rugby world and form a division. Sometimes it's almost like we're half-pariahs and half-saviours.'

It is Lyle's expert view, though, that marrying imported expertise with natural American can-do spirit could still prove a potent mix.

'We have 1,000 universities and 627 men's universities who play rugby. Harvard, Yale, Cal . . . they have $20–30 million endowments for rugby. We just haven't tapped into that conversation.' Surely those institutions can produce a clutch of half-decent rugby players before 2031? As Lyle says, 'If they just graduate 10 rugby guys a year, that makes 6,000 collegiate rugby players. Per year. Let alone all the other talent that slips through the net.'

But if better talent ID and a proper development conveyor belt are crucial, so is an enhanced international fixture schedule. Lyle reckons it is time to accept that New Zealand making a lucrative trip over to thrash the American national team 104–14 (as happened in Washington in 2021) is counterproductive. 'I don't want to play a tier one country for the next four years. They can play against the Six Nations and SANZAR teams, whoever they're making the most money from. But why not tell them they're not going to come into America unless they can make money *and* America can make money?

'You've got to make it a meritocracy and say to them, "We don't make money going to your stadia, so why are you complaining you don't make enough money here? And we're not going to make money here if you're going to beat us by 90 points because our team hasn't been able to assemble in advance and guys are unavailable."'

In other words, everyone needs to be smarter and work together. If not, says Lyle, nothing will ever change. 'If you continue to have a dull mentality, that's going to keep you in a tier two structure for all time. What if England played Ireland on the East Coast, for example, on their way to the southern hemisphere? That's a $20 million game. Make it a double-header with USA v Canada as well. Boom. Or New Zealand could play Australia or South Africa on the West Coast on their way up to Europe. There's more Australians and South Africans in southern California than anywhere else in the world, outside of their own countries. Our double-header there would be USA v Fiji. I mean, you could sell out the Rose Bowl if you make the fixtures scarce enough.'

Lyle also has no doubt whatsoever the 2031 World Cup in the USA will be a hit. 'If you were to ask me if 2031 will be a financial success in America, I'd say, "Hands down." Every match will be a home match because we have so many ex-pats in America. We don't even need people to travel. And you'll be talking 50,000 people at each game. Soccer and rugby are not sports you should draw parallels between very often. But you can in terms of selling out stadiums for big events. Everyone wants to be part of something that's unique and authentic. When people say they're sceptical about American rugby, I hear them, but I don't hear them on the World Cup. It's going to unlock a lot of sponsors and commercial people who want to get into the game. Done right it should incubate more sustainable structures.'

Lyle has only one caveat: he believes clashing with the American football season would be a mistake and thinks the tournament would be much more likely to fly in July and August. 'As long we can move it from September–October it will be a success.' In every other respect, though, he is adamant World Rugby has done the right move in giving the States their big chance.

'Alan Gilpin and others pushed all the sceptics and naysayers aside and said the sport needed to open up America, based on what happened in Japan in 2019. We have to open up a new flank for rugby. And, in the interim, figure out the economics, structures and fan base etc., which are in jeopardy everywhere. Every sport is having those issues right now because there's so much choice out there.' Spot on. If conquering America was easy, rugby would have cracked it years ago.

20

ALLEZ LES BLEUS!

*I was the captain of France and I'd never done a
weights session in my life.*

Everyone has their defining image of French rugby. For years it was Serge
Blanco's exhausted celebration after scoring the late try to beat Australia in
the last moments of the 1987 semi-final at Concord Oval in Sydney. Then
there was the late, much-missed Christophe Dominici, streaking clear to
break All Black hearts at Twickenham in 1999. Or Jean-Baptiste Élissalde's
euphoric diagonal dash towards the touchline after the 2007 quarter-final
over the same opposition. Drama everywhere, intertwined with glorious
possibility. Or maybe we were just sucked in by the divine madness the
best French sides always possessed? Almost serene backline elegance with
a pack full of knuckle-dragging giants riding shotgun.

The other day someone posted some online footage of the French side
waiting in the tunnel before heading out to face England at the Parc des
Princes in 1988. You could smell the danger. The forwards were already
glistening with sweat and liniment, the air of menace palpable. More
recently the former Sale no. 8 Sébastien Chabal exuded similar menace: an
almost biblical hair-and-beard combo supplemented by superhuman
strength and reach. His teammate Christian Califano used to joke that
'Sea Bass' had such long arms he could not only turn the light off when
lying flat in his bed but, rather than using the switch, could simply unscrew
the bulb. Others referred to him as a *cartonneur*, or 'box-maker' in English.
In real life, however, the pantomime villain squeezed into a Smart car to
drive to work in Manchester and possessed a dry sense of humour. 'I don't
like running round a training pitch . . . I'm about as much use as a baked
bean,' he once told me, before wondering aloud about a curious local

sport he had just encountered. 'Why do English people like cricket? The only reason for going seems to be to have a few beers? I find it strange. Surely it would be simpler just to go to the pub?'

It reminded me of something the great Jean-Pierre Rives once said, when asked about his old mate Blanco. 'I love him because he's a little "cuckoo" – and I love the cuckoo.' Can you imagine Bill Beaumont murmuring something like that about Dusty Hare? Or Owen Farrell using similar language to describe Ellis Genge? Something rather wider than a stretch of water divides French rugby culture from its British and Irish – and particularly Anglo-Saxon – equivalents.

There is, even so, plenty of mutual Anglo-French respect. The former Saracens player, Thomas Castaignède, is among those who retain a genuine soft spot for *les rosbifs,* despite one or two slight culinary issues back in the day. 'Jelly was the worst – or meat cooked the English way so it's like the sole of a rugby boot.' Now living in Biarritz – 'I miss London and the UK . . . I really like the atmosphere and the spirit of the English' – his time in London has also given him a first-hand perspective on how the game has evolved on both sides of the Channel since professionalism, initially as a player and pundit and more latterly as an administrator.

For those who never saw him play, his YouTube highlights reel remains a delight. In many ways he was the Antoine Dupont or Romain Ntamack of his day, a twinkling star in the *rouge et noir* jersey of Toulouse and a natural-born crowd-pleaser in a blue French jersey. On the subject of defining Gallic images, many would still choose the footage of a happy Castaignède, with his tongue sticking out and doing a high-kneed jig of celebration, immediately after landing the crucial drop goal to beat England 15–12 on his Five Nations debut in 1996. In any pecking order of impish, matador-style playmakers, Thomas would be prominent on the podium.

My abiding memory of him will always be the last game of the 1998 championship. France had achieved a clean sweep in 1997 and were now looking to become one of the rare teams to have claimed back-to-back Grand Slams. Their final fixture was against Wales at Wembley, with the stadium in Cardiff then being rebuilt. France's 51–0 win did owe something to their opponents' shortcomings, but Castaignède delivered a truly masterful performance, slashing the Welsh defence to red ribbons.

For France it also ranked as an achievement that has stood the test of time. 'Successive Grand Slams have not been done many times. It was a very big moment for French rugby. On the day everything went right for us. I remember the sun was shining and we played in the way we loved to play. By the end I think even the Welsh were cheering for us. But when you play rugby you're only a champion for one day. It's like turning the pages of a book. The following year Wales were better than us and won in Paris. Winning is difficult, but the hardest thing of all is to keep winning. When you reach a certain level, everyone wants to beat you. That's hard.'

'When you play rugby you're only a champion for one day. It's like turning the pages of a book.'

And when you invite Castaignède to nominate the individuals who best encapsulate French rugby for him, he does not hesitate. 'I would say two guys. They were top, top players, yet every time you meet them they still keep a low profile. One was Philippe Sella. To play against him when I was a kid was really amazing. But my "god" is Serge Blanco. He has been a very successful player and businessman and I love speaking to him. He took Biarritz to the top level both as a player and the president, without the club having a huge amount of money. Some people criticise him, but I think they should remember what he has done for the game in France. He is a legend of French rugby.'

Ah, Blanco. So good that generations of hacks still call their blank receipts after him. What I really want to hear from Castaignède, though, is why French rugby is now flourishing. Even without taking into account the financial bonanza heading their way as the hosts of the 2023 World Cup, the entire game in France seems to be in Moulin Rouge mode, twirling its skirts and performing the metaphorical cancan more enthusiastically with every passing year. True, uncomfortable off-field questions have been raised by the corruption case involving the FFR president Bernard Laporte and Mohed Altrad, the billionaire owner of Montpellier, who were both handed suspended sentences in December 2022, but the rude health of the Top 14 domestic league and the national team's upturn in fortunes are undeniable.

These days Castaignède is employed by the insurance giant AXA – 'Unfortunately I didn't play football, I still have to work' – but he was a board member at Toulouse for four years and currently sits on the 16-strong board of the Ligue Nationale de Rugby, the powerful body representing the French clubs. Despite Toulouse's fabled history, he says the financial impact of COVID was substantial. 'Even when you think you're dealing with big clubs, everything is still fragile, especially the financial part . . . Toulouse weren't too far away from having big troubles.'

The heritage of club rugby in France, though, has been a major factor in driving the kind of revenues that others, including England's Gallagher Premiership, can only dream about. While the national team remain the most visible symbol of French rugby abroad, the TV rights deal with Canal+ that promotes club rugby to a huge nationwide audience has also been pivotal.

In 2021 the French broadcaster signed a four-year deal worth a whopping £390 million, dwarfing the current three-year £110 million domestic rights agreement between BT Sport and the Premiership, which is due to expire in 2024. 'Canal+ has supported French rugby massively and I think that was key,' suggests Castaignède. 'As a result, rugby has been exposed to nearly everyone. Maybe one of the things that hasn't worked in English rugby is that when you sign a big contract with a satellite broadcaster you largely lose your terrestrial platform. If that happens, it becomes difficult.'

The steady rise of clubs from outside the supposed elite has been another factor, helping to draw new fans to games and extending rugby's tentacles beyond its traditional south-west heartlands. Even Castaignède has been taken aback by the club game's growth. 'Every week you have full crowds nearly everywhere. That's massive. The best example of French rugby's success is La Rochelle. It's not just about the rugby. It's about how you create the support, how you create links with your sponsors, how you manage to attract players. It's not only about the game itself, it's about how you treat people and how they train. That's why the French team is so good now: it's a product of the hard work of the clubs and the federation that has created this success.'

Times have also changed appreciably since France's 48–19 loss to England in 2001, after which Laporte suggested his players should 'give up red wine and cigarettes'. Teams at both international and club level can play for the full 80 minutes (and beyond, if necessary). 'French rugby has now understood that while French flair was very important, so is preparing yourself physically,' confirms Castaignède. 'People have been abroad and seen what the expectations are. We have also seen some foreign coaches come here. All of it has made us realise we had to work harder.'

And when you marry innate skill and flair with improved fitness, physical strength, a vibrant, competitive domestic league with a well-policed salary cap and a good relationship between club and country, the results tend to be impressive. 'The players are much better prepared than before and we have a very good generation of talent, too. Antoine Dupont, Thomas Ramos, Julien Marchand, Romain Ntamack, Damien Penaud. Previously the best French players were not always the key players in their club teams. Now they are. Even if we bring in some foreigners they're not as important as these guys.'

All of which begs a question: precisely how long will this modern oval-shaped French renaissance last? Castaignède can certainly see a tell-tale glint in their eyes. 'Now we really believe we can achieve things. In the past we maybe thought we were outsiders. We weren't as confident of our potential. Rugby was different then, too. The rules have maybe helped us, the clubs are now well organised and the players know they are going to be looked after.

'Previously we've had a sense of expectation going into big tournaments, but this time we really believe in our team. We have lost the kind of fear we used to have. When you only play the big teams maybe once every two or three years, you could be scared. Now you play them all the time. That's why Argentina and Georgia are getting better . . . the more you play the better sides, the more competitive you become. That will be the key thing for rugby in the next few years. If you always have the same teams, with just four or five countries who can win the World Cup, it will be boring. That's why people love football. Any team can successful.'

Before he retreats back to the beach in Biarritz – 'It's very tough, but we wanted to live in a place where we could be sure the kids would come and visit us' – the engaging Castaignède also leaves another interesting theory hanging in the breeze. As a self-confessed Anglophile – he spent seven years at Saracens – he has long felt there is a rarely discussed elephant in the room when it comes to English rugby. 'The English are punished by having two different codes of rugby,' he says, flatly. 'Maybe it's a gift to have two professional rugby codes and very nice for the population to watch two different games. But I'd be really interested to see if the two games ever came together how good the English team could be. I'm pretty sure the addition of some talented league guys would be amazing for English rugby, as Jason Robinson has proved. We don't have the same degree of competition in France.'

The impact of Shaun Edwards' coaching style on the French national team – along with the defensive tutelage of Dave Ellis before him – further reinforces his point. French rugby league fans will rightly point out there is a very good reason for this, namely the ban on *rugby à treize* by the wartime Vichy government. In recent years, however, the penny has certainly dropped. 'All these rugby league tricks and training have helped French rugby massively,' says Castaignède. 'We've learned a lot from English rugby union over the years, but we've also learned a lot from English rugby league. I watched the 2022 rugby league grand final and I've seen how quick it is.' Either way, he reckons the English XV could still come good sooner rather than later. 'I don't think you're too far away from achieving something special. You've got some talented players. They just need to gel together.' *Plus ça change,* Thomas, *plus c'est la même chose.*

* * * * *

Even Castaignède, though, cannot match his friend Philippe Saint-André when it comes to stellar achievements on both sides of the Channel. Not only did Saint-André captain his country and score 32 tries in 69 Tests for Les Bleus but he coached his national team and also won both the English Premiership and the French Top 14 titles with Sale Sharks in 2006 and Montpellier in 2022 respectively. He played a significant part, too, in two of the greatest international tries ever scored, against England in London in 1991 and against New Zealand at Eden Park in 1994.

Those of us lucky enough to be there to witness the Twickenham *tour de force* had the perfect press box view of the daring breakout from behind the French posts led by Blanco, followed by the pitter-patter running and deft cross-kick by Didier Camberabero almost right in front of us. 'When Serge sniffs the wind in the air and seeks out possibility, you know that it is going to produce a beautiful scent,' as Saint-André later put it. Modestly he downplayed his own crucial role; without him sprinting down the middle of the field to gather the bouncing ball and score at the other end, there would have been no try. 'It started behind the posts at Twickenham and finished under the other set of posts 110 metres later. It's still a good memory.'

Whenever they replay the footage nowadays, Saint-André much enjoys the feedback he receives from the younger generation. 'People don't realise I was fitter and had hair on my head once.' What has not altered is his continuing regard for his thrill-seeking full back Blanco. 'He symbolised French rugby at the time . . . when somebody kicked the ball to him, he would start to run and we didn't know where he was going. I'm not sure he knew either. He could create something from nothing. I think people are thinking about him when they start talking about "French flair".'

Ultimately, though, France lost the game 21–19 and England clinched the Grand Slam. As Saint-André says, 'When you are a player or captain of your country, you remember the games you win more than the ones you lose.' If he had to choose one, he would nominate the match featuring the so-called 'Try From The End Of The World' in Auckland three years later when he launched a similar long-range raid when New Zealand were leading 20–16 and only three minutes were left on the clock. Sixty-five seconds and a dazzling sequence of phases later, it yielded a score for Jean-Luc Sadourny to ensure a 23–20 victory and clinch a first series win by a single northern hemisphere union against the All Blacks.

There is much more to Saint-André, though, than an eye-catching CV. His grandfather, also Philippe, was a hero of the French Resistance in the mountains of central France, near Grenoble, until he and 15 of his compatriots were shot dead in July 1944 after an SS patrol discovered their limestone cave hideaway. The German soldiers subsequently headed for the nearby village where his grandmother lived and burned it to the ground, leaving her with nothing except a few pictures.

No wonder it meant so much to their grandson whenever he stood for the anthems before an international game. 'You are very, very proud to be picked and to be representing your country. And for me to be captain despite being a winger, which doesn't often happen. And because of my personal history. To sing *La Marseillaise* and to make your family and your dad proud is something very special. I think it's still the same now. All the young generation love sport: they love rugby, they train hard to be a professional and to represent their country at the top level. It's difficult to describe, but you feel the passion, the crowd behind you and then the anthems stirring your blood. It's an amazing feeling.'

'In France we were amateur. I left France to go and be a professional player.'

Which is the moment it strikes you: is there anyone worldwide better equipped than Saint-André to identify precisely where the soul of rugby beats strongest? Probably not. He played either side of the game going professional and became the first high-profile modern French international to come over and try his luck in English club rugby. When he pitched up at Gloucester in 1997, he encountered a parallel universe. 'I learned a lot when I played in England. I found that everyone at Gloucester was strong and bench-pressing 140 kg. I was the captain of the French team and I'd never done a weights session in my life. People couldn't believe the captain of the French team, with over 60 caps, had never lifted anything. In France we were amateur. I left France to go and be a professional player. To enjoy my passion but to improve as well. For me it was an adventure and something amazing.'

It says much for Saint-André that he swiftly graduated to the role of Gloucester's director of rugby. As a player he sometimes felt that performing in front of the Shed, home to the most vociferous of Cherry and Whites supporters, was as intense as a Test match. As he once put it, 'Coming back to France after that is like going from eating caviar to having a baked potato.' A shrewd eye for an influential player has remained a consistent strength, and no one has ever doubted his enduring passion for the game, despite a tricky time as French national coach. 'For me it was much easier to be captain of the French team rather than the coach. When I was captain, I won over 70 per cent of the games. When I coached France, it was less than 50 per cent. When you are in charge of the French team as a coach, you have a lot of responsibility. It is a happy day if you win and a very, very tough day at the office if you lose.'

Saint-André, though, was ahead of his time in seeking greater collaboration between the French federation and the clubs. He also believes the recent improvement in the national team's fortunes has underlined the transformation in attitude within French rugby. 'When I was playing, we were very good when it was an unstructured game but we were missing discipline, both in terms of organisation and structure. It was more about fast play, passing the ball being quicker than running, trying to find space in order to keep the ball alive and enjoying the game.

'But French rugby over the last 10 years has changed completely, as you can see with our national team now. It used to be "Jouez, Jouez", but now rugby is professional, the kids are skilful and well coached and everything is well organised. Rugby used to be completely different in England, in New Zealand, in South Africa and everywhere else. It is quite uniform across the world now.'

Regardless of the outcome of the World Cup, Saint-André also foresees a bright mid-term future for French rugby, both at club level and nationally under the guidance of his old teammates Fabien Galthié and Raphaël Ibañez. 'Rugby is huge in France and the Top 14 is growing bigger and bigger. Each week the stadiums are full. Rafa and Fabien have a plan, they have the resources and we have a great generation of players. I hope Antoine Dupont stays fit . . . it helps when you have the best player in the world playing in your team. You can be a good coach, but with great players you can be a great coach. It's one of the best generation of French players we've had for a long, long time.'

The best, perhaps, since Saint-André and friends were in their prime. But will Dupont, Ntamack and Penaud develop the same warm relationships with some of their English counterparts that Saint-André still has with *les rosbifs* of his vintage? 'I enjoy it when I go to England and I see guys like Will Carling or Rory Underwood. We are quite good mates now and we talk about the moments we loved most. At the 1995 World Cup, after we'd beaten England in the third-place play-off, we finished the evening all together in the same bar. One of the English props was scrummaging against one of the French props. It was the last of the amateur days and the beginning of a new era of professional rugby. I enjoyed the whole period. Now it's different.'

You can only hope the example of people like Saint-André and Castaignède rubs off on those who follow. The future of the game, if so, will be secure regardless of any wider issues. Our chat is winding up, but Saint-André insists on a shout-out, alongside Blanco and Sella, for another totemic French skipper. 'I didn't play with him, but Jean-Pierre Rives was the ultimate captain. Blond hair, covered in blood, winning grand slams, fighting over six inches to bring the French side to the top of Europe.'

There have been precious few like Rives, before or since. But Saint-André still discerns a similar spirit in today's dressing rooms to that he experienced as a player. 'I think it's still strong. We beat Racing 92 recently. We fought hard and stuck together until the final seconds to get the win. It was a privilege to be in the changing room afterwards. We had a room full of players of all nationalities, laughing and smiling together. This is rugby, this is sport. In rugby you can't be too selfish. You need to give a lot in order to receive anything. That's why rugby is an amazing, unbelievable sport.'

EPILOGUE

It is the first Thursday in February and hundreds of us are gathered in Abergavenny's Market Hall. Over to the right is the familiar profile of Sir Gareth Edwards. Up ahead is Jonathan Davies. All around are familiar rugby faces, media types and locals, squeezed into rarely worn suits and ties. We are here to remember Eddie Butler, the former Wales captain and BBC commentator who also wrote for the *Observer* and the *Guardian*, and to be reminded what rugby is ultimately about.

Eddie, like Bill McLaren before him, instinctively understood that rugby is more than just a game. I was lucky enough to be his long-time colleague and particularly admired the way he traversed the tricky line between being a recognisable public figure and one of us hacks. We tended to gloss over the fact he was significantly more intelligent than we were and better read, as well as able to speak more languages. When he passed away in September 2022, I wrote that simply basking in the reflected glow of his talents was enough for most of us.

He also taught us that rugby's sweetness and occasional sourness were two sides of the same coin. He could write and speak with sensitivity but he packed a punch as well. Even his hard-bitten teammates at Pontypool remembered him as fearless in an era when the ping of metal stud on bone was a regular backing track. 'We did lose rather a lot of games,' Eddie once wrote. 'Not on the scoreboard necessarily. We were just struck off other clubs' fixture lists.'

Later, following the memorial service, a few of us returned to Abergavenny RFC where the former 'Pooler' wing Goff Davies told us another evocative story. In the Pontypool dressing room before games Davies would often sit directly across from the club's illustrious all-Welsh international front row of the late Tony 'Charlie' Faulkner, Bobby Windsor and Graham Price. Most weeks he would look up and see the same frightening sight: Faulkner removing his false teeth, the fearsome Windsor geeing himself up for more mayhem and Price looking as coolly forbidding as ever. A few seats up would be the craggy Terry Cobner, also tucking his false teeth away in preparation for the brutal battle ahead. One day, Davies recalled, Butler chose this moment to wander down from the far end of the room, lean over to him and murmur in his ear: 'I don't know about you, but I've never felt so handsome.'

Beauty and the beasts. If this book has reinforced one eternal truth it is that rugby is a game for all sorts. What they nearly all have in common, though, is the ability to locate humour amid the darkness. One of the classic examples was on the 1974 British & Irish Lions tour to South Africa when a major fight broke out in the third Test in Port Elizabeth. The Scottish lock Gordon Brown threw a punch at his nearest Springbok opponent, the hulking Johan de Bruyn, and dislodged the latter's glass eye. At which point the match had to be halted as both teams and the referee dropped to their hands and knees to search for it. When it was finally found and De Bruyn popped it back in, there was – as Brown loved recounting – a piece of grass sticking out of the socket.

Brown was also famous as one of rugby's more endearing characters. When he died aged 53 after being diagnosed with non-Hodgkin's lymphoma, there was a global outpouring of affection. Gavin Hastings, the former Scotland captain, used to tell the story of the 1991 World Cup semi-final when his missed penalty at Murrayfield enabled England to advance to the final. Up in the commentary box, Brown had just told his audience he would eat his hat if Hastings was off target. When that turned out to be a touch impractical, he spent a day dressed up as a morris dancer instead.

Time and again, rugby produces individuals whose humour in adversity inspires millions. Andy Ripley, the long-striding former Rosslyn Park and England no. 8, was another classic example. He died from prostate cancer aged 62, but his attitude to life was beyond wonderful. Aged 50 he even tried to row for Cambridge University in the Boat Race. When rugby went professional in the mid-1990s, he explained why, for him, amateurism held a deeper resonance. 'I want to have heroic figures out there,' he told one interviewer. 'If they're chasing a few quid like me,

I don't like it. It devalues them. It means they are marionettes, puppets, manipulated by people with money.'

His attitude, not surprisingly, found favour with his old opponent Jean-Pierre Rives, whose admiration for the Englishman never wavered. 'Rugby needs people like Andy. You can still meet people like him in the game and that proves to me that rugby still has spirit.' The remarkable Doddie Weir was an equally life-enhancing presence until his death in November 2022. And what about Kevin Sinfield, now England's defence coach after a stellar career in rugby league? On behalf of Weir and his good friend Rob Burrow, he has been running ultra marathons to raise funds to aid research into motor neurone disease.

Of course, rugby does not have a monopoly on remarkable people, but it does seem to generate more than its fair share. Something about it strips away selfishness and reveals the individual within, for better or worse. And overcomes supposedly immutable boundaries. For the men and women of Ulster to be part of a proudly all-Irish team, for instance, remains a shining example of rugby's ability to bring opposing factions together.

To be at Twickenham or Murrayfield on a Six Nations Saturday is also to sense something else. Twickenham is so vast and unashamedly corporate that romanticism can dissipate quicker than you can say, '£130 for a ticket?' But then the anthems start and the soaring noise tells you that, right now, nothing else matters. In those rousing moments big can finally be beautiful.

Rugby badly needs to preserve those warm, fuzzy feelings of shared communion. The game is being assailed from all sides by assorted violent cross winds, both financial and societal. At the time of writing, the national unions of Wales, Scotland, England and France are all working to erase damaging perceptions of one kind or another, just when rugby had been hoping to show its best face to the world. At a pivotal juncture in the game's history, even devout believers need fresh reasons to keep the faith.

Imagine, though, if you could bottle rugby's essence. The visceral thrill of a great try securing Calcutta Cup glory, the crackle of history at Croke Park when England visited in 2007, that first mini-rugby experience, the majestic power of any British & Irish Lions series decider. Or even just strolling back through, say, Edinburgh's Old Town on a Six Nations evening, the strains of 'Take Me Home, Country Roads' drifting out from the cosy-looking pub on the corner. Travelling revellers, easy fellowship, simple pleasures.

And right there is why so many are still irresistibly drawn to the game. For the spirit, for the craic, for the *esprit de corps*. You could be in Murrayfield, Munster or Montpellier and still be channelling the same force. Or even sitting alone in front of your television, struggling to comprehend where all the missing years have gone. Can it really be 50 years since Sir Gareth dived headlong into immortality? Not many sports have seen so much change and yet, somehow, remained essentially the same.

Rugby, in short, is as much about humanity and humility as it is anything else. As Brendan Venter, Richard Beard, Gus Pichot and others have already identified, it is not just a question of on-field success. When sport is at its most satisfying, there is almost a spiritual element that transcends all else. Which sounded like a theory that a proud Frenchman like Philippe Saint-André might confirm. So I suggested to him that Peter Sellers' character in *Being There* had it almost right; that rugby, as well as life, is a state of mind. 'Exactly,' he replied quietly. 'Exactly.'

Journey's end at last. From Bennett and Duckham to Ntamack and Dupont, greatness is not simply defined by talent. Or the scoreboard. Or the size of a stadium. It is about possessing the mental resilience and bravery to enter the emotional furnace and emerge the stronger from it. It is about retaining a sense of perspective when everyone else is losing their shit. And, if possible, laughing in adversity's face. Rugby is not for everyone but, once hooked, it shapes you for life.

ACKNOWLEDGEMENTS

This book would not have been written without the generous assistance of numerous people. Rugby union has its problems but it also has a disproportionate number of remarkable individuals. I really hope these pages reflect that enduring truth.

I am particularly indebted to the following (in chronological chapter order) for sharing their personal memories and reflections with me: Sir Gareth Edwards, David Duckham, Alastair Hignell, Mark Ella, Phil Kearns, Michael Lynagh, John Rutherford, John Jeffrey, Sean Lineen, Simon Halliday, Stuart Barnes, Paul Ackford, Will Carling, Jonathan Davies, Jason Robinson, Gill Burns, Liza Burgess, Lawrence Dallaglio, Austin Healey, Sean Fitzpatrick, Edward Griffiths, Brendan Venter, Sir Clive Woodward, Alan Quinlan, Ronan O'Gara, Richard Beard, Jacques Burger, David Campese, Brian O'Driscoll, Carl Hayman, Phil Pask, Bill Ribbans, Dame Farah Palmer, Maggie Alphonsi, Ben Ryan, Dan Leo, Eddie Jones, Robert Maes, Alan Gilpin, Agustín Pichot, Dan Lyle, Thomas Casteignède and Philippe Saint-André.

I am also most grateful to David Davies, Julia Hutton, Donal Lenihan, Dominic Rumbles, Catherine Stewart, Dave Swanton, Tom Whitford and the following organisations: the Rugby Football Union, the Scottish Rugby Union, the Welsh Rugby Union, New Zealand Rugby, BT Sport and Progressive Rugby.

Heartfelt thanks, too, to Matthew Lowing and everyone at Bloomsbury for backing the concept so enthusiastically, to Nick Walters at David Luxton Associates for his expert guidance and to my editors at the *Guardian* – past and present – for allowing me to travel the globe and to write about rugby union for one of the world's finest newspapers. Some passages in this book have previously appeared in the *Guardian*, the *Observer* and *Rugby Journal* while several other publications have been invaluable for research purposes.

Stephen Bale and Robert Woodward both deserve special mention for their keen-eyed assistance, as does everyone else with whom I have shared wintry press boxes over the years. Without your unfailing good humour and comradeship, it would have been much less fun. Finally, I would like to say a big thank you to my family. To Fiona, Alex, Louisa and Greg, I remain eternally grateful for your patience, support and catering skills. I love you all – and this time I really do promise to clear out that shed.

BIBLIOGRAPHY

Behind the Dragon: Playing Rugby for Wales; Ross Harries; Polaris, 2019

Behind the Rose: Playing Rugby for England; Stephen Jones and Nick Cain; Polaris, 2014

Blindsided; Michael Lynagh; HarperCollins, 2015

Campese: The Last of the Dream Sellers; James Curran; Scribe, 2021

The Captains; Edward Griffiths; Jonathan Ball, 2001

City Centre: High Ball to High Finance; Simon Halliday; Matador, 2013

The Complete Rugby Union Compendium; Keith Young; Arena Sport, 2015

Endless Winter: The Inside Story of the Rugby Revolution; Stephen Jones; Mainstream, 1993

Finding My Feet: My Autobiography; Jason Robinson; Hodder & Stoughton, 2003

Gareth Edwards: An Autobiography; Gareth Edwards; Stanley Paul, 1978

Giants of Scottish Rugby; Jeff Connor; Mainstream, 2000

The Grudge: Scotland vs. England, 1990; Tom English; Yellow Jersey Press, 2010

Knife in the Fast Lane: A Surgeon's Perspective from the Sharp End of Sport; Bill Ribbans; Pitch Publishing, 2020

Lions of England; Peter Jackson; Mainstream, 2005

Mud, Blood and Money: English Rugby Union Goes Professional; Ian Malin; Mainstream, 1997

Muddied Oafs; Richard Beard; Yellow Jersey Press, 2004

My Life and Rugby: The Autobiography; Eddie Jones; Macmillan, 2019

Our Blood Is Green: The Springboks in Their Own Words; Gavin Rich; Zebra Press, 2019

Pumas: A History of Argentine Rugby; Rex Gowar; Polaris, 2022

Ronan O'Gara: My Autobiography; Ronan O'Gara; Transworld Ireland, 2008

The Rugby War; Peter FitzSimons; HarperCollins, 1996

Scrum Queens: The Story of Women's Rugby; Ali Donnelly; Pitch Publishing, 2022

Sevens Heaven: The Beautiful Chaos of Fiji's Olympic Dream; Ben Ryan; Weidenfeld & Nicolson, 2018

Smelling of Roses: A Rugby Life; Stuart Barnes; Mainstream, 1994

The Test: My Autobiography; Brian O'Driscoll; Penguin Ireland, 2014

This Is Your Everest: The Lions, the Springboks and the Epic Tour of 1997; Tom English and Peter Burns; Polaris, 2021

Unholy Union: When Rugby Collided with the Modern World; Michael Aylwin with Mark Evans; Constable, 2019

The Winning Way; Bob Dwyer; Rugby Press Ltd, 1992

Winning!; Clive Woodward; Hodder & Stoughton, 2004

Winter Colours: Changing Seasons in World Rugby; Donald McRae; Mainstream, 1998

INDEX